Water
and the
Landscape

Water

and the Landscape

A LANDSCAPE ARCHITECTURE Book

Edited by Grady Clay
Editor, **LANDSCAPE ARCHITECTURE** Magazine

McGraw-Hill Book Company
New York   St. Louis   San Francisco   Auckland   Bogota
Dusseldorf   Johannesburg   London   Madrid   Mexico
Montreal   New Delhi   Panama   Paris   Sao Paulo
Singapore   Sydney   Tokyo   Toronto

Cover: At Redditch, a new town in England, Billing Brook has been saved from the usual fate of urbanized streams and formed into a series of small lakes connected by wooded corridors along the stream. Rustic footbridge in distance connects housing areas on either side of the stream valley. Photograph provided by Benjamin J.W. Smith, author of the article beginning on page 40.

The production editor for this book was Susan Rademacher Frey.

Printed and bound by Halliday Lithograph.

Library of Congress Cataloging in Publication Data

Main entry under title:

Water and the landscape.
    Includes index.
        1. Water in landscape architecture.   I. Clay,
Grady.
SB475.8.W38   714   78-19206
ISBN 0-07-036190-8

1234567890 HDHD 7865432109

Contents

Preface

It was no accident that in a national design competition for landscape architects in the 1970s, the jury chose among 18 winning projects 11 having to do with water-related development of the landscape. It was no accident that the world's first desertification conference was held by the United Nations in Nairobi, also in the 1970s—or that water shortages as well as record-breaking floods plagued many parts of the world with sudden intensities during this decade.

All these events derive from our growing use and waste of water, our steady population drift toward the shores of waterbodies large and small—and thus to the increasing value we now place upon our access to this marvelous, miraculous liquid which unites all of life on earth.

Our attitudes toward water have been oddly warped. Much of early American life consisted of getting rid of surplus water: the pioneers' East was full of swamps, muck and mire, their early lives miserable in the mud. East of the Mississippi, successful politics often consisted of providing roads, drainage canals, wooden sidewalks and pumps to get whole towns out of the mud. West of the 20 in. rainfall line, laws were passed and then perverted so as to water the Great American Desert—a dry and dusty reality which generations of Westerners pretended wasn't there by wiping it off their maps and histories.

By the 1970s, legal battles over water rights were moving from West to East, and in 1977 the citizens of Washington state voted on a revolutionary proposition to put a 50-year limit on irrigation water rights—which normally ran with the land in perpetuity.

Along with the discovery that even in the humid East water was a diminishing resource came the widespread realization that waterfront land was growing more scarce; and that old derelict waterfronts deserved to be reexamined as assets long buried underneath dumps, railroad tracks and bulk-using industries. Already in the 1960s, hundreds of urban renewal projects had begun to reclaim bits and hunks of old waterfronts made derelict in the previous century.

Quickly it has become apparent that urban waterfronts, whether natural or artificial, are now prime pieces of real estate, essential ingredients in forming a community image, invaluable stages for architectural display, and great places for public recreation.

Recycling waterfronts has become a wide-spread civic enterprise, just as recycling water has become necessary to many a water-short community.

Peter Drucker, the noted economist, has written brilliantly* about "the first great revolution technology wrought in human life seven thousand years ago when the first great civilization of man, the irrigation civilization, established itself. First in Mesopotamia, and then in Egypt and in the Indus Valley, and finally in China, there appeared a new society and a new policy: the irrigation city, which then rapidly became the irrigation empire." He sees irrigation civilizations as "the beginning of history," if only because they brought about the invention of writing, standing armies, the concept of man as a citizen, organized trade, and organized knowledge, and not least, the individual as a focal point of the emerging concept of justice. Not a small yield.

What can we say of today's society but that it is struggling to become a recycling civilization? We are rapidly learning how to recycle hundreds of basic resources: principal among these are water and water-served sites. And nowhere on the American scene is this transformation so apparent as in water-related developments such as are described in this book. For here is where a small and often-unheralded profession of landscape architects are doing what they do expertly, which is the analysis, design and management of the dynamic living landscape. Some of these places were close to death: a shore badly battered by flood or hurricane, a marsh foolishly filled by a generation of dumpers, a watercourse concreted and turned into an open-land sewer by the earlier established wisdom of engineering; or riverbanks wasted and littered for a long century before.

Now, thanks to expanding techniques for landscape analysis, the watershed is emerging as a rational planning unit. (TVA tried to tell us that in the 1930s, and Patrick Geddes in an earlier generation, but few would listen.) Today, thanks to expanding population pressures, the city's edge of river, bay and ocean is being examined for its recreation potential.

Not all these places can be or *should* be developed. It takes the wisdom of artist and technician combined to tell us that most difficult lesson to learn: *where not to build.* Those of us who have watched over these projects, either personally or editorially—during the years 1970-1978 in which they were originally published—hope they will serve a growing public awareness of the scarcity, fragility and wonder that is to be found in water—and of our need skillfully to protect and design water in the future landscape.

Grady Clay

*In "The First Technological Revolution and Its Lessons," *Technology and Culture*, vol. VII, no. 2, Spring 1966, p. 143.

Water
and the
Landscape

1
Watershed Planning and Design

Towards Zero Runoff: All the Rain that Falls on Me is Mine. Right?

As a solution to floods, soil erosion, drought and other afflictions, "zero runoff" sounds ideal. You keep the water on your land from running off, right? All rain that falls on me is mine, right?

Zero runoff is getting increasing attention, the term having been dramatized by the Texas Soil Conservation Service. This service has helped the owners of some 500 cattle feed lots to redesign their land and its drainage so that no manure-fouled waters run off their land. What doesn't evaporate goes back into the ground via irrigation.

Which goes down well enough for individual landowners — but only so long as the creeks don't dry up. So long as all the upstreamers don't keep all the runoff to themselves and leave the downstream folks with zero water.

Now, hold up just one cottonpicking minute! Let's look at this Texas proposition again. The prospect of millions of landowners in North America scrambling singly and collectively to achieve zero runoff over the next two decades gets pretty spooky.

Suppose you're one of 2000 landowners in the upper reaches of, let us say, Beargrass Creek, an urbanizing stream that starts among septic tanks and soon becomes an extension of the suburbanites' alimentary canal. You and your 1,999 fellow landowners are running out of cheap water, so you organize to capture all the rain that falls on your land — Your Rain! — and hold it in aquifers, seepage pits, catchbasins, reservoirs, retention ponds, etc. But what happens to people downstream who find that, except after unusual rainstorms, there's no stream left?

What usually happens is they hire a lawyer and go to court, for it is well-known that under either Western (prior appropriation) water laws, or Eastern (riparian rights) laws, downstreamers need to be protected. Consequently, with or without zero runoff, the managing of water-rights lawsuits and the writing and processing of new legislation has become a minor growth industry. So much so that the legal, engineering and land planning and design professionals are deeply involved in a struggle . . . not so much with each other, but to sort out the rights of all parties, including the right of the landscape itself to survive man's use of it.

The Editor

A Strategy for Watershed Development . . . that Beats the Bulldozer by Using Land-Sale Profits to Preserve Greenspace

By JOHN RAHENKAMP, WALTER SACHS and ROGER WELLS

Survival is our stake in the land-development process. And survival requires that the natural environment continue to function as development proceeds.

Conservation therefore can be defined as good development — and the best development is that based on natural systems. But conservation often becomes a battlecry, a slogan against any and all development. Inevitably, the demand for new housing brings the bulldozer, and at that point the chance for rational controls is often lost.

Since a primary objective of good planning is to accommodate good development while protecting the integrity of natural and social systems, we are trying a new method in the Wissahickon Watershed outside Philadelphia. We believe it is a new and unusual example of conservation through controlled development.

Wissahickon Creek winds its way through the gentle slopes of suburban Montgomery County, flowing into the Schuylkill River in the heart of Philadelphia's Fairmount Park. It is a pleasure-ground for a large city and suburban area, and offers a logical place for a regional park.

The watershed itself covers 34,000 a. beyond Fairmount Park, and is directly in the path of major development thrusts. Since the 19th century, railroad lines encouraged the growth of small farming communities which, with large estates, dominated the scene. Now construction of expressways has stimulated widespread subdivision which threatens the environment of the valley.

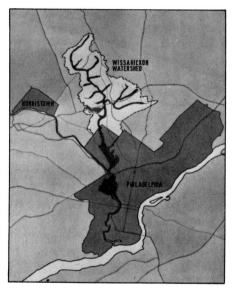

In an effort to preserve a greenway along the creek, residents formed a Wissahickon Valley Watershed Association, and asked Rahenkamp, Sachs, Wells and Associates, a Philadelphia-based planning firm, to develop a strategy.

It quickly became apparent that if a citizen group is to stay ahead of the cookie-cutter development pattern, it must know where to act and what to seek. It must have a comprehensive up-to-date information base for the whole watershed, know which areas have the highest conservation value, and where development pressure is most likely to build up immediately. Knowing all this, the association can take steps to obtain logical restrictions on new development, working with local government and private developers

to do so. Vigilante-style brush-fire action is usually negative and ends in failure.

A park is not just a 300 ft. greenway along a creek. And to protect a creek one must exercise some form of control over floodplains, swamps, steep slopes, erosion, siltation and removal of cover. Our studies showed that a "Wissahickon Valley Park" would necessarily include more than 4800 a. plus controls on adjacent land. Such a large concept required that we evaluate what we call conservation demand.

The first step, therefore, was to map the whole watershed in terms of conservation demand. We considered six major criteria (see below), assigning each a value based on its relative importance to the maintaining of conservation standards. Such a value system ranks each factor, and relates it to an overall conservation composite which shows areas of maximum, minimum and moderate conservation values. The six factors are:

> Existing open space
> Forest cover
> Visual corridor
> Erodible soil
> 15% slope
> 170-year flood plain
>
> Total possible value

Clearly, the association couldn't control all important conservation land at once. They needed an evaluation method to determine priorities. Therefore the next step was to evaluate development demand. This showed where development pressure was likely to be felt immediately.

THE METHOD

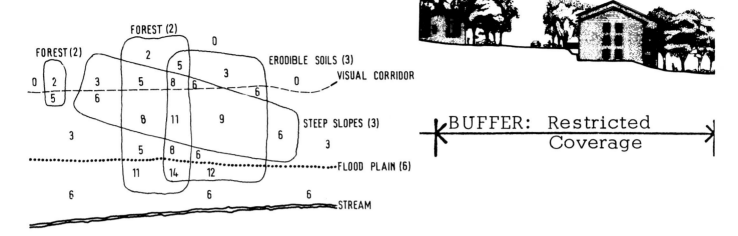

FOREST (2)

FOREST (2)

FOREST (2)

ERODIBLE SOILS (3)

VISUAL CORRIDOR

STEEP SLOPES (3)

FLOOD PLAIN (6)

STREAM

BUFFER: Restricted Coverage

This involved considering both positive and negative elements. First, those which encourage development — water service, sewerability, potential highway capacities. Next, a composite of natural building restrictions, viewed from a developer's viewpoint (such as depth to bedrock, 1-3 ft. slopes over 20%, 50-year floodplain, seasonal and permanent water table). The sum of values against development was subtracted from the sum of values encouraging development. The result was a "demand composite" picture of priorities which located areas of development demand.

This *demand composite* showed the association its priorities — where should they act at once? The composite of course requires updating, so as to serve as an up-to-the-minute guide for action.

But the association must also consider political climate, tax bases and costs of local public services — so as to stay within the give-and-take of local politics.

It is also possible — and essential — to evaluate manmade constraints — access, sewer, water, schooling and market demand. The sum of all these evaluations is what we call a dynamic development impact model. This is a rational basis for making decisions about development; it respects both natural and social systems in any locality.

In two important ways, using this D/I/M differs from traditional town planning practice. First is its basis on the local natural and economic re-

sources. Secondly, it is not fixed; it suggests logical patterns of open space and development; and it can be used at township, regional, and statewide levels. It is a way of "test-flying" a design — before it leaves the drawing board.

With such tools, how do we protect 34,000 a. where values are $10,000 per acre and more? The association quickly saw that traditional methods would not work. At this point, our firm's experience in planning cluster housing developments reminded us that land value can be doubled by rezoning, and still leave 20-50% open space. Why not apply a similar technique to the entire watershed? Why not enlist private enterprise for public purpose — using landbanking and computer capability to do so?

Acting on our proposal, the association received a private local grant of approximately $500,000 toward the creation of a Wissahickon Valley open space program to implement what we proposed in our basic study. This was essential because of the weakness of the usual government tools: condemnation is prohibitively costly in such a wealthy area — as well as being politically untenable. Traditional zoning would only embroil the association in devastating political squabbles, and would be inappropriate anyway since the zoning usually encourages the cutting of open space into private yards.

Three conventional methods remained. We estimated that they

would produce the following amounts of land needed:
1. Public purchase . . 15%
2. Public action (easements and restrictions) . . 20%
3. Philanthropy 10%

Total by conventional methods 45%

Clearly, other methods must be found.

At that point we looked into the effects of the usual development process on land values — the upward push. If private developers got rezoning, their land would go up in value. If the association sought conservation restrictions, values on nearby lands would continue to rise.

Why not permit the association to share in the overall increase in land values, while at the same time getting land-use controls essential to the park? It was then estimated that with comparatively little seed money — $480,000 — the association could begin a land-banking operation. It would buy land, put conservation control on the valley lands, re-sell upland properties to developers and thus acquire funds for park maintenance. This proposal was accepted by the association.

But this was not enough. If the association is to use its data base, the information must be both accurate and up-to-the-minute. The need for computer capacity soon became obvious.

First, we had to map information for computer programming on a grid. To standardize, we chose the

GREENBELT: 300' Wide Minimum ✕ BUFFER: Restricted Coverage ✕ Controlled Development

1000 m. Universal Transverse Mercator grid (UTM) divided into 64 parts, each unit being 3.86 a. All information could then be mapped on this grid for computer input. (We later checked its accuracy against the ¼ a. grid used for site studies within the watershed. Our watershed grid was accurate within 90% of the site-specific grid.)

Land-banking with a computer information base is vital to the Wissahickon project. It is projected to break even after 4½ years and reach its goal of land control and conservation development in 25 years. By that time, the association will have obtained, controlled and replanned 3600 a. at an average cost of $10,000 per acre. After replanning, this land will be sold with a 30% restricted open space (1,080 a.) at an average of $14,000 per acre. These operations will result in a $4,000,000 profit.

This program requires the W.V.W.A. to become active in local leadership to plan and execute a total open-space program. At this point (March 1971) the association is investigating several sites, each of 100 a. or more, to initiate the regional plan. Let's look at the site-planning strategy involved for one of these 130 a. sites.

First, we evaluated conservation criteria as they applied to this site, mapping the restrictions on a ¼ a. site-specific grid. The resulting table shows that 25% of the site is minimally restricted, 28% moderately restricted, etc. (Minimum restriction means that buildings may

EVALUATION SYSTEM NO. 1: Including visual corridor

Feature	Wt.	Definition	Categories	Value	Total
Visual Corridor	5	Open contiguous area from ridge to ridge or interceding tree line (natural enclosure).	Views within property	10	50
			Views outside property	8	40
Cover	3	Tree association type, density, stability and enclosure capacity.	Forest - prime	8	24
			hedgerow - 2nd	6	18
Topography	4	Slopes highly susceptible to erosion (stream siltation) and increased runoff (flooding-water table recharge).	15% + - severe	8	32
			10-15% - moderate	6	24
Water	2	Natural flood and seasonal high water table conditions (natural reservoirs - water table indication).	0-6" SHWT	8	16
			0-18" SHWT	6	12
Soils	1	Prime agricultural land, soil structure susceptible to erosion by wind or water.	erosion - severe	6	6
			erosion - moderate	4	4

cover only up to 20% of that area; maximum means no more than one per cent site coverage.) The sum of allowable coverage for each level of restrictions indicates that 14.3 a. of this 130 a. site may be covered by buildings and other impervious cover.

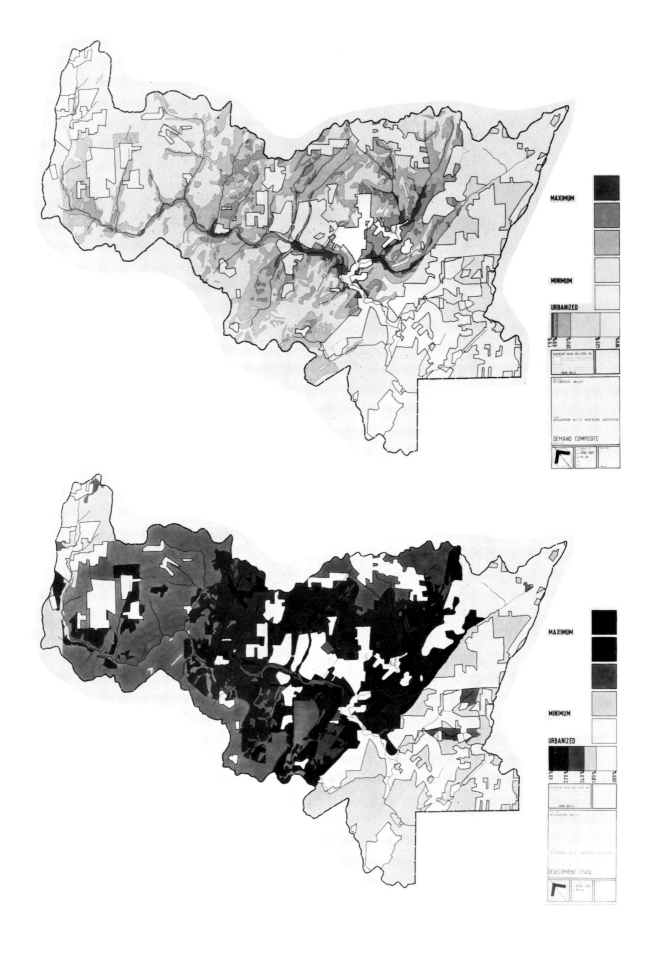

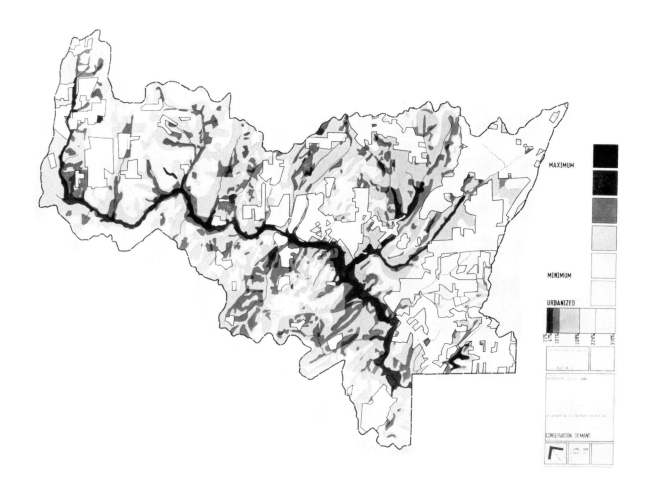

MAXIMUM

MINIMUM

URBANIZED

Development Impact Model

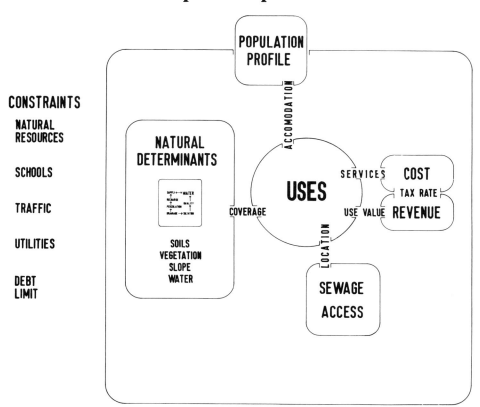

CONSTRAINTS

NATURAL
RESOURCES

SCHOOLS

TRAFFIC

UTILITIES

DEBT
LIMIT

POPULATION
PROFILE

NATURAL
DETERMINANTS

ACCOMODATION

USES

SERVICES

COST

TAX RATE

COVERAGE

USE VALUE

REVENUE

SOILS
VEGETATION
SLOPE
WATER

LOCATION

SEWAGE

ACCESS

USE-DENSITY-RETURN SUMMARY

No.	H.R.	G.A.	T.H.	S.F.	Density	Value
1	1233	—	—	—	9.5	$1,849,500
2	131	131	210	53	4.0	852,000
3	98	97	156	39	3.0	626,100
4	73	—	—	290	2.8	718,500
5	—	616	—	—	4.7	739,200
6	—	—	411	—	3.2	739,800
7	—	195	156	39	3.0	596,700
8	—	237	190	47	3.65	725,100
9	—	78	176	137	3.0	683,000
10	—	—	65	259	2.5	660,900
11	—	—	—	130	1.0	819,000

KEY EVALUATION

No.	Approval	Return	Marketability
1	Difficult		
2, 3, 4	Difficult		
5, 6	Difficult		
7	Possible	Lowest	Moderate
8	Difficult		
9	Possible	Moderate	Moderate
10	Easy	Low	Low
11	Easy	High	Lowest

ALLOWABLE COVERAGE FOR ALTERNATE USES BASED ON SITE ANALYSIS NO. 1.

Restrict. % area	Min. 25	Low 11	Mod. 28	High 29	Max. 7	Totals 100%
20%	33 ac. 6.6					
15%		14 ac. 2.1				
10%			36 ac. 3.6			
5%				38 ac. 1.9		
1%					9.0 ac. .09	

% cover	Gross acres x % cover =	130.0 acres
	Net acres of coverage =	14.3 acres

Having established that 14.3 a. is the maximum to be covered, we then calculated the number of units for those portions of the site, and the dollar return based on development by high-rise, garden apartments, townhouses, or single-family units. We found that high-rise units would bring the greatest return on the current market, but such exclusive development has the least likelihood of zoning approval at this time. We then evaluated various mixes in terms of marketability, dollar return, and local approval.

The table, Land-bank Profit Distribution, shows how we arrived at the most suitable mix. It respects the natural restrictions on the site, as do all the listed alternatives. It stands a good chance of approval because the municipality will reap a large tax profit. This tax advantage comes from the reduced number of children in townhouse and garden apartments, as well as from the decreased utility and road-service costs for cluster development. This chosen mix provides a moderate return to the developer, and includes a sufficient variety of housing types to be quickly marketable.

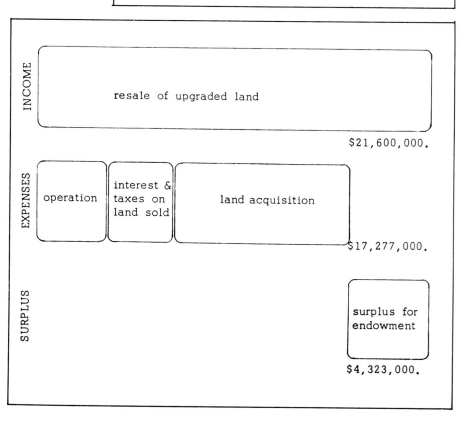

INCOME — resale of upgraded land — $21,600,000.

EXPENSES — operation | interest & taxes on land sold | land acquisition — $17,277,000.

SURPLUS — surplus for endowment — $4,323,000.

Thus this is a strategy which respects the existing natural systems of the site, as well as the economic systems of the community, and of the developer. From this beginning, the association has a site-evaluation program which may be implemented by the methods outlined above.

In summary, the W.V.W.A. is a citizens' group practicing private enterprise for a public purpose. It uses land-banking technique and computer capability to carry out an open-space-park program determined by an up-to-date regional information base. Its activities start from the realization that all concerned must participate with local government to get good development that implements their original conservation goals. Gains from this policy are measurable in the acres of greenspace preserved, and in the pleasures of future generations that can enjoy the park's woodland and the Wissahickon waters as they rush downstream.

One of the most familiar techniques and diagrams from American land-use planning of the 1960s is basic to the Wissahickon program: the grouping of cluster housing, and pooling of the remaining land for community open space.

SINGLE FAMILY

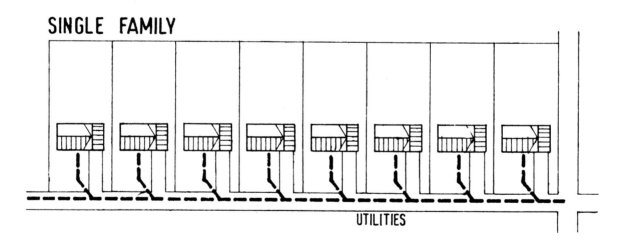

UTILITIES

TOWN HOUSES

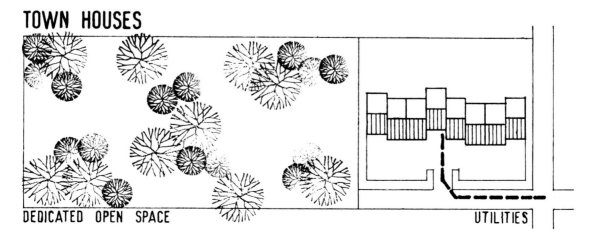

DEDICATED OPEN SPACE   UTILITIES

Early Warnings: The Trigger Effect of Upland Irrigation

By TITO PATRI, DAVID STREATFIELD and THOMAS INGMIRE

Suburban residents who irrigate their lawns have been the first intruders to exceed the water-carrying capacity of soils in the Santa Cruz Mountains of California, as reported by Patri, Streatfield and Ingmire in *Early Warning System.** Their analysis of the highly diverse, complex, and dynamic ecology of this region shows that suburban development . . . "has caused numerous problems in the destruction of watersheds. One example is the ubiquitous use of irrigated lawns which has introduced an excessive amount of imported water into a naturally semi-arid landscape which is adapted to long droughty periods in the summer. The soil is unable to absorb all the water and the surplus flows as direct runoff into streams and creeks, many of which are ephemeral. The additional water either changes these drainage channels into perennial water courses or else causes the growth of lush herbaceous and woody vegetation.

"In either case, the flood hazard can be greatly increased because the channel is unable to contain the winter flood waters. The additional volume of water then spreads over the flood plains at the foot of the hills. Since all flood plains are nearly level and present no obvious problems for building they are usually occupied by residential or other forms of development. Thus, what was originally conceived of as an improvement to the landscape in the form of beautification has added considerable hazard to a part of the community. This usually results in the creation of a Flood Control District which then builds flood-control structures and concrete channels.

"One extreme example of this particular problem is a golf course which is normally kept watered all the year round. The net effect is to create conditions similar to a paved surface in which there is little or no infiltration into the soil. In such instances streamflow and turbidity may be greatly increased.

"A further probable by-product of irrigation is the triggering of landslides. The water which does infiltrate into the soil considerably exceeds what would occur under natural conditions and can often act in concert with naturally stored ground water to trigger landslides. Landslides have been destructive in this manner by moving large quantities of soil and weathered rock downhill sometimes completely destroying structures in their path . . . The collapse of part of Potrero Hill in 1967 was due to the alignment of the Bayshore Freeway through the center of a very large landslide."

Postcript 1978 by Tito Patri

The original study of the Santa Cruz Mountains and San Luis Obispo County, California, under a Ford Foundation grant, involved light table overlay mapping techniques, but was also designed as a prototype to be used with computers. This is an important capability since the time investment in compiling base, natural resource and user interest pattern mapping and its interpretation in the design of various models of natural resource dynamics under differing potential land use and intensity patterns is considerable and costly. If a permanent, comprehensive data bank is desired, then the investment warrants an Early Warning design and computer capabilities. Early warning tests of the impacts of different development potential according to land-user attractiveness indicators and the resultant natural resource performance patterns can then be displayed easily and economically in graphic form. This is very important since many public agency planning departments are already overburdened with familiar tasks and, under normal circumstances, have trouble responding quickly to redevelopment proposals. There is precious little time to do light table analysis to create a data bank if retrieval is cumbersome as would be the case. As an EWS example, the Morro Bay Study is of particular relevance since runoff and sedimentation models were used to determine the quantitative impacts of future development patterns on the fragile coastal estuary which is presently under intense development pressure. All local governmental jurisdictions along California's coast are required by the state's 1976 Coastal Act to prepare Local Coastal Programs (resource use plans) and the EWS techniques as refined in the Morro Bay study including EWS data banks could become key tools helping to make such programs meaningful and enforceable. The basic strategy which could be used is illustrated in the accompanying diagram from the Morro Bay study.

*The Santa Cruz Mountains Regional Pilot Study EARLY WARNING SYSTEM. A report by Tito Patri, David C. Streatfield, and Thomas J. Ingmire, based on a study made possible by a grant from the Ford Foundation. Department of Landscape Architecture, College of Environmental Design, University of California, Berkeley. August, 1970.

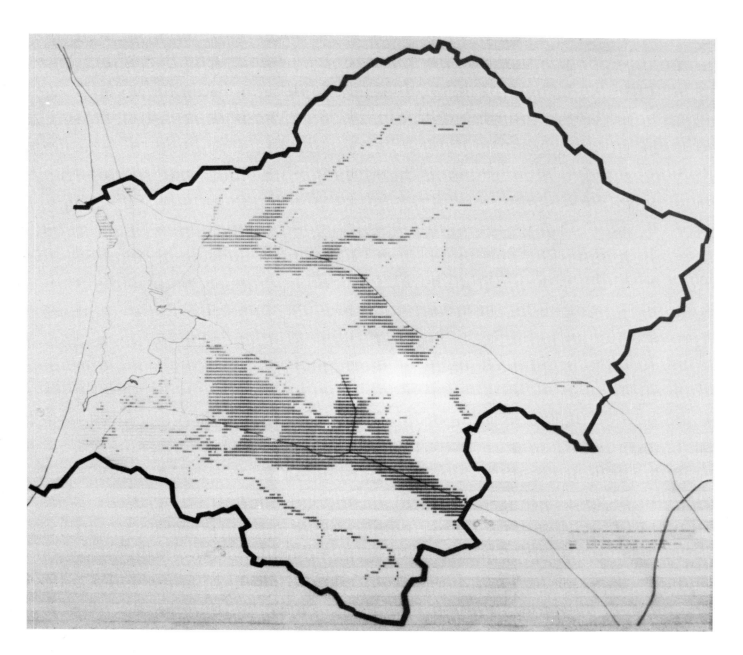

The computer maps out dark areas which depict development in conflict with ground water recharge areas in the Morro Bay study.

Disney's Other World: Mickey-Mousing with Florida's Water Supplies?

By WILLIAM H. GALCHUTT and WILLIAM J. WALLIS

Ten years ago sleepy central Florida could boast of several peaceful hamlets built around the lakes, swamps, and streams that pockmark the region. Its most important export was water, the life source for much of the state.

This crucial zone in central Florida includes the Central Florida Aquifer Recharge Area, the Green Swamp, and the headwaters of the Kissimmee River. The Central Florida Aquifer Recharge Area absorbs water into the Floridian Aquifer before its subterranean flow outward toward Tampa and St. Petersburg to the west; Ocala to the north, and Daytona, Melbourne and Titusville to the east.

The Green Swamp is the headwaters of all three major rivers that flow to the west coast of Florida — the Peace, Hillsborough and Withlacoochee rivers. It is also the headwaters of the Ocklawaha River, which flows northward into the St. John's River and then on to Jacksonville and the Atlantic Ocean.

The third water resource can be best described thus: from the Windermere chain of lakes flows Cypress Creek; which empties into Bay Lake; which feeds Reedy Creek; which flows southward 25 mi. to empty into Lake Hatchineha; which empties into Lake Kissimmee; which feeds the Kissimmee River; which flows southeast to Lake Okeechobee; which spills over the south rim into the Everglades sweeping across Palm Beach, Broward and Dade counties; while feeding the Biscayne Aquifer (water source for the cities of Fort Lauderdale and Miami); and finally flowing through the Everglades National Park and out into Florida Bay and the Gulf of Mexico

It was precisely at this critical

ecozone — within the confines of the Kissimmee headwaters region and within a short distance of the Green Swamp and the Central Florida Aquifer Recharge Area — that Walt Disney Productions secretly assembled 27,000 a. for Disney World. Cautiously they proceeded, so that local land prices were not upset before the giant parcel was pieced together at a low price, said to be $185 per acre. The storm clouds began to build over Orlando.

The first and loudest thunderclap pealed through Florida skies when Disney announced construction plans for a $400 million amusement park, larger and better than its counterpart in Anaheim, California. The intensity of that storm has not subsided since; it continues to rumble ominously on.

Disney officials are not entirely to blame for the resulting chaos in central Florida. They had warned that 10 million visitors were expected in the first year of operation . . . that huge, unprecedented traffic tie-ups would come if the transportation situation were not improved upon. Their warnings were largely unheard. Little more than bad publicity and minor improvements came from this: the resurfacing of two roads and the initial paving of two others. The Reedy Creek Improvement District was established by the Florida legislature, creating separate jurisdictional power over the giant parcel controlled by the Disney crowd. This was necessary to accomplish the construction of certain portions that were far in advance of the Southern Standard Building Codes, as well as to give the Disney organization full sway over their property. It effectively removed them from county and city jurisdictions.

The adverse publicity had little effect in the long run. When Walt Disney World opened to insignificant crowds, relaxing the city of Orlando, the word was soon out that the traffic mess hadn't materialized. So Floridians and tourists gathered up the kids and headed for the attraction.

Gradually the crowds grew closer to capacity daily as news media communicated the story of this fantastic playground of plastic and artificiality. On Monday, October 25, the long-awaited official Grand

Opening Day of Walt Disney World was held, followed by a national TV broadcast of festivities the following Sunday. Crowds began to swell and finally the bubble burst. Thanksgiving weekend of 1971 shall not be forgotten by thousands of frustrated Florida motorists. The *St. Petersburg Times* called it a "30 mile mousetrap." Disney World gates were slammed shut at noon. Capacity had been reached for the first time. Now Florida realized what it would be like for years hence. Thousands were stranded on Interstate 4 in bumper-to-bumper traffic 15 mi. eastward toward Orlando, and 15 mi. westward toward Tampa-St. Petersburg. The situation was worse over the Christmas holidays.

It was only then that Florida "discovered" what any map would have shown — the total lack of alternate routes. John Volpe, Secretary of the

U.S. Department of Transportation, estimated that it would cost upwards of $150 million to unsnarl the traffic with new highway links and mass transit lines. The public would have to foot the bill, equal to almost half the price of the original Disney attraction.

The Magic Kingdom has not come out of this chaos untarnished. Stormy sessions between Disney officials and the Orange County Commission are becoming the rule in Orlando. On April 7, 1972, Disney officials asked for the widening and straightening of their two employee entrance roads. When told the situation was under study by the commission, the Disney spokesman retorted: "Gentlemen, how are we to get something done? I should have brought a tennis ball." When he asked what the Disney crowd could do to help this situation he was

Night scene of Main Street, opposite top, at Walt Disney World. Opposite center, Orlando, with Interstate 4, right. Disney traffic jams have stretched 30 mi. east and west. Doomed grove, opposite below, surrounded by theme park parking lot. State Road 535, below, a crooked farm road, is one of two inadequate employee entrances overloaded daily. Nearby, a mobile-home community.

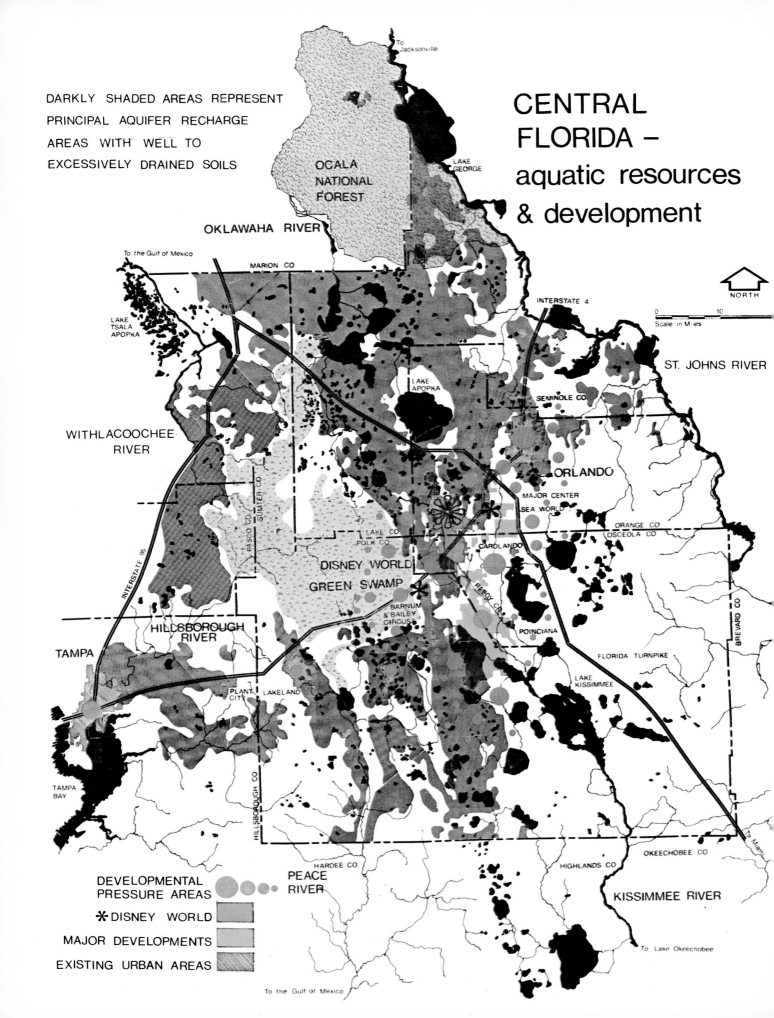

CENTRAL
FLORIDA –
aquatic resources
& development

DARKLY SHADED AREAS REPRESENT
PRINCIPAL AQUIFER RECHARGE
AREAS WITH WELL TO
EXCESSIVELY DRAINED SOILS

DEVELOPMENTAL
PRESSURE AREAS
* DISNEY WORLD
MAJOR DEVELOPMENTS
EXISTING URBAN AREAS

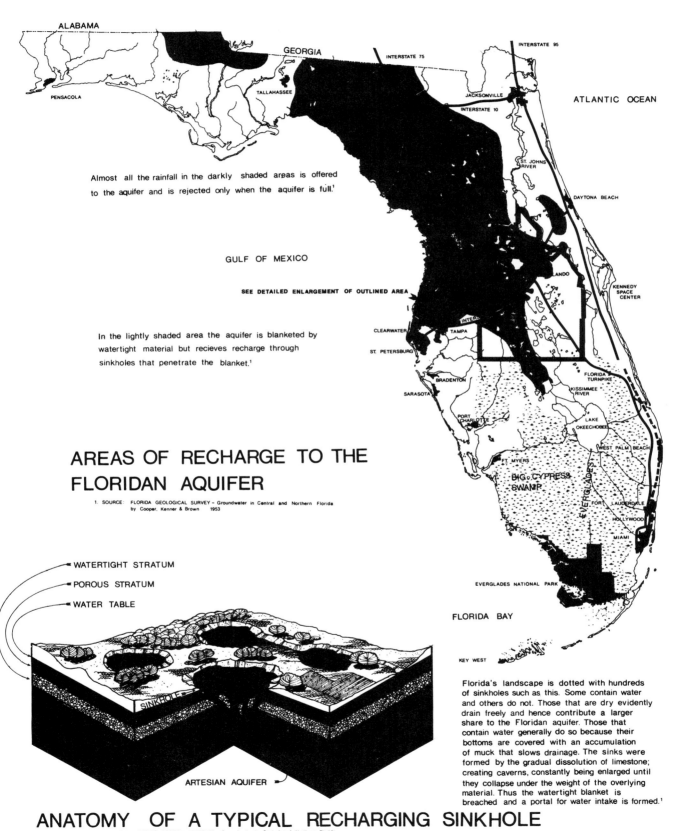

ALABAMA

GEORGIA

INTERSTATE 75

INTERSTATE 95

PENSACOLA

TALLAHASSEE

JACKSONVILLE

ATLANTIC OCEAN

INTERSTATE 10

Almost all the rainfall in the darkly shaded areas is offered to the aquifer and is rejected only when the aquifer is full.[1]

ST. JOHNS RIVER

DAYTONA BEACH

GULF OF MEXICO

ORLANDO

KENNEDY SPACE CENTER

SEE DETAILED ENLARGEMENT OF OUTLINED AREA

In the lightly shaded area the aquifer is blanketed by watertight material but recieves recharge through sinkholes that penetrate the blanket.[1]

CLEARWATER

TAMPA

ST. PETERSBURG

FLORIDA TURNPIKE

BRADENTON

KISSIMMEE RIVER

SARASOTA

PORT CHARLOTTE

LAKE OKEECHOBEE

AREAS OF RECHARGE TO THE FLORIDAN AQUIFER

1. SOURCE: FLORIDA GEOLOGICAL SURVEY – Groundwater in Central and Northern Florida
   by Cooper, Kenner & Brown   1953

WEST PALM BEACH

FT. MYERS

BIG CYPRESS SWAMP

EVERGLADES

FORT LAUDERDALE

HOLLYWOOD

MIAMI

WATERTIGHT STRATUM
POROUS STRATUM
WATER TABLE

EVERGLADES NATIONAL PARK

FLORIDA BAY

KEY WEST

SINKHOLE

ARTESIAN AQUIFER

Florida's landscape is dotted with hundreds of sinkholes such as this. Some contain water and others do not. Those that are dry evidently drain freely and hence contribute a larger share to the Floridan aquifer. Those that contain water generally do so because their bottoms are covered with an accumulation of muck that slows drainage. The sinks were formed by the gradual dissolution of limestone; creating caverns, constantly being enlarged until they collapse under the weight of the overlying material. Thus the watertight blanket is breached and a portal for water intake is formed.[1]

ANATOMY OF A TYPICAL RECHARGING SINKHOLE

ADAPTED FROM A SIMILAR SECTION FOUND IN – Groundwater in Central and Northern Florida

Walt Disney World Theme Park, looking east.

answered by a commissioner: "Write a check." After this suggestion was turned aside, another commissioner sputtered, "Many county residents have been waiting 10 to 12 years for completion of their secondary road projects. Some of them would take exception if we re-aligned priorities for someone who deliberately decided to use inadequate facilities" (State Road 535 and Reams Road). It should be noted that State Road 535 is no more than a crooked country farm road. Congestion on it will be unbearable when the five hotels at Lake Buena Vista open late in 1972.

The roadway proposal was attacked by local conservationists because of the development that would accompany it, causing incorrigible damage to the Central Florida Aquifer Recharge Area in that vicinity. At that point, State Senator Ralph Poston Sr. (D-Miami), chairman of the Senate Transportation Committee, retorted that he "was elected to serve the people and not the birds and the alligators" — as though to say that protection of the direct freshwater source used by Tampa, St. Petersburg, Lakeland, Winter Haven, Clearwater, as well as

the indirect water source for Jacksonville and Miami-Ft. Lauderdale, was less important to the residents of these cities than it is to the birds and the alligators.

Immediate warnings came from the Disney officials and others that unless development is restricted to the north of the Disney parcel, the downstream area of Reedy Creek (the site of Poinciana, a new development by GAC, and Kissimmee) will eventually face serious flooding.

Will this warning also go unheeded as was the last one? The greatest danger comes not from Disney alone, but from all the supporting development that will inevitably surround the Disney property.

Two more gigantic attractions have announced plans since Disney: Barnum and Bailey will construct "the world's largest permanent circus," and "Sea World" is already under construction in the area. Massive convention facilities are planned at Carolando, directly across from the entry road into Disney World. Major Center, 13 mi. north, will build "a city of hotels"

while the Lake Buena Vista area on Disney property sports four new highrise hotels. Literally thousands of smaller resort projects, hotels, motels, hot dog stands and filling stations are either planned or under construction in the area. Land development projects are also springing up. GAC plans two in the area, Poinciana and River Ranch.

Recently the property owners surrounding Disney incorporated to form the Land of Oz, Inc. The intent of the corporation reads as follows from their membership application:

"To study, develop and promote the planning of an environmentally sound, economically viable community, protected to the greatest possible extent against damages to the natural resources of the area, providing the maximum benefit to landowners of Lake, Orange, Osceola and Polk Counties, Florida."

Those are big words. To back them up with action is difficult anywhere, and especially here.

The corporation president has been quoted as saying: "Some of them (planners) think we'll have a bust after this boom — that we're building too many hotel rooms. But they ain't seen nothing yet."

Utilities will prove to be the greatest problem to the Land of Oz members: "It is obvious that to let each property owner dig his well and put in his own sewage treatment plant is the wrong way to go about it, from the standpoint both of ecology and money. The land, 309 sq. mi. of it, lies over the Floridian Aquifer, the critical water recharge area in Central Florida."

Another Land of Oz member, Frank Malfa, is building a Holiday Inn, franchised Trav-L-Park next to astronaut John Glenn's Holiday Inn franchised hotel facility. There are three such Holiday Inn franchises planned on Route 192 alone. Mr. Malfa, treasurer of the Land of Oz corporation, has said:

"We don't want another South Orange Blossom Trail, with honky-tonks and topless joints, or another West Colonial Drive, with signs so thick that you can't read them. Either we'll have planning or we'll have chaos."

Route 192, "the main drag of the Land of Oz," is off to a good chaotic start. Mr. Malfa has erected the first sign for his Trav-L-Park, and there will be at least three Holiday Inn signs.

Speculation has reached the point of frenzy. One Milwaukee mortgage firm, obviously disturbed by the number of applications from the area, called the East Central Florida Regional Planning Council in Winter Park to ask: "We've got five or six applications from the area. We know all about Walt Disney world, but is it really that big?"

Jack Glatting, director of the council, has said, "In the past three months there have been daily announcements of new projects in the study area (four corners of Orange, Osceola, Polk and Lake counties). All evidence at this time suggests that this trend will continue for some time."

Within all this chaos the Orange County Commission, undoubtedly the strongest in all counties involved, has tried to "avert" a crisis situation that already exists. It adopted a stringent land-use policy for its affected areas, but in so doing condemned the entire portion of the county to single-family residences at a density of one per acre, and to "planned development," thus increasing sprawl problems in the area. Since this area is so ecologically important as an aquifer recharge area it would be wiser to leave the more critical areas undeveloped.

Once again, the promise of an expanded tax base preceded development. Once again it has proved to be a falsehood. The cost of living in Orlando has shot up. Disney employees earn around $5600 per year, an income category that pays less taxes than the urban services it demands. Most residential construction in the Orlando area will be in the $30,000 range, far above the budget of thousands of new Disney employees. Disney World has proved itself to be an economic drain on its locality, which has little power over it since it was removed from their jurisdictional and taxation powers.

The true scope of this can be revealed only under the banner of planning on a state scale, since the impact of this development truly crosses all county, municipal, and regional boundaries.

Had we carefully planned the location of this one attraction, as well as its services and environs, we could have avoided the headaches of today and the problems of tomorrow in central Florida.

How many more Disney Worlds can we allow, before we begin to plan rationally for them; before they are located and constructed? As this is written, the city of Jacksonville has acted to approve another Disney World-type deal, specifically a giant industrial district proposed* by Westinghouse-Tenneco for building package offshore nuclear facilities — to be built in the salt marshes of the St. John's River. This "paves" the way for 11,000 employees, 1000 more than Disney World, with an impact surely of similar nature.

How many more, before states begin to buy up lands ahead of the speculative price increases? The state of Florida could have then afforded to sell developable parcels to the inflated market, and with the sales monies could have afforded all the necessary improvements, while maintaining total control over the situation. They could have then planned rationally, conserving the important ecological areas and controlling the quality, and scope of the surrounding development.

Until this happens, all of central Florida and the rich tourist regions to the south exist under the threat of pollution and irremediable damage to the state's greatest aquifer — an example of speculative anti-planning at its gaudiest and most dangerous.

---

*and later abandoned. (Ed.)

Ponding Against the Storm

By ALFRED OBRIST

Damming a Narrow Ravine

At the suburban Community General Hospital, in Syracuse, New York, adequate storm water coordination had never been attempted. In fact, the natural water route had been blocked by an athletic field and high school.

The only existing outlet from this 15 a. site was a highway culvert which could accept an additional load of only five cubic feet per second (cfs.). Since runoff from the roof and paved area was estimated at 57 cfs. on the basis of a 50-year storm curve, some viable solution had to be found to prevent flooding and erosion.

We calculated that a pond of 202,000 cubic foot retention capacity could store peak flow and allow storm waters slowly to disperse by damming a narrow ravine, using materials from the site. Tests indicated that the soil had over a 20% content that would pass a 200 mesh sieve. This silt and clay, when compacted to a density of 95%, would be suitable. The outlet was designed to limit overflow to five cfs. An emergency spillway was also provided. The maximum impoundment is eight feet. However, since esthetic considerations were important, a minimum water level is retained in the pond at all times. Seeding, planting of the slopes, and retaining all the existing vegetative cover possible were prime design concepts.

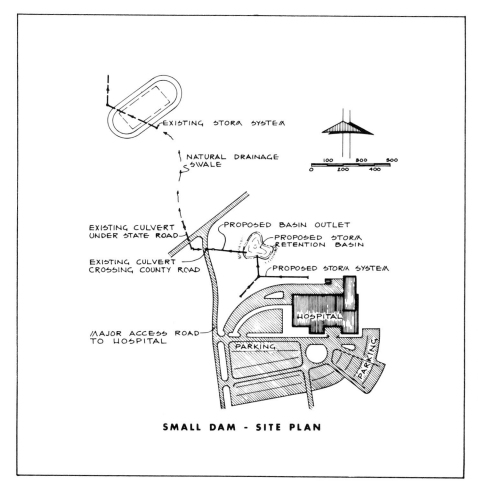

SMALL DAM - SITE PLAN

EXISTING STORM SYSTEM

NATURAL DRAINAGE SWALE

EXISTING CULVERT UNDER STATE ROAD

PROPOSED BASIN OUTLET

PROPOSED STORM RETENTION BASIN

EXISTING CULVERT CROSSING COUNTY ROAD

PROPOSED STORM SYSTEM

MAJOR ACCESS ROAD TO HOSPITAL

HOSPITAL

PARKING

PARKING

100 200 300 400 500 0

Site plan, left, shows relationship of Community General Hospital to existing storm system and retention pond which allows stormwater to disperse gradually.

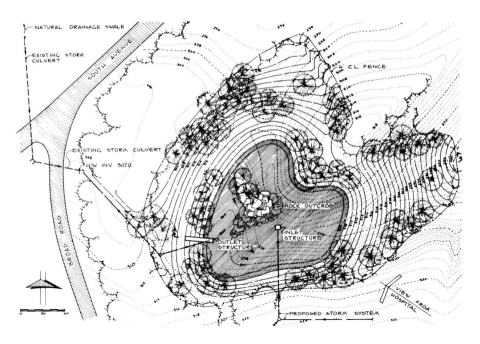

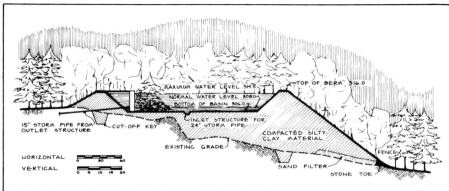

Detail, left, and cross-section, center, of hospital pond area demonstrate how it receives stormwater and allows it slowly to run off. Pond for Adirondack High School, bottom, holds stormwater for a short time.

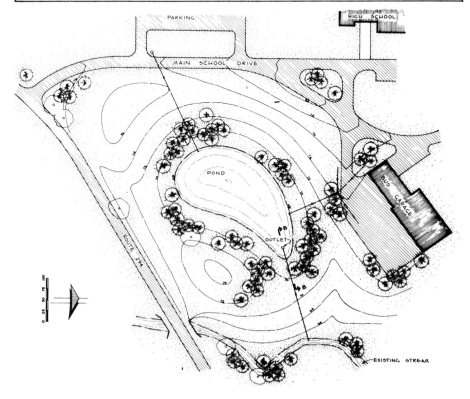

Rising Above the Flood

At Adirondack High School in Booneville, New York, an .82 a. pond retains the peak flow of storm waters before they reach an adjoining stream. The existing high water table keeps the pond filled to its normal level.

Storm water discharge from school and paved areas was calculated at 18.4 cfs., retained in the pond for a short time avoiding the usual result of loading the stream with a heavy surge. The outlet limits the rise to 6-12 in. during a heavy rainfall.

Excavated earth from the pond was used to raise the level of the athletic fields above flood level of the adjacent stream. Thus, the pond solves a storm water problem and also provides students with an opportunity for nature study, ice skating in winter and visual enhancement.

Stemming the Overload

Syracuse's Loretto Rest Geriatrics Center is located on a sloping plateau bounded on the west by a steep hillside with residential properties below. The hillside has several springs feeding a creek which passes through these properties. The creek has a flooding history; any additional storm water would only aggravate the situation. It was imperative, therefore, to avoid any further load.

A stormwater sewer connection was available, but since economics dictated the design be based on a 10-year storm curve, some accommodation was necessary to avoid any overflow. The stormwater runoff was calculated as 16.2 cfs. based on a 10-year storm curve. It was felt that protection based on a 25-year storm curve would be more realistic.

When the sewers are overloaded, stormwater would back up at the inlets, would run overland and eventually reach the lowest portion of the site. Here, a temporary ponding basin was designed for 12,000 cu. ft. based on the difference in runoff between the 10 and 25 year storm curves.

In severe storms excess water from the paved areas would eventually reach this shallow basin and be held until it could drain via the normal storm system. The basin appears to be merely a grassy bowl with planting along its edges.

Creek flooding was stopped at Loretto Rest Geriatrics Center, below, by grassy bowl which temporarily ponds rushing rainwater.

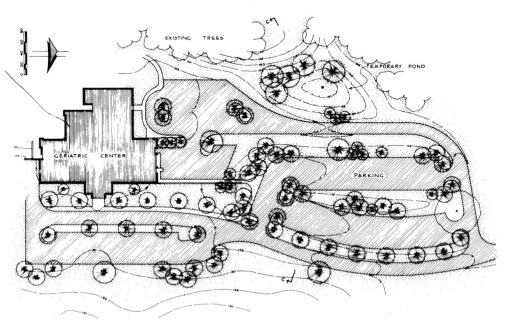

TEMPORARY POND - SITE PLAN

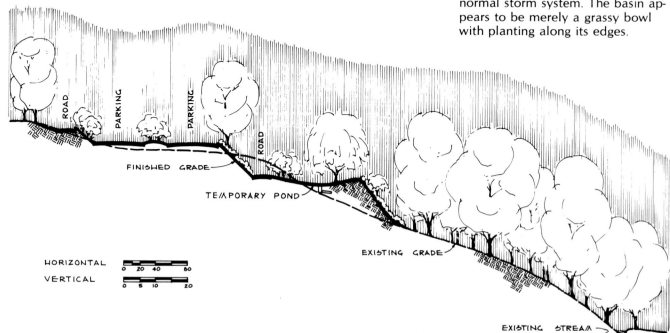

HORIZONTAL

VERTICAL

Architectural credits: King & King, Community General Hospital, Syracuse, and Adirondack High School, Booneville; Finnegan, Lyon, Colburn, Loretto Rest Geriatrics Center, Syracuse.

Drainage Plans with Environmental Benefits

By HERBERT G. POERTNER

The Finger Lakes Solution

Reliable flood protection and satisfactory drainage are extremely important to Earth City, a new town being built in the Missouri River Bottoms, St. Louis. Flood protection is provided by a levee built by the U.S. Army Corps of Engineers. Drainage must be provided not only for the runoff from the project area, but also for runoff from hillside streams which discharge across the bottoms. Providing for drainage of stormwater without providing storage was found to be uneconomical because of the large facilities required to handle peak flows.

The developers of Earth City, Missouri, incorporated a chain of detention ponds surrounded by open space in the initial planning of this new 1500 a. (6.07 mm.^{2}) "total community."

Several plans for detention storage were studied and a system of interconnected, oblong finger lakes having a total area of 51 a. (206 km.^{2}) was selected. This drainage system will cost $2 million exclusive of land costs — resulting in a considerable savings when compared to the $5 million cost estimated for a system without storage provisions.

Using design criteria of the Corps of Engineers, the consulting engineers (Horner & Shifrin, Inc.) chose a 15-year storm for the design of the interior drainage system, and a 30-year storm coincident with the 19.5 ft. (5.9 m.) stage of the Missouri River for the drainage system to the River. At this river stage, the water must be pumped from the lakes into the river. Below this state, the lakes will drain by gravity. Normally, the lakes will be maintained by elevation 433 ft. (132 m.), and the maximum water elevation will be 439 ft.

(134 m.). At this elevation a maximum of 42 ft. (12.8 m.) of shoreline width would be flooded in residential areas, and about 45 hours would be required to drain the stored runoff.

Besides providing for storage of stormwater runoff, the lakes will enhance the esthetics of the community and serve for boating, fishing and passive recreation. The lakes will also provide a visual corridor between the central urban plaza and the outlying areas.

Plaza and Rooftop Ponding

In the planning of its 80 a. Skyline Urban Renewal Project in downtown Denver, the Denver Urban Renewal Authority (DURA) took action in 1970 to require private redevelopers to temporarily detain (on-site) rainfall directly falling on their properties. The purpose was to reduce the surcharging of the storm drainage system in the downtown area until tributary areas have been drained.

The DURA criteria described two distinct types of ponding: one includes elevated plazas, pedestrian malls, arcades, and other extended flat areas in which a minor amount of ponding at designed locations would not cause a serious inconvenience. For these areas, the design assumed a rate of runoff of one inch (2.5 cm.) per hour, which should result in a maximum depth of ponding during a 10-year return frequency storm of approximately 3/4 in. (1.91 cm.) of water.

The second type of ponding is on rooftops, parking lots, structures, and other areas where a greater depth can be tolerated. The design assumes a run-off rate of 1/2 in. (1.27 cm.) per hour which, during the 10-year return frequency storm, would result in a ponding depth of approximately one inch. During the 100-year return frequency storm the ponding depth would not exceed three inches (7.62 cm.).

DURA is also approaching complete separation of sewers in the redeveloped areas, and the installation of a storm sewer system.

The complete 25-story office tower of the Prudential Insurance Company in the Skyline area was designed to detain rainfall on its roof and plaza area. A specially designed ponding ring for rainfall-detention was installed surrounding each roof-drain conductor head. It is designed to operate in accordance with DURA drainage criteria.

The Park Central Bank and Office Complex in the Skyline renewal area incorporates rooftop ponding in plazas. Detention ponding is also being provided in the adjacent depressed parkway.

All other new construction in the project will include provisions for detention storage of rainfall wherever feasible. Some buildings' flat roofs were modified to hold rainfall and were permitted to remain when the area was razed.

All this was done at extremely low cost and with little inconvenience to land developers and the public.

The Ski and Skate Retention Basin
Melvina Ditch, the detention reservoir constructed by the Metropolitan Sanitary District of Greater Chicago at a cost of $892,000, is in a flood-prone area with particularly heavy damage to lands downstream of the site selected. This project is unique, not only in terms of its size and multipurpose nature but because it has a pumping station rather than gravity outflow from the reservoir. This basin, 21 ft. (6.4 m.) deep,

covers 11½ a. (46.5 km.²) and has a capacity of 165 acre-feet (204 km.³)of storage. It serves a principally residential four sq. mi. (10.4 mm.²) drainage area, and was designed to accommodate a 10-year storm. Actually, it is the 100 cfs. (2.83 m3/5) discharge capacity of the downstream ditch which limits the potential of the reservoir. Planned improvements of this ditch and an additional reservoir upstream will enable this system to accommodate the runoff from a 100-year storm.

The basin was dug out of a clay soil which provides a tight seal. The bottom is grass, and the grassy sides with 4:1 slopes are enclosed with an eight foot (2.44 m.) chain link fence. The pumping station, located at one corner of the basin, contains three 66 cfs. (1.87 m3/5) pumps and two 7½ cfs. (0.21) low-flow pumps. These pumps could empty the full basin in 12 hours; however, because of downstream flow limitations, a period of 24 hours is currently required. After most storms (which do not fill the basin), the basin is pumped dry in four to six hours.

Storm sewers draining the tributary area carry the runoff into the basin through a concrete inlet structure located at a corner of the basin, remote from the pumping station. Upon being discharged from the inlet into a sloping concrete chute, the flow is directed to a 100 ft. (30.5 m.) by 200 ft. (61.0 m.) concrete-paved area installed to prevent erosion of the basin bottom. At low flow, the runoff drops through a grate in the inlet structure and is guided to the pumping station through a 60 in. diameter underground pipe. This allows low flows to by-pass the basin, leaving it dry during low-flow periods, thus

enhancing the multi-purpose of the facility.

A reverse-crowned concrete roadway, located in the bottom of the basin, extends from the basin inlet to the intake of the pumping station. This serves as a roadway for maintenance trucks and as an erosion prevention channel for runoff inflows that exceed the low-flow capacity of the underground pipeline. When the basin begins to fill, the paved areas become completely submerged; with further increase in basin water depth, the inlet structure is also submerged.

The detention reservoir was designed to serve as a recreation facility in addition to its primary function of reducing local flooding. Steps were constructed down the basin side slope. Winter activities include tobogganing and skiing on a large earth mound formed in one corner of the basin using excavated materials. The concrete paved area (erosion-prevention section at inlet) is flooded during winter months as an ice-skating rink. During summer, it is used for volleyball, basketball and general play. All recreational activities are supervised by the South Stickney Township Park District under an agreement between the park and sanitary districts for use of the property for recreational programs.

The reservoir was built as part of a cooperatively financed general drainage improvement in the area. When completed, the improvement will consist of: (1) storm sewers upstream of the reservoir provided by the South Stickney Township Road District at a cost of $4.5 million; (2) the Melvina Detention Reservoir and downstream channel modifications provided by the

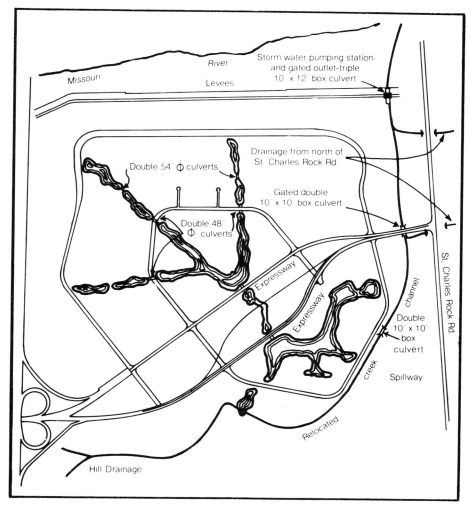

At Earth City, Missouri, Missouri River bottomland was developed with intersecting finger lakes providing stormwater detention. The lakes also improve aesthetics, offer recreation and separate the urban plaza from the rest of the community.

detention basin cost about one million dollars less than it would have cost to construct large storm sewers to an adequate outlet located about two miles (3.22 km.) away.

Conclusion

The general public, as well as public officials, planners, drainage engineers and land developers, should develop an understanding for the need to provide storage space for the runoff that inevitably results from storms. They must be convinced that the developments in metropolitan areas should be guided in part by decisions regarding stormwater drainage and flood control. On-site detention of runoff is a very effective means of handling runoff in upstream areas without adding to downstream flooding. Appreciable cost savings can be realized and, often, esthetics improved and recreation facilities provided in the bargain.

Sanitary District at a cost of $1.9 million; and (3) downstream channel modifications provided by the Village of Oak Lawn, at a cost of $500,000. Without these improvements, programs for street paving with curb and gutter, elimination of roadside ditches, and general upgrading of neighborhood conditions would have been impossible.

Since completion of the Melvina Detention Reservoir, no flooding has occurred downstream or upstream of the facility. Recently, this basin took runoff from a 10-year storm lasting six hours, with the pumps inoperable. There was no downstream damage. It is estimated that this

The Power of Water in Planning
A New Synthesis for Regulating Land Development

By ROGER WELLS

The Problem

Some years ago our firm (Rahenkamp, Sachs, Wells and Associates) began to look for ways to use natural systems in the design of large scale residential projects. We sought a method which would employ each site to its best natural advantage — a technique that would get the most out of nature without destroying it. Ultimately we became convinced that the behavior of water is the best indicator of successful conservation. If the drainage systems of a watershed have been managed properly, erosion, siltation, and flooding should not be problems. If provision has been made to recharge the water table, water resources will be protected and natural vegetation will thrive. In short, good conservation requires planning with the context of the natural hydrologic cycle.

This is easier said than done. The natural hydrologic cycle is a complex mechanism affected by weather, slope, soils, vegetation, geology and surface drainage. Precipitation, which activates the cycle, can pass through it in a number of forms. The real question for the land planner is how to use this dynamic model as a design guide.

The critical factor is direct run-off, the water that runs directly into the surface drainage system without seeping into the ground. Excessive direct runoff will cause erosion, down-stream flooding, and silting, and may also mean less base runoff, a lower water table, and irregular surface drainage flow. Direct runoff, which is usually 15% or less in forest areas, is increased by

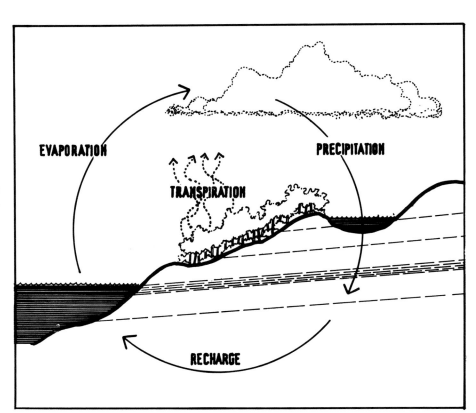

Hydrologic cycle

buildings, driveways, and roads. In cities, where these kinds of impervious surfaces predominate, direct runoff can account for 90% of the annual precipitation. To reduce direct runoff, impervious surfaces must be regulated in accordance with a site's natural capacities.

Standard zoning and subdivision ordinances do not adequately regulate impervious surfaces. A town's concern is with quality, but its codes regulate quantities in a fixed and absolute manner so as to protect the landowner and his right to equal treatment under the law. Expressway-sized roads are the norm, with piped runoff which is passed on downstream as someone else's problem. Faster moving and more destructive runoff is the result. We believe current zoning laws do not do much to recognize environmental constraints and represent a narrow reading of public and private interests. To replace these laws with environmentally sensitive legislation will require an efficient and objective way of quantifying change in the natural hydrologic cycle. What we see as necessary is a model which sets specific limits to the amount of impervious cover — houses, driveways and streets — permitted on any site and which is based firmly on the capacities of that site. We consider our cover model a step forward in this direction.

The Method
The work of the United States Soil Conservation Service made feasible the design of a cover model for national use on a uniform basis. The SCS has standardized data classifying 4000 soils in the United States and has developed the formulae necessary to calculate both annual direct runoff and peak discharge. Working with these tools, the necessary site specific information, and a properly programmed computer, the planner can generate coverage coefficients for the site, municipality, or watershed.

The concept is simple:

1. Lands with various natural and artificial cover absorb rainfall differently while the remainder runs off. The quantity of annual direct runoff generated by given vegetation and soil conditions can be determined according to reasonably reliable equations based on local rainfall intensity and frequency.

2. Slope and watershed size do not affect the amount of annual runoff. They do affect its speed, however, and, therefore, the peak discharge from the watershed. If the model is to be an effective flood control device, these are essential ingredients.

3. To relate the model to existing zoning controls, a legally defensible minimum standard for increased runoff as the result of proposed construction is necessary. This will assure the protection of the landowners' constitutional rights but allow a regulation system that can react flexibly to the variety of nature.

In combination, these three factors will generate coverage coefficients. The fact that the data and calculation techniques upon which this model is based have been standardized by a widely respected government agency, in our view,

establishes a firm base for performance-standard ordinances and progressive court decisions.

The Formulae
The basic SCS formula used in the cover model is the direct runoff equation

$$Q = \frac{(P - .2S)^2}{P + .8S}$$

where Q is the quantity of runoff, P is the amount of precipitation and S is the maximum water retention potential as defined by soil type and vegetative cover. Since "S" values can have a dramatic range, the SCS has assigned each possible combination of ground cover and soil type a curve number (CN) which is an index of the infiltration potential (S) of the soil-cover complex. For the convenience of calculation, tabulation, etc., CNs are on a 0 to 100 scale with actual values as low as near zero (almost no direct runoff — deep gravel) and as high as 98 (almost complete direct runoff — impervious).

For use in the cover model the SCS equation is solved repeatedly substituting for "P" annual rainfall data and for "S" the values corresponding to each curve number encountered in site analysis. This process generates Q or direct runoff value for each curve number as shown on page 26, top.

To establish coverage constraints, it must be determined to what degree new development will be permitted to increase the Q values. Clearly, this issue involves some elements of social choice and cannot be resolved satisfactorily without reference to existing legal controls. For the Wissahickon Watershed Study an increment for run-off values was developed on the basis of Federal Housing Administration minimum dwelling size standards. Based on these standards including minimum assumptions for accessory paving, an impervious cover of about six percent on a one acre lot appeared to be the bottom limit. Since current local zoning law seemed to guarantee the landowner the right to build one unit on any one acre lot, the Wissahickon model took six percent coverage as the absolute minimum it could enforce (ex-

clusive of wetlands which are now protected by floodplain zoning and coastal wetland laws). Any lower limit might amount to confiscation. Practically, this meant a six percent coverage increase on the most restrictive sites: soil-vegetation conditions with a curve number of 80 (low retention potential) and buildable slopes in excess of 25%. The annual runoff increment caused by this intensity of development under these conditions was taken as the increment permissable throughout the study area.

This process is represented by the equation

$$X_{t_M CN_M} = \frac{Hm}{Dm}$$

where X is the acceptable increment in runoff caused by the minimum house size (Hm) at the minimum density (Dm) on the most restrictive slope (t_M) and soil-cover conditions (CN_M).

Once determined, the acceptable increment is added to each of the annual runoff values (Q) which were derived using the direct runoff equation. Each new incremented "Q" value corresponds to a new CN called CN'.

With CN and CN' known, establishment of a cover constraint is a simple matter. The operation

$$\frac{CN' - CN}{98 - CN} \times 100$$

(identified as the coverage calculation) renders a coverage constraint for a given CN on a 0-3% slope.

To adjust the coverage coefficient to steeper slopes, four slope adjustment factors derived from the SCS peak discharge charts are used. Slope has no significant effect on the actual amount of runoff generated which is a function of the soil-vegetation types and quantity of rainfall. Steeper slopes do increase the speed of runoff, however, as measured by peak discharge from a watershed. SCS has measured and tabulated peak discharge by field observation. Using a 1000 a. watershed and a three-inch rainfall as typical, we calculated the percentage of increase in peak discharge for the CNs as slopes became steeper. For each slope category an adjustment factor was identified by averaging the percentage of increase in peak discharge for selected curve number values.

This process roughly indicates that water will run off a 25 + % slope about 3.2 times faster than it will off 0-3% slopes and with proportionally less speed off the intermediate slopes. Cover on steeper slopes is restricted accordingly by the adjustment factors as shown right.

An Example

The following graphic series depicts the mapping process we go through in developing our cover limitation numbers for any given site. The example shown represents approximately 247 a. This has been divided into 64 data cells of 3.86 a. each. We use the Universal Trans Mercator system as a standard to insure future data collection compatibility and ease of reference. A nested or halved system permits data analysis to be in keeping with the level of the project. With interlocking and compatible systems, state-wide planning could become a reality. We have found the four acre cell to be sufficiently accurate in most large-scale public or private projects unless unusually diversified

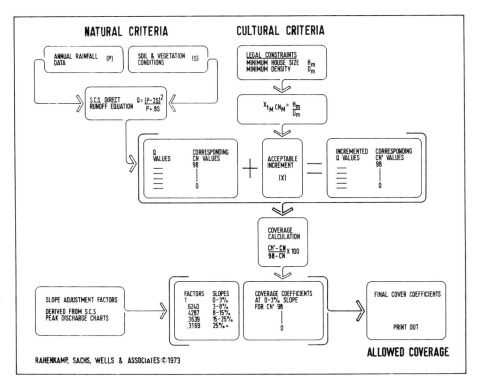

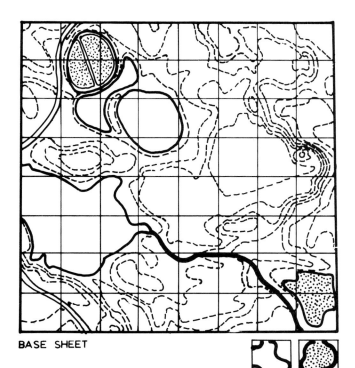

BASE SHEET

SURFACE WATER BOGS

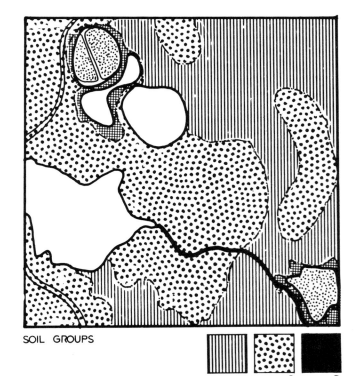

SOIL GROUPS

B   C   D

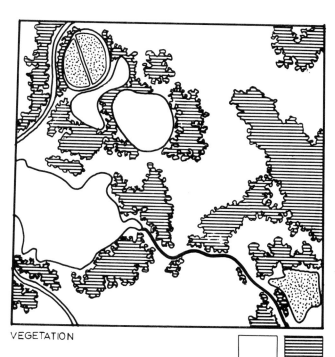

VEGETATION

	GRASSLANDS	FOREST

FIG. 3-C

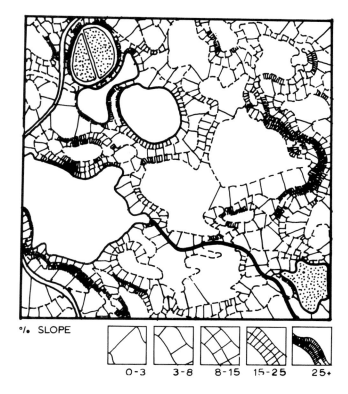

% SLOPE

0-3	3-8	8-15	15-25	25+

	A	B	C	D	E	F	G	H
1				12.8	15.9			
2			21.58	17.93	18 05	18.05	15.55	
3	15.3	11.1			16.83	24.33	13.93	11.95
4	8.2	9.8	10.13	10.9	12.33	31.2	28.58	9.2
5			11.5	22.13	29.5	16.2	21.35	10.35
6				10 6	17.23	8.5	10.75	12.4
7	10.8	8.7	15.9	14.3	14.13	26.35		
8		9.67	10.75	11.48	16.13	36.5		

COMPUTED COVERAGE GRID: TOTAL COVERAGE = 15.6%

SINGLE FAMILY SUBDIVISION

WETLANDS

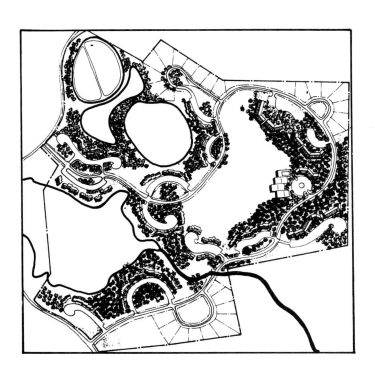

Open space community

COMPARISON						
A. LAND STATISTICS						
1. TOTAL SITE AREA				167.9 AC.		
2. SURFACE WATER			35.4 AC.			
3. WET LANDS			10.5 AC.			
4. UNBUILDABLE LAND				45.9 AC.		
5. BUILDABLE LAND				122.0 AC.		
B. LAND USES			S.F.D.	O.S.C.		
1. 1 AC. LOTS			106	0		
2. 1/2 AC. LOTS			0	27		
3. TOWNHOUSES			0	152		
4. GARDEN APARTMENTS			0	92		
5. TOTALS			106 DU	271 DU		

C. PROJECT SUMMARIES	TOTAL DU	GROSS DENSITY	IMPERVIOUS COVER	COMMON OPEN SPACE LAKES	LAND	%
1. SINGLE FAMILY SUBDIVISION	106 DU	0.63 DU/AC	15.7%	35.4 AC	7.3 AC	25.5%
2. OPEN SPACE COMMUNITY	271 DU	1.61 DU/AC	15.9%	35.4 AC	62.1 AC	58.1%

Development Impact Model

CONSTRAINTS

NATURAL RESOURCES

SCHOOLS

TRAFFIC

UTILITIES

DEBT LIMIT

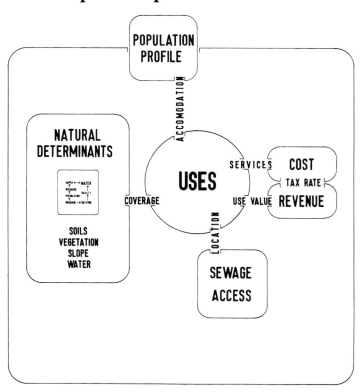

topography is encountered. Soils, slope and cover data is then collected and mapped in its most accurate free-form state.

Having mapped the data in its natural state the next step is to determine the percent of each soil, slope and cover type in each cell. After a minute or two of computer time, a graphic output is produced showing the recommended impervious cover limit for each cell.

This cover number then permits evaluation of any proposed plan and its relative conservation merits for each four acre cell as well as the entire parcel under consideration.

The position is clear: conservation is not necessarily served by uniform zoning but rather performance standards applied on a site-by-site basis.

In this way the inherent differences of the natural landscape can be recognized and properly dealt with.

In Retrospect
We have used the cover model in connection with three regional/municipal projects and a half dozen private developments. An early version of the technique was developed for the Wissahickon Watershed Study and has since been refined in connection with municipal master planning projects in several towns. At the site level we have found the model to be a reliable and useful land use allocation technique. The major drawback has been that, even with a computer, the computations are time-consuming. For the large site (1000 a. plus) the time is worth-

while and can be somewhat reduced if standard weather input calculations are assumed for large regional areas. The logical solution to this problem is to encourage more states, river basin commissions, and municipalities to have this basic information available.

As shown in the Development Impact Model, our economic and feasibility computer models tie into the impervious cover numbers for a proposed plan. By comparing these figures with those of the cover model we can gauge the ecological impact of possible land uses and mixes and recommend alternatives to the client.

The options this process make available to a town are illustrated below. Note that all options have roughly the same ecological impact while the economic consequences vary. This provides a solid base for countering the frequently used argument of the conservationist that large lot zoning protects the environment. At the same time it illustrates the fiscal impact of unbalanced zoning as a result of this so-called environmental position.

We have also found that soils with extremely high infiltration rates (like the glacial till encountered in Duxbury, Massachusetts) have created some problems for the model. We are in the process of developing other constraints, based on septic restriction and aquifer recharge areas, to augment the coverage coefficients and hope to report on our progress in the near future.

Another approach, taken by some municipalities in the Wissahickon Watershed, is a "zero-runoff" policy. Although the technology to support this position (retention ponds, turfed swales, diversion ditches, energy dissipators, etc.) is clearly available even for a small site, the risk of potential legal exposure as a confiscation of a landowner's constitutional rights seems high to us. It remains to be seen how the courts will react.

In any event, the fact that planners and municipalities are recognizing the natural hydrologic cycle as an indicator of good planning and developing ways of working with it, is alone very encouraging.

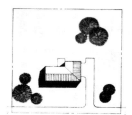

SINGLE FAMILY

COVERAGE	16%	TAX YIELD	$1200.00
DENSITY	1 DU/AC	MUNICIPAL COST	1050.00
VALUE	$40,000.00	SURPLUS	$150.00

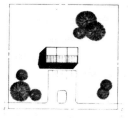

TOWNHOUSE

COVERAGE	16%	TAX YIELD	$2250.00
DENSITY	3 DU/AC	MUNICIPAL COST	1650.00
VALUE	$75,000.00	SURPLUS	$600.00

GARDEN APARTMENT

COVERAGE	16%	TAX YIELD	$3240.00
DENSITY	6 DU/AC	MUNICIPAL COST	1700.00
VALUE	$108,000.00	SURPLUS	$1540.00

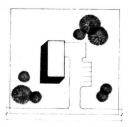

INDUSTRIAL

COVERAGE	16%	TAX YIELD	$1200.00
VALUE	$40,000.00	MUNICIPAL COST	60.00
		SURPLUS	$1140.00

Tools for a Land Use Guidance System:

The Development Land Unit
The Public Land Trust
Stormwater Runoff

By RICHARD R. WILKINSON

1. In 1970, Mr. David Springer of the Point Farm in Mocksville, North Carolina, filed a suit against Schlitz Brewing Company of Winston-Salem, North Carolina, for allegedly discharging untreated sewage into the Yadkin River and causing a serious fish kill in the river, of which Mr. Springer is a riparian owner. Schlitz' brewery uses the Winston-Salem sewage treatment plant, which at the time was charged as being seriously overtaxed and not capable of handling the effluent of the brewery. Mr. Springer has filed for punitive damages and the case went to Federal District Court.

2. In April of 1971, the Raleigh, North Carolina, city council voted to approve a zoning request along a major arterial highway serving the city. This approval, in conjunction with other recent decisions by both the city planning commission and city council, prompted the *Raleigh News and Observer* to comment "that may just about finish off mobility along the stretch of [U.S.] 70 running from Raleigh past Crabtree Shopping Center. It will also help hasten the transformation of a green and placid Beltline into another unsightly, overdeveloped highway . . ."

3. The Legislative Research Commission of the General Assembly of North Carolina, under the direction of Senate Resolution 975 of the 1969 General Assembly, was authorized to study public water supply systems in the state and prepare legislation for their control and regulation.

The original draft of the ensuing bill presented to committee contained a clause requiring all plans for altering or introducing water supply systems to include evidence of coordination of water supply planning with land use planning and regulations in the affected area. This clause was deleted from the bill during committee hearings.

Each of these vignettes is a common occurrence of everyday life in America. They are the results of the normal processes of land development, but need not be accepted as the norm. There are solutions that deprive no one of their basic rights and that can leave the community with a gain in the quality of its environment.

The basis of land developments' negative influence on environmental quality is the dual system that separates land from the landscape. Most states view land solely as property. In North Carolina the statutes describe land in the following terms: "Land means real property, buildings, space in buildings, timber rights, mineral rights, rights of way, easements, options, and all other rights, estates, and interests in real property."

This is a legal view. It does nothing to recognize that land as property is part of an integrated natural system comprised of inextricably linked components. It does not give credence to the fact that alteration of any property is going to cause reverberations throughout the entire system of the landscape very similar in effect to the dropping of a pebble in a still pond. This would not be such a great problem if there were government machinery to adequately control and manage the consequences of each independent land act. There is not. In fact, most governments are in the business of encouraging property development for its own sake.

The province of government is not to limit change, but rather to limit its consequences in such a way that the community as a whole is in control of its own destiny. My argument is based on the need to resolve the disparity between property rights and the landscape in the interests of the present and the future.

A New Land Trusteeship
The substance of a modern land policy is the trusteeship of property rights and not the question of the right to hold interest in land. Rights of private citizens to have and hold property rights is one of the basic motivating forces of our country's success. It has become clear over time, however, that these are not exclusive rights and the role of government cannot be passive.

Property rights are held in trust by private citizens. There are two basic principles involved: (1) every legitimate use of the land has spillover effects on the rights of others that limit its scope and use; and (2) the limit of one's right is measured by the ability of one's neighbors to make a reasonably productive use of his own property.

These principles have given us the land use regulatory powers that we have today. It is not difficult to prove they are inadequate. Zoning and other controls falling under the police power are almost totally contrived to support monetary value of property. The impact of a private citizen's use on the systems of the natural environment that affect others indirectly and over time are not accounted for. This is not to say that zoning and similar controls are totally inappropriate; they must be added to and evolve.

A proper role for state government is the establishment of a modern land policy based on the trusteeship of real property rights. As a by-product of encouraging and facilitating development, state governments in the past have collected various interests in land. This

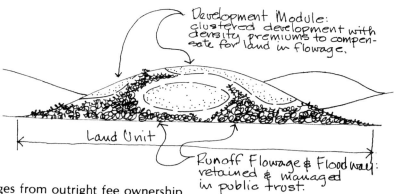

Development Module: clustered development with density premiums to compensate for land in flowage.

Land Unit

Runoff Flowage & Floodway: retained & managed in public trust.

ranges from outright fee ownership of rights-of-way for roads and utilities, parks, public buildings and facilities to easements and partial ownerships. The most primary responsibility of the states, however, is the trusteeship of the common property resources of the people, water, air, beaches, marshes and segments of the environment that are beyond ownership. The states have the obligation to organize this responsibility into a land use guidance system that will prevent land use change from exceeding the capability of the landscape to sustain them. Conservation of water quality requires that incremental change not be permitted to gradually and irreversibly destroy the common property of the people.

Water Rights as 'Leverage'
To achieve this status the accumulated rights and interests of the public in common property need to be organized into a management trust that guides private development and prevents deterioration of the landscape into smaller and smaller unrelated land use units. The basis for public management to meet this objective is the relationship between land use and water quality. The state can establish water quality standards and use them as a lever to exact more orderly land use development. The relationship is clearly viable but requires an organized instrument such as a Public Land Trust with the following objectives:

1. Conservation of the common property resources of the people.
2. Guidance of the land use change process through more strategic use of present control devices (zoning, development regulations, right-of-way locations, location of parks and other public facilities, etc.)
3. Responsibility for the con-

sequences of land use change.
4. Protection of private property.
In order to accomplish the task with any success, it requires severe alteration in the current process of development. Disjointed decisions to create land use changes must be brought into a uniform format and viewed in a total context. The most readily available tool is the land unit. Such a unit is defined as the land between drainage courses with the crown or ridge of the land as the center.

This is the reverse of the normal drainage basin unit used in water management circles, but which has little effective relationship with the land development process.

Land units exist in varying scales in all physiographic regions. Effective management of the public trust requires that such a unit be designated as the least component of both the natural and man made systems in order to bring about the necessary adjustments. Each land unit based on its hydrologic characteristics has a measurable capacity for various types of land uses.

The Public Land Trust can force the organization of land into units and deal with them as the minimal increments of land use change. A transition strategy from the present Euclidian zoning format to a land-use-intensity format is theoretically possible. Presently each zone has a maximum capacity for use. Each land unit could also be evaluated as a Euclidian zone to determine its present value as real estate. It would then be a matter of design to translate this capacity into integrated clusters and then to stage the development in such a way that it did not exceed the capacity of the natural systems to sustain it.

There are several devices in the present system that can be used by

the Public Land Trust to make the process work. The principal tool is the ability to pre-locate road and utility rights-of-ways and easements. These are features that would be owned and operated by the Public Trust. Rather than continue to permit their installation to be activated merely by market demands for land, they should be used as prestructuring components.

Another device is a facet of water law in most states. Storm runoff water is the only water which is now treated as private property. This is because of its inherent capacity to create property damage which must be assignable in case of litigation. Rather than retain this negative role, it should be used positively. If it is property, it can be condemned through eminent domain, along with its natural flowage, to create and consolidate the developable modules within the land unit.

Conceptually the entire process is based on the evolving nature of property in the United States. Land is valuable only in terms of its proximity to other land uses. The value of service station, factory or commercial sites is related most directly to other land uses if services are available. Land in the real estate business has little to do with its natural characteristics. By recognizing this and reinforcing it through integrated development complexes we could at once reverse the sprawling discontinuity of urban growth and gain an ascendent position in the management of the landscape.

If environmental concern and the search for quality is to move from the rhetoric to an action stage it will take strong action. The Public Land Trust with a broad mandate to conserve common property can guide the development process into an orderly and manageable sequence. Land Units as a basis for relating real estate and landscape afford a technically possible format that would deprive no one of their prerogatives. Essentially it is a path to the only true measure of environmental quality that we can articulate: When it comes about it will only exist because it satisfies the legitimate aspirations of every segment of the community including the conservationists and the developers.

The Rise of Porous Paving

By THE EDITOR

For decades there has been a rising chorus of complaints about "asphalt desert" parking lots and excessive run-off caused by paving large areas for human settlements. Recent new developments of special paving blocks and porous paving are beginning to have an impact on landscape design, representing changes long overdue.

Varieties of porous pre-cast concrete paving block with perforations have long been used in Europe. The parking lot at the Stuttgart, Germany international exhibition grounds is "paved" in these perforated blocks. Enough soil and water exist in the perforations to support a healthy stand of grass and shade trees throughout the lot. At least two of these European blocks have been franchised in the United States. A variation in the form of an oversized perforated brick developed by the Structural Clay Products Research Institute (now the Brick Institute of America) has also had limited use in the U.S.

Porous paving, while no universal panacea, seems now to have reached the point in technical improvement where many varieties are on the market in patented and other forms. Be prepared for a proliferation of fancy names: "Grassy grids," "permeable concrete," "environmental surfaces," etc.

Recently given widespread publicity are porous-paved parking lots, one at the University of Delaware, Newark, designed by the firm of Edward R. Bachtle, ASLA, landscape architects of Wilmington, Delaware. The other is at the new town of Woodlands, Texas. Bachtle reports his is "the first practical application of porous asphalt paving as researched and developed by the Franklin Institute, Philadelphia; in cooperation with the Office of Research and Motoring of the Environmental Protection Agency." Edmund Thelen of the Institute was chief researcher.

According to Bachtle, "the surface wearing course is similar to an ordinary non-porous asphalt surface. The difference is in the gradation of aggregate — no fine materials are used in the mix; a slightly higher amount of asphalt is used as a binder, 5½-6% by weight. Strength of the material comes from the friction of the large particles trying to slide over one another. The very fine particles do not seem to have much to do with the overall strength of the material. The in-place density of the materials is 123 lbs./cu. ft.

"Absence of fine particles in the asphalt-aggregate mix leaves channels for the water to pass through. The base material is composed of *graded crushed stone;* by using coarse material a large void space remains for storage of water until it percolates into the soil beneath at whatever rate the soil will take it. (The University of Delaware parking lot has approximately 40% void space in the base material.)

"At this site we used a 12 in. stone base in accordance with the subsoil boring indication of a medium permeability. The stone was layered as shown in the section mainly for stabilization of the stone base. The layer of smaller stones, Delaware State Highway Specification crushed stone gradation #107 (3/8-1/2"), was used to bind the large stone. Del. #106 (basically 1 1/2-2"). The top layer of small stone (Del. #107) was also required so that the asphaltic concrete laying machine could lay the paving on a smoother, and more maneuverable surface."

Adds Bachtle: "It is important to stress that each individual site will determine the design of the porous pavement and that a thorough examination of the site is of primary importance to the working of the pavement. Test borings should be taken to determine the character and permeability of the soil. The ability of the soil to transmit the water passing through the pavement will determine the thickness of the base reservoir needed; or in some cases where permeability is extremely poor, an alternative approach is removal of water from the base reservoir to the water table where it is ultimately headed.

"The point is that each case is different depending on site and particularly soil conditions, on the wear expected on the surface itself, and on the objectives of the particular use of the porous surface — ground water recharge, reduction of runoff or flash flooding, preservation of natural drainage patterns, etc.

"In regard to effects of freezing and thawing on porous asphalt pavements, researchers expect such problems to be minimal because of the large void space (35% ±) in the base reservoir which will allow room for freeze/thaw without undue stress on the material, and the high porosity of the surface itself.

"Our experience during the first winter indicates that ice and snow conditions and snow removal are the same as for any other paving. Porous pavement does freeze over in severe ice storms and freezing rain and additional water runs off the surface. However, as soon as the ice on the pavement melts, the porous paving again allows water to pass through to the base reservoir. No problems are expected with regard to ice heaves if the underlying soil is free-draining. Swelling clay-type soils could present difficulties and should be avoided.

"Asphaltic porous paving material costs somewhat more than regular non-porous standard plant mix. However, actual installation of a porous paving project is at least 20% less in cost when you consider that a drainage collection system requiring structures, pipes and sewers can be eliminated, as well as curbing and other elements in the parking lot related to the standard drainage system."

At the Technical University of Ulm, Germany, right, this perforated concrete block has been used successfully to surface parking and exhibit lot. Perforations permit grass to grow. Below, a cross-section of porous paving which allows water to soak through. Illustrative site plan, bottom, shows multiple facilities for holding and directing stormwaters.

SECTION/POROUS ASPHALT PAVING⁎

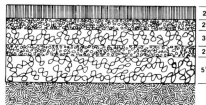

2 1/2" **Porous asphalt surface**
2" A
3" B **Graded crushed stone base**
2" A Stone gradation
A = 3/8" – 1/2"
5" B B = 1 1/2" – 2"

Undisturbed subgrade

⁎AS USED AT THE UNIVERSITY OF DELAWARE, NEWARK. DELAWARE

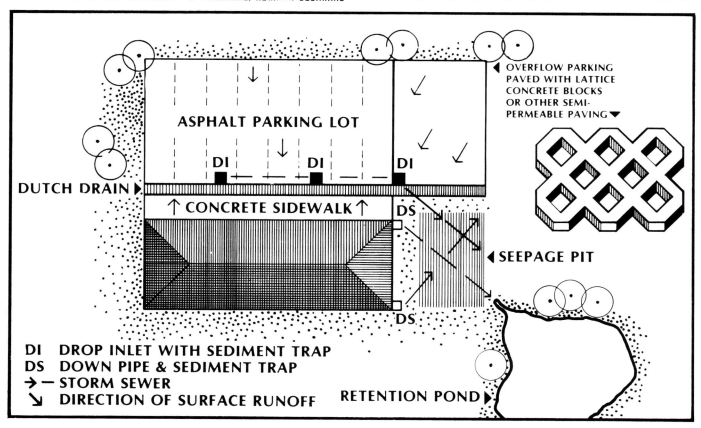

OVERFLOW PARKING PAVED WITH LATTICE CONCRETE BLOCKS OR OTHER SEMI-PERMEABLE PAVING▼

ASPHALT PARKING LOT

DI   DI   DI

DUTCH DRAIN▶

↑CONCRETE SIDEWALK↑   DS

DS

◀SEEPAGE PIT

DI   DROP INLET WITH SEDIMENT TRAP
DS   DOWN PIPE & SEDIMENT TRAP
➔─ STORM SEWER
↘ DIRECTION OF SURFACE RUNOFF

RETENTION POND▶

2
Communities and Rivers

Outrage and Energy at the Riverside

No balance is so delicate, so easily upset as that between a stream and the community alongside it. Few streams can survive communalizing, for it is a rare community that leaves either a stream or its edges more livable than before. Thus it goes almost without saying that to communalize a stream is to deprave and despoil it. American communities in particular have developed the capacity to mess up a stream far quicker and on a larger scale than any society on record. Our towns and cities are proud of their industrial capacities — and one of those is the ability to take a beautiful stream and quickly to render it unfit for drinking, swimming, boating or even for smelling.

But the litany of lost opportunities need detain us no longer at the water's edge, peering at vagrant Chlorox bottles and poking at flotsam from distant dumpers. For on the following pages we chronicle the exceptions, the works of brave reclaimers, of determined improvers who are our authors showing us and their home-owners that all is not lost, that life can begin again at the waters' edges, just as surely and sometimes as swiftly as it was once wiped out.

Few scenes can be more promising than those along a city waterfront being brought back to life and beauty after a half-century's burial underneath industrial dumps, tracks, filth and pollution. Few sights offer the promise of a better urban future more certainly than a long, wide expanse of riverfront now — after years of abuse — being converted into a community park/marina and recreation retreat.

Practically speaking, the act of waterfront reclamation usually requires consummate skill on the part of the reclaimers — skill at assembling land held under many owners and jurisdictions; the ability to envision a future waterfront of beauty that might emerge from its present dereliction; and adeptness in carrying out the complex improvements required.

Everyone who examines an urbanizing river closely soon comes to realize that river policy is essentially land policy; that the condition of a river and its shores reflects the land-using policies and traditions of the towns and cities along the bank. To look at the quality of a city's stream is to look into the value system of that city and its people. No quicker clue can be found to guide a visitor to understand the depths of degradation to which a community has sunk than to examine what it has done with its streams and their margins.

It takes energy and outrage combined to roll back history, and few communalized waterfronts can enjoy such a combination until professional planners and designers join forces with political groups to bring about the changes. Many contemporary success stories come from just such combinations as have occurred at Spokane, along the Connecticut River's Great Meadows, and other waterfronts revisited on the following pages.

The Editor

35

Gently Flowing Through the Village

By ROY WINTER

This stream was not culverted but allowed to keep its natural line as a major open space corridor.

One of the most difficult tasks facing the designers of new towns is to create an atmosphere of permanence and "place," and it is probably in the landscape design where the greatest contribution can be made. In this context "landscape design" must mean total design and not merely the later addition of greenery.

In many towns and cities it can be seen that the most successful growth and renewal is gained by a retention of the patterns of movement, activity, and enclosure, even though the structures may be new. The same applies to the imposition of new uses on old landscapes, such as in the building of housing on farmland. The structure and pattern of the landscape can have a continuing meaning and function if they are woven into the fabric of the total design.

Redditch new town possesses a wealth of natural and man-made beauty and it is the policy of the designers to build upon this framework in the creation of new settlements.

The preservation of mature trees is now commonplace in newly developing areas, but little thought seems to be given to other elements such as hedgerows and water courses, which to a large extent form the framework of the landscape. It is not difficult to fit the pattern of development to an old field pattern, making full use of the hedgerows as boundaries, footpath routes and space definers. A more difficult task however is to make full use of an existing open drainage pattern, the tendency being to disregard its potential and to pipe all the flows into a new system. It has been proved that this exercise is an extremely costly one, and very often troublesome. In the area described, a success has been made of in-tegrating an existing natural drainage line into the pattern of development and realizing its recreational potential.

The Matchborough housing area, having a density of 67 persons per acre, contains a small unpolluted stream which rises in the high land to the northeast of the town, and which served as the main drainage line to the surrounding farmland. An early decision was made in 1968 that the stream should not be culverted but should be retained on its natural line with provision for excess flows to be taken into the new surface water drainage system. The potential of the stream as a basis for the main open space provision was to be utilized.

Some doubts were expressed at the time concerning the viability of such a proposal. Danger of flooding, pollution, safety and maintenance were the main causes of concern, but were the most easily overcome by technical skill. Perhaps the most lingering doubt in the minds of the designers was the unknown reaction of the future occupants of the area. Many newcomers would not have had any experience of living close to water and would possibly be afraid of its presence. It was felt, however, that the benefits of the proposal in the close contact of man and nature outweighed the doubts, and the scheme proceeded.

A thorough survey of the entire half-mile stream course was carried out to determine its source and flow characteristics, particularly as much of its catchment area would be cut off by new development. The stream now floods three or four times a year, rising from a nine-inch to two-foot depth. The state of the banks and the stream bottom was recorded and a survey of the existing vegetation plotted.

From this survey a plan was drawn up which integrated the stream into the total design. It was realized from the outset that a generous amount of open space should be provided on one or the other side of the stream course, not only to allow sufficient recreation space but to ensure the survival of the retained vegetation and to cater for periods of minor flooding due to blockages. The vegetation consisted mainly of hawthorn, willow, alder and elm growing closely on the stream banks. To avoid hidden dangers to children, some of this vegetation was cleared to enable regrading to be done and to open up the stream to view.

Where there was no access to the banks — no paths directly along the edge — or where private gardens abutted the stream, the vegetation was undisturbed and reinforced with further planting. A regrading exercise was carried out on the banks to eliminate steep areas liable to erosion, and to allow the adjacent open spaces to flow down to the water's edge. The whole of the stream bed was covered with a layer of rounded stones found on the site, to facilitate access and maintenance.

The stream enters the housing area from the northeast, having passed by a local shopping center, where it supplies a small lake in a public park. The entrance is marked by a small pine wood and from this point the course meanders through the side of a public open space which is grassed and planted with trees and shrubs in informal groupings. This space also contains several play features, in particular a timber structure and slide with a stone bench which gives access into the water. The line then skirts the primary school and meeting hall, crossed at many points with simple timber footbridges. At the crossing of the main estate road the stream is

piped underneath, but the road is dipped down over the pipes to provide a ford in times of high flow. The ford, in conjunction with a rough granite sett surface provides an ideal "rumble strip" at this point.

The main footpath system follows the stream course corridor and along the remainder of its length the stream runs through a narrower, more enclosed space where the house frontages often are placed quite close to the stream banks. Again, in this area, play beaches in cobbles and sand have been placed on the banks. Planting in the narrower corridor has been confined to groups of standard trees, and naturalizing drifts of narcissus, while the existing vegetation has been selectively thinned.

No special or excessive maintenance is needed on the stream and its surroundings. Grass areas are cut to the top of the banks, and where the banks remain steep they are reinforced with additional shrubs. In the rougher bankside areas, naturalizing waterside plants and nettles are allowed to flourish, but are enlivened by the addition of the daffodils and occasional cornus and willow. Regular clearing of rubbish deposited in the stream is carried out, but over the three years since completion this problem has been diminishing as the residents become familiar with the feature. The stream is of course an immense attraction for children for paddling, fishing and general play, and this in no way appears to affect the bird and animal life that also uses the stream.

Complaints are now few and are mainly triggered off by children who get wet or dirty in the water, thus causing their parents some inconvenience.

The whole project was carried out by the building contractor, and the corporation estates department for the planting. The cost was contained within the housing cost yardstick.

The success of the project is due in no small measure to the high quality of maintenance carried out by the estates department without whose efforts establishment would not have been possible.

Willows shade the stream, left and opposite below, as well as a playground for older children which is visible in background. Play area, below, makes full use of water as an element of play.

Smoother Waters for the Next 110,000

By BENJAMIN J.W. SMITH

Historic Northampton, home of the English Parliament during Norman and Plantagenet times, is now an expansion town increasing from 120,000 population in 1968 to 230,000 in 1981. Midway between London and Birmingham, it has a countryside of rolling hills, woodlands and streams running north and south.

Since urbanization, which began in 1969, increases surface water runoff considerably, it became necessary to develop a combined open-space and flood control system to avoid flooding the valley.

The Welland and Nene River Authority stipulated that the flow of Billing Brook through the site of a major new housing development should not be more than 11,640 litres per second. In order to achieve this, three balancing lakes were constructed along the length of Billing Brook to catch stormwater runoff from roads and roofs. This flows into the stream and lakes via gasoline interceptors, which prevent pollution by floating off and segregating oil and gasoline wastes.* The alternative would have been culverts which although similar in cost could not provide the amenity values of lakes and open water. Although the flood-control system alone is not unique, the extent of landscape design and provision of amenities-plus flood control is unusual.

Work commenced in 1971 with the excavation for the lakes. Engineers worked closely with landscape architects and later with other consultants. The construction of the banks was either shingle beach or Malayan Kerume revetment. In order to provide a more suitable habitat for fish the centers were deepened, their clay bottoms not requiring lining.

Footpaths around the lakes are linked to other facilities, such as schools and shops. Adjoining the main footpath, a play area was constructed and sitting areas developed using natural York stone and cobbles. Footpaths are of a standard macadam construction although gravel was bonded to the surface by a bituminous resin. The footpaths thus appear to be gravel but can carry emergency vehicular traffic.

Shrubs and trees planted around the lakes follow two distinct forms: indigenous species around the middle lake with its mature woods on one side; and more exotic species around the lake surrounded by houses. The latter include *Arundinaria nitida, Corylus maxima purpurea, Phormium tenax, Phalaris arundinaria picta* and *Rheum palmatum.* Aquatic plants introduced include *Caltha palustris, Metheuccia struthiopis, Iris sibirica* and *Rumex hydrolapathum.* The development corporation is monitoring the rate of spread of indigenous aquatic plants within the lakes. None so far appear likely to become a major problem.

---

*Petrol/gasoline interceptors work on the opposite principle to silt traps. Runoff from roads containing petrol and oil flows into a series of chambers; the oil, being lighter than water, floats to the surface. The outlet from the first chamber is positioned at the bottom so that any remaining oil floats to the top of the second chamber. Four chambers in each interceptor means that there is little chance of contaminated water reaching the lakes.

Starting at lower end of a Billing Brook lake, opposite; the camera moves upstream the following summer, left; then to the head of the lake, bottom, photographed when background was still open land.

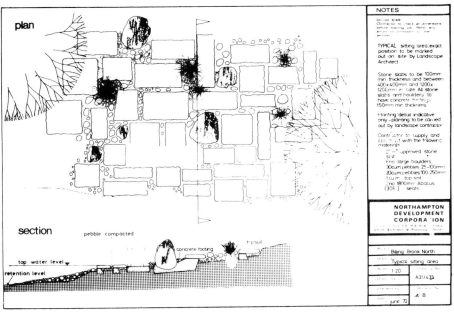

NOTES

Do not scale
Contractor to check all dimensions
before starting work. Refer any
errors or omissions to the
architect.

TYPICAL sitting area, exact
position to be marked
out on site by Landscape
Architect

Stone slabs to be 100mm
min thickness and between
400 x 400mm and 1200 x
1200mm in size. All stone
slabs and boulders to
have concrete footings
150mm min thickness

Planting detail indicative
only - planting to be carried
out by landscape contractor

Contractor to supply and
construct with the following
materials:
20 m³ approved stone
slab
Fine large boulders
30cum pebbles 25 -100mm
20cum pebbles 100 -250mm
1 cu m top soil
2no 1800mm Abacus
(306) seats

NORTHAMPTON
DEVELOPMENT
CORPORATION

Billing Brook North
Typical sitting area
1 20
A31/433
A B
June 72

plan

section   pebble compacted

concrete footing

typical

top water level

retention level

BILLING BROOK LAKES

Woodlands and wooded stream valley become the visual-functional spine that follows Billing Brook in this development model of the Eastern District. Typical sitting and duck-feeding area is shown in photo and sketch, top.

At an early stage of the work, the corporation retained the services of a consultant freshwater biologist, Dr. M. Pugh Thomas. The main concern was the growth of algae in the shallow lakes. Although some growth has occurred it has not yet been necessary to resort to chemicals. To counteract flies, the lakes have been stocked with roach (Rutilus rutilus), bream (Abramis brama), tench (Tinca tinca) and carp (Cyprinus carpio), and the water area is becoming rich in wildlife. There are restrictions against boating, fishing, or swimming; and notices, barriers and other paraphernalia are kept to a minimum. Considerable feedback information has been obtained and will prove valuable in the development of future lakes and water parks which the development corporation hope to carry out.

River Walk Generates 'Strong Positive Response'

By CLARE A. GUNN

This study analyzes the response to an outstanding design and development of a park-business complex along a natural river in the heart of a major city, the San Antonio River Walk. The research includes both those who visit and those who control or influence its development.

The River Walk refers to a horseshoe bend in the San Antonio River covering an area about four by six blocks in size in the central business district. This portion of the river lies in a deep cut, about 25 ft. below street level, and is flanked by huge trees, lush plant growth and many shops, restaurants and hotels. A continuous promenade parallels the river on both sides and the 50 ft. river is bridged many times, providing both automobile and pedestrian crossing.

The visitors' use and image of the River Walk was surveyed through visitor response to interview — using social survey techniques at nine stations along the River Walk. The survey was conducted on weekends for a full year.

Results of the survey reveal a single encompassing conclusion — the River Walk design and development are evoking an unusually strong positive response. This response is consistent over a wide range of ages, incomes, and occupations of visitors. Visitors describe the River Walk as very beautiful, moderately large, passive, uncrowded, safe, very interesting, cool, and uncommercial. At the same time, they make diverse leisure use of the area. Some find solitude and others find excitement and gregariousness. Some shop and others do not. Some prefer to walk and others like the specially designed sightseeing barges. A wide range of personal

satisfactions appear to be coming from a relatively small development.

In order to gain some insight into the strength of the voter support of the San Antonio River Walk, the registered voters of the city were surveyed. A statistical random sample of 2,001 of the 216,100 registered voters was drawn and was mailed questionnaires. A total of 414 usable responses was returned, which constitute the basis for the following analysis:

76.6% have visited River Walk in the last year.

96.6% consider it a tourist attraction; 80.7% consider it to be of economic benefit to the city; 74.9% consider it to be of benefit to them as residents of the city.

42.5% consider downtown traffic a problem; 64.5% consider downtown parking to be a problem;

only 15.7% believe that the entrances to the River Walk are difficult to find; 11.6% say that they could not get a ride to the River Walk if they wished to go there.

76.6% consider the building on River Walk to be attractive; 50.2% consider the River Walk to be lighted well enough at night; 47.1% consider the River Walk to be safe; 48.3% do not consider the river water to be clean.

62.3% would favor increased recreational use of River Walk; 55.1% favor a man-made channel connecting with the Alamo; 79.7% favor improving the remainder of the San Antonio River northward to the Brackenridge Park, while 62.8% favor improving southward to the city limits.

45.4% would be interested in living in an apartment along the river if

The horseshoe-shaped River Walk is at mid-left in airview, San Antonio, Texas.

The Chamber of Commerce Building, below, Hemisfair river extension. Design theme of the River Walk reflects heritage culture dating from the century of Spanish rule, an era when Texas was an integral part of Mexico.

Contrast of landscape character along River Walk extension. Temperate climate, microclimate zone below street level allow semi-tropical plantings.

available in their price range.

56.0% would vote for a bond issue to expand river development even if it raised taxes slightly; 25.6% favor if it would not raise taxes; 4.8% against if it raised taxes; 2.7% against even if it did not raise taxes. (10.9% were undecided.)

The survey of controlling agencies revealed a unanimity of policy toward the River Walk even though they are not bound officially. A high degree of collaboration and cooperation is taking place. When questioned, not one was interested in greater power, believing that the present management was working well.

The contiguous owners of property did not reveal future plans but generally were in favor of the present River Walk development. Some were in favor of land use and building controls and others believe them to be overly restrictive. About 70% of the owners do not have land uses that face upon or utilize the amenities of the river at the present time.

Conclusions:
1. The River Walk is unique.
2. The River Walk is a unified whole.
3. The River Walk contains diversity.
4. A delicate balance between park and commercial exists.
5. The River Walk is of great social and economic value.
6. The River Walk is a cohesive whole with dynamic internal forces.

For other urban river areas:
7. The River Walk has an atypical setting
8. A refocus upon downtown can become a powerful social force.
9. A small amount of water can become a powerful social force.
10. Composite management can succeed.
11. A business-park mix can be functional.
12. Diversity is successful.
13. Internal and adjacent land uses must be compatible.
14. Both tourists and local citizens can participate.
15. Can provide state tourism stimulus.

How to Handle Environmental Threats: The Great Meadows of the Connecticut River

By JULIUS GY. FABOS

THE GREAT MEADOWS

The planning study for the Great Meadows of the Connecticut River was an outgrowth of both citizen and government concern for the future of the Meadows. By the summer of 1967 it was clear that the quality of the Meadows was deteriorating. Several severe encroachments had been perpetrated, most visibly the use of the Meadows as a dumping ground, for sand and gravel extractive pits, and for gasoline tank "farms." Along the borders unattractive tract housing had been constructed. Nevertheless, the majority of the Meadows remain as open and scenic landscape and most of the historic houses along the borders have been preserved. Given impetus by the Capitol Region Planning Agency, interested citizens of the three towns on the borders of the Meadows came together to form the Great Meadows Committee. One of its members summarized the committee's purpose as follows:

"Our challenge is to find a way to maintain the character of as much as possible of this area, which is of great historical significance . . . and yet make room for inevitable development." To achieve these goals the committee determined first to sponsor a detailed study of the resources of the Meadows and their optimum land use potentials, and second to establish a land trust for the preservation of the Meadow lands.

The Landscape Architecture Department of the University of Massachusetts was chosen to undertake the study. The department was fortunate in obtaining grants from America the Beautiful Fund, the three towns and private donors. Students in the department and specialists in law, ecology and economics assisted in the preparation of the study. Further cooperation from the officials of the three towns and from the committee itself proved invaluable in formulating the

"On the edges of the cities there are still enclaves of countryside with great scenic potential that should be tremendously enjoyable but . . . are not, because people do not see them. The most beautiful expanse of open space in New England is the (Great) Meadows, a natural expanse of park-like pasture land bordering the Connecticut River, complete with white steeples in the background. Here, only six miles from downtown Hartford, is the epitome of what the New England landscape should look like."*

*William H. Whyte, *The Last Landscape*

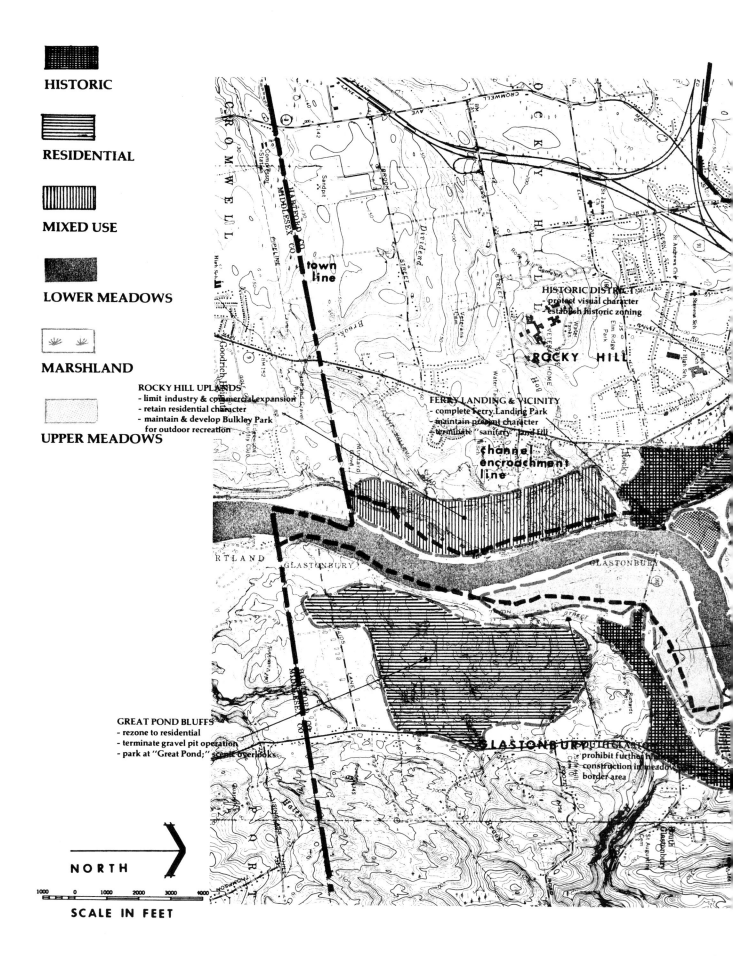

HISTORIC

RESIDENTIAL

MIXED USE

LOWER MEADOWS

MARSHLAND

UPPER MEADOWS

ROCKY HILL UPLANDS
- limit industry & commercial expansion
- retain residential character
- maintain & develop Bulkley Park
  for outdoor recreation

HISTORIC DISTRICT
- protect visual character
- establish historic zoning

FERRY LANDING & VICINITY
- complete Ferry Landing Park
- maintain present character
- terminate "sanitary" land fill

channel
encroachment
line

GREAT POND BLUFFS
- rezone to residential
- terminate gravel pit operation
- park at "Great Pond;" scenic overlooks

SOUTH GLASTONBURY
- prohibit further
  construction in meadow
  border area

NORTH

1000 0 1000 2000 3000 4000

SCALE IN FEET

HISTORIC DISTRICT
- protect visual character
- maintain historic zoning

FOLLY BROOK
- preserve natural area
- ecological research
- nature study

WETHERSFIELD

TRAP ROCK QUARRY & BLUFFS
- scenic overlook
- park facilities or well designed residential development with quality design control

NORTHERN MEADOWS
- preserve rural atmosphere & farming where possible
- walking and bicycle paths
- picnic sites
- playing fields
- control excavation

RIVER'S EDGE
- trail system
- natural scenic area
- open views to river

RIVER COVES & CONN. RIVER
- abate pollution
- water recreation
- boating, fishing, swimming

SOUTHERN GLASTONBURY
- prohibit commercial and industrial expansion
- present mixed use
- further study need

HISTORIC DISTRICT
- protect visual character
- establish historic zoning

GLASTONBURY BLUFFS
- residential developments with controls

goals of the study and in obtaining factual information.

To achieve the specific aims of the study, namely to give guide lines (recommendations) for the conservation and development of the Meadows, the following inventory and analysis were conducted.

Settlement of the Meadows area: The uniqueness of the surrounding three historic towns is a very important determinant in deciding future land use alternatives.

The relationship of the Meadows to the urban center of the region-Hartford: The mere location of the Meadows and the realization of its uniqueness based on the quality and scarcity of open space within the larger region provided us with some essential planning constraints.

Natural resources and features: The evaluation of the geology, soils, the topography, the hydrology of the river, and ongoing ecological processes illuminated the most important use opportunities and limitations of the Meadows. For example, filling or diking for industry would have a detrimental effect on the entire Connecticut River Valley since the meadows serve as a major storage basin during floods. The soils are excellent for agriculture, which also provides the visual amenities of a rural landscape.

Cultural features and resources of the Meadows: The relevant areas of study included analysis of land types, present land uses, its quality as open space, transportation and the economic considerations. The sum result of man's activity in the Meadows resulted in both compatible and incompatible land uses.

The above described inventory and analysis was sufficient to illuminate the existing limitations and resource values (natural, cultural and visual). The next major portion of our study aimed *to project and evaluate the consequences of potential uses.* The final outcome of this portion of the study has grown out of the meetings we had with the Great Meadows Committee, regional and local planners and town officials. As a result of our collaboration the following aspects were evaluated.

Effect of urban expansion on the Meadows: This portion of the study merely projects the increase of present activities into the future, e.g. building of subdivisions, cutting off public access, using the meadows for dumping grounds. The study raised the question: is there any means to stop this trend?

Effectiveness of present land use controls on the Meadows: This chapter illuminates the lack of sufficient controls to curb encroachment, dumping or other incompatible uses. For example, the established channel encroachment line would allow up to 10% development of the Meadows, but because of many unknown incremental developments, the eventual percentage might result in a much greater percentage of Meadow area lost.

Incompatible land uses and land use determinants: These related aspects of the study aim to summarize and dramatize all outstanding opportunities and limitations of the Meadows and its surroundings. The beautiful marshland depicted in the report suggests preservation of that resource. The auto graveyard on the riverbank suggests reclamation of the bank. The summary description of the land-use determinants sets forth the most significant constraints for future utilization of the natural resources, e.g., quality as a flood storage basin.

Analysis of the present planning for the Meadows: What we expected we found: there is no lack of planning for the Meadows. Numerous federal, state and local agencies with little or no coordination and acting upon superficial information are busy trying to determine the future of the Meadows. The essence of the most important plans are presented in our report with the evaluation of the compatibility of their proposals.

Alternative types of development and their impact on the Meadows: In carrying the above evaluation further, in this section we aimed to describe the costs and benefits of the potential uses proposed by the various plans for the Meadows. What we give up and gain if we maintain the status quo, or trade off for low intensity or high intensity development, is evaluated.

At this point we had sufficient information from which we were able to develop some sensible recommendations which recognize the visual and cultural opportunities and the numerous natural limitations of the Meadows. The concept map summarizes our recommendations and the accompanying chapter explores the reasons for those recommendations. In short, the recommendation represents "what" should happen; the final item remained to suggest "how" this ideal use would happen. We, therefore, described management and legal devices for implementation of our recommendations. These are now being carried out.

Revival at the River:
Spokane

By ROBERT L. WOERNER

Spokane, Washington is completing plans for a riverfront park on the site of Expo '74 which will utilize structures, paving, plant material, and more importantly, open space developed for the recent international environmental exposition.

What makes the project unique is the long range planning which led to development of a riverfront plan for this community of 180,000. Expo '74 provided a means to realize an urban river park, part of the comprehensive plan for the entire Spokane River within city limits.

Spokane is fortunate that 34% of the 3800 a. in the riverfront conservancy area is publicly owned. Beginning in 1900, riverfront property was acquired whenever possible by the Spokane Park Board. The state of Washington acquired a large area which is included in Riverside State Park. Fort George Wright, a military post for many years, accounted for another large public holding. Since the closing of this post, riverfront parcels and a 500 a. reservation

In the throes, Expo '74 railroad yards were cleared for fair and eventual downtown riverfront park.

have been made available for public use and incorporated into the city and state park systems.

From 1911 to 1913, Olmsted Brothers, of Brookline, Mass., prepared plans for several Spokane parks and made a study of the park potential of the city. The firm commented on the unspoiled beauty of the Spokane River below the Expo site and urged its protection and development for public recreation. Fortunately, the river gorge that was so much admired has been preserved, but the Expo site was buried under commercial and industrial development, including extensive railroad yards.

But the Park Board and the Plan Commission never lost interest in the river. In 1958 the City Plan Commission undertook a study of the central river area, and in May 1961, the City Council adopted the Havermale

area (site of Expo '74) as a cultural center. At the same time, local business interests engaged the national engineering firm of EBASCO to develop a plan for the central business district which encompassed the same area. In 1965 the Parks and Open Spaces Plan was adopted as a part of the City Comprehensive Plan. Spokane landscape architects contributed to the formulation of this report. The establishment of a riverfront district and the preparation of a riverfront program was recommended.

The team for the riverfront plan included landscape architects, architects, engineers and planners; the riverfront property involved more than 1100 owners. The final plan provides the basis of the required shorelines program for environmental protection. Rezoning of some of the river area is being studied and implemented. The riverfront program objectives are to focus attention on the river, guide development of public land, enhance the use of private land, develop economic potential, benefit the entire community, and reclaim the river.

What made Expo '74 and the post-Expo riverfront park possible was the cooperation of the Spokane railroads. The central business district had been walled off from the river. Viaducts and bridges carried rail traffic along and over the river. An essential step was a merger which resulted in the Burlington Northern Railroad, along with consolidation of all rail traffic on the major line south of the business district and away from the river. Donation of much of the riverfront land by the railroads and the Washington Waterpower Company, and the purchase of adjacent land made Expo '74 possible. The demolition of tracks

Fait accompli: Circular structure is U.S. pavilion. Upper left-hand portion of photo shows Washington State pavilion which will house an opera house and art galleries.

and trestles followed, and a feasible site became a reality.

Expo '74 has been sponsored and underwritten by the Expo Board and the business community. The city pledged $5.7 million for riverfront park development, guaranteed by a business and occupation tax. Housing and Urban Development open space funds were used to acquire and develop those portions of the site earmarked for parks and open space. The state of Washington provided $7 million for the Washington pavilion which will later become a permanent opera house and convention center. The state also provided $1.4 million for the Washington Street Bridge and tunnel, a major arterial change which permits the open space to flow over the arterial in a continuous park area. The U.S. provided funds for its $12 million pavilion. The Canadian government developed Cannon Island, the smaller of the two islands in the site, into a permanent park area as its share of the exposition.

Master planning for the Exposition involved studies of feasibilty, financing, and programming by a number of national firms. A consortium of local architects was employed to prepare development plans for the fair under the direction of Thomas R. Adkison, A.I.A. The general concept plan for landscaping the Expo site and the post-Expo park was prepared by landscape architect Robert Perron of Portland, Oregon. Two local landscape architects, L. Keith Hellstrom and Robert L. Woerner, served as consultants to the Expo architects and were responsible for the planting designs and contract drawings for the project, exclusive of exhibitor areas and Canada Island. Over $1 million was expended in landscaping the exposition, much of which will remain in place or be relocated as a part of the riverfront park.

Most of the 3000 trees planted on the site were purchased by the city in advance of contract awards to insure availablity. Principal deciduous trees were Thornless honeylocust (*Gleditsia tricanthos inermis*), London planetree (*Platanus acerifolia*), Quaking aspen (*Populus tremuloides*), European birch (*Betula verruculosa*), and Washington hawthorn (*Crategus phaenopyrum*). A number of species

Old Burlington Northern clock tower, below, is a Spokane landmark and frequent meeting place. The dome of the U.S. pavilion is in background. "Butterflies" (i.e., plastic sails) are free at the fair. Wing-like constructions encircled by colorful plantings were a visual theme at Expo.

and varieties of hawthorn, crab-apple, maple, linden, plum, etc. were used in smaller quantities.

Coniferous trees were used in six foot, 10 ft., and 18-24 ft. heights to produce effective natural groupings with deciduous trees and the underplanting of over 10,000 shrubs. Species used included Douglas fir *(Pseudotsuga menziesii)*, Balsam fir *(Abies balsamea)*, White fir *(abies concolor)*, Norway spruce *(Picea abies)*, Ponderosa pine *(Pinus ponderosa)*, Scotch pine *(Pinus sylvestris)*, Austrian pine *(Pinus nigra)*, Lodgepole pine *(Pinus contorta latifolia)*, Shore pine *(Pinus contorta)*, and Eastern hemlock *(Tsuga canadensis)*.

Deciduous and evergreen shrubs were selected from a list of readily available species and varieties, since the quantities needed and the time limits of the project were a major consideration. Shrubs were supplied and installed without difficulty, although the impact of Expo was felt throughout the northwest. In addition to the shrubs, some 60,000 annuals were grown under contract and programmed for use. Petunias were planted for the opening on May 4, 1974 despite the risk of early frost. Some plantings were changed, marigolds were added about June 1. A second planting in late July rejuvenated flower beds on the site. One of the theme features of Expo was the use of colored "butterflies" or large sails of plastic in the form of wings. Planting circles at the base of these sculptures featured annuals in red, magenta, yellow, purple and mixed colors.

Expo '74, with its theme of "Man Living in Harmony with his Environment," was an outstanding success. The impact of the Spokane River, particularly in the spring when cascades of white water dominated the site, the new open space in an urban area, and the abundant plantings on the site fulfilled the fair's concept. Seldom, if ever, have visitors to an international exposition had the opportunity to view so many excellent environmental exhibits in the heart of a busy city — a central area developing according to a long range plan and dedicated to open space and an urban park.

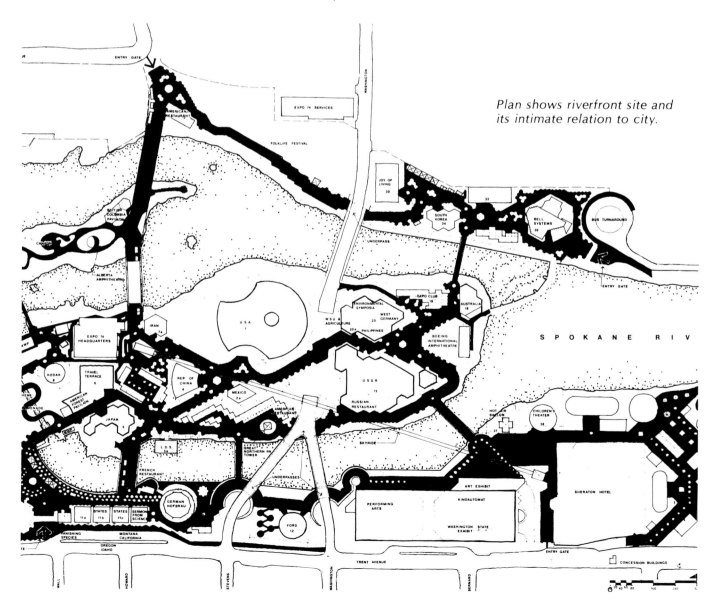

Plan shows riverfront site and its intimate relation to city.

To Save a River

By THE EDITOR

A 99 mi. bicycle trail along the White River's West Fork from Winchester, Indiana, to within 1000 yards of the state capital at Indianapolis, used by 1/4 to 1/2 million people a year, is the key to a proposal by Daniel Bazil Young, while professor at Ball State University (BSU).

The plan's long-range aim is rejuvenation of the entire White River watershed, through establishment of environmental planning boundaries and goals. Cyclists enjoying the proposed beautified trail would trigger public interest in the region's ecology and support the restoration of the abused river, Young and BSU believe.

Establishing the trail, an eight foot asphalt path on a 20 ft. easement almost entirely on submarginal agricultural land, would bring high benefits per mile cost, according to Young's report. These include increased adjacent property values, reduced pressure from the automobile, increased physical fitness and awareness of the environment including that of the major cities, towns, hamlets, and parks it would traverse.

Young's research base involved his students in practical applications of their ecology studies as they searched for the White River's identity. This was their professor's belief in the cultural value of the river in establishing a genius loci in a monotonously flat landscape whose communities are losing identity in the economic crush for urbanization. "The corollary between the socio-economic health of a city and the strength of its sense of place is measurable," Young reminds his classes. "The Lynds observed in their 1929 study, 'Middletown,' that 'in 1890 when timber still stood on its banks, White River was a pleasant stream for picnics, fishing and boating, but has shrunk today to a creek discolored by industrial chemicals and malodorous with the city's sewage.' "

Earlier, the Muncie region's first white settlers needed to dig only 18 ft. for an excellent supply of ground water. The water would rise to water-table height and was withdrawn by windlass or wooden bucket. By 1880 the population of Muncie had reached 5,208, and the need for a water supply system became apparent. In 1885, by contract of city fathers and private water company, a water plant and piping system was constructed using wells as a source of supply. The discovery of a natural gas reservoir in the area in 1886 caused a tremendous influx of people and industry,

> **Muncie, Ind.**
> The soft-pedaled effort to beautify a seven-county, 99 mi. stretch of White River lands was spearheaded by a former Ball State University faculty member who taught his students ecological applications of their studies by involving them in hefty projects.
>
> Daniel B. Young, Principal, D.B. Young & Assoc., Inc., Landscape Architects, said the college has been working on studies in connection with the river for about seven years — since he has been at Ball State. But he said he learned through funded research in July 1971 there still is too little ecological information to support any urbanization planning along the river.
>
> "One of the problems I discovered was a tremendous apathy, a lack of public awareness about White River as one of the major organizing systems," he said.
>
> "We decided what we were doing was kind of inappropriate," he said. "We decided a bicycle trail may be one of the ways to come through the back door to achieve public awareness." [By United Press International].

and by 1900 the population of Muncie was 21,000. Well supply became inadequate and a filter plant was constructed utilizing the White River. In 1905 salt pollution of the river caused by gas well drilling forced the company to abandon the river supply and build the Buck Creek pumping station and pipeline. This auxiliary system was used for 11 years before the river returned to a usable state. The river was used as the prime source for water until 1960, when the Prairie Creek Reservoir was constructed to supplement the low water flow.

Young applied in 1971 for a grant to inventory and map the natural systems base in portions of the 800 sq. mi. upper watershed of the river. Two sub-unit areas in Randolph and Delaware counties were studied that summer. He hoped to use the data as a basis for a "White River Coordinating Council" whose members would represent all state and regional groups interested in river basin planning. But nobody cared.

Obliged to seek another direction to use the research results, Young and BSU hit on the bicycle trail idea to focus attention on the river as a prime resource, a recreation corridor, and a vehicle for developing a regional planning strategy.

Statistics support the bike proposal, as Young has observed*:

"In 1965 the national average number of bicycles was 0.275 per person or 54 million bicycles. By 1970 the average had jumped to .33 per person and in 1970 there were 75 million bicycles or 0.368 per person, and by 1980 there will be approximately one bicycle for every two persons in this country. In 1960 bicycle sales in the United States were estimated at 3.7 million; by 1970 there were seven million; and by 1975 they are estimated to be 10 million in number.

---

*"A Strategy for the Recovery of a River," by Daniel Bazil Young, No. 3 in Ball State University Faculty Lectures 1971-72.

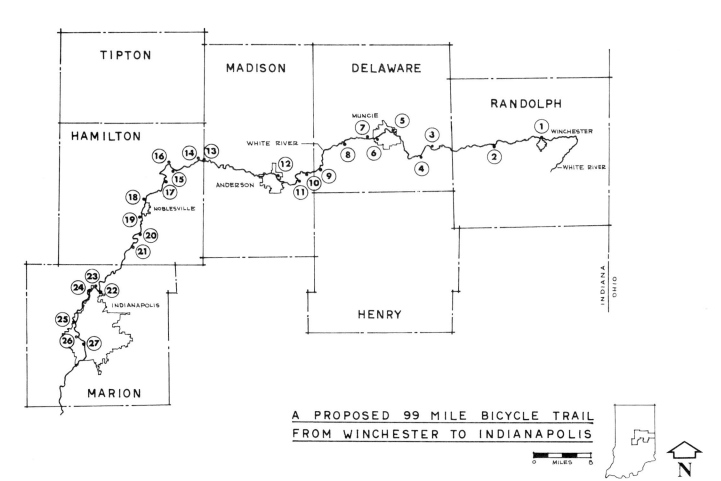

TIPTON

MADISON

DELAWARE

RANDOLPH

HAMILTON

MUNCIE

WHITE RIVER

ANDERSON

NOBLESVILLE

WINCHESTER

WHITE RIVER

INDIANA

OHIO

HENRY

INDIANAPOLIS

MARION

A PROPOSED 99 MILE BICYCLE TRAIL
FROM WINCHESTER TO INDIANAPOLIS

0   MILES   8

N

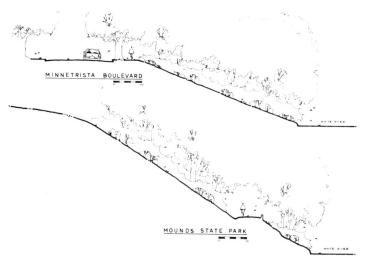

MINNETRISTA BOULEVARD

MOUNDS STATE PARK

"In the Muncie-Anderson region there are approximately 53,000 bicycles and virtually no bicycle paths or trails as such designated. Ball State in Muncie and Anderson College in Anderson report approximately 30% of the students enrolled own bicycles, and the rate is increasing by four percent per year.

"The 99 mi. trail system, including construction of an eight foot path on 20 ft. easement, with minimal grading, and appropriate trail graphics could be built for between $12,000 to $15,000 per mile (an estimated national average for similar conditions). For the 22.5 mi. segment between Muncie and Anderson, the construction cost would be roughly between $270,000 and $340,000, exclusive of land fees, design fees, and optional rest, picnic and camping facilities. Many of these facilities may already

exist, but a detailed inventory of available resources would discover facility needs and these could be met in a subsequent project-phasing strategy as part of a master plan.

"Implementation would include public awareness action, government agency funding, development and a maintenance program. Federal programs are available on a 50/50 cost-sharing basis. The U.S. Department of Housing and Urban Development Housing Act of 1949, as amended, provides an Open-Space Land Program which would allow a 50/50 cost sharing for development of bicycle trails. The Land and Water Conservation Trust Fund Act administered by the Bureau of Outdoor Recreation could also provide matching funds for qualifying applicants.

"In 1971 Oregon enacted trend-setting trail legislation (HB-1700), which provides that one percent of the money received from the state gasoline tax be used for the establishment of footpaths and bicycle trails. Many cities provide supplementary revenues for such development through bicycle registration fees. If, for instance, this fee were two dollars per bicycle per year, the city could make half available for the development of physical facilities. In Muncie, with approximately 25,000 bicycles, a fee of $50,000 might be collected in registration fees, with one-half, or $25,000, available for development and maintenance of bicycle trails and paths each year."

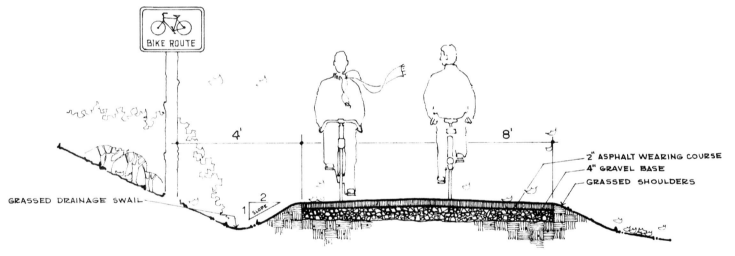

TYPICAL 8' WIDE TRAIL CROSS SECTION

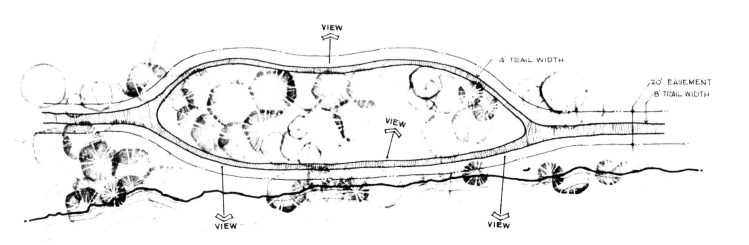

WHITE RIVER

TYPICAL SPLIT TRAIL PLAN SHOWING EASEMENT

Soil Conservation & Urban Design

A New Downtown Concept

By ROBERT WELDON BAIRD

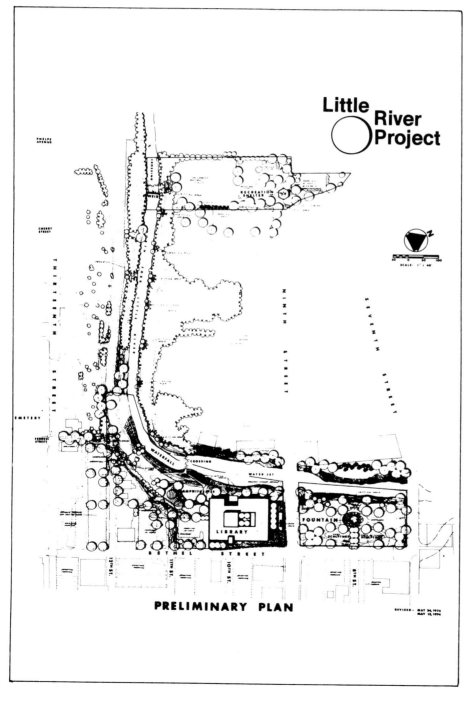

Little River Project

PRELIMINARY PLAN

What happened in "Hoptown," as the central Kentucky town of Hopkinsville is called, appears a classic textbook example of linking soil and water conservation practices with modern urban design, and getting a new mid-city river park somewhat on the San Antonio model.

This venture was the nation's first to be developed under the Soil Conservation Service's resource-conservation and development program. (RC&D).[1] The transformation took place at a former eyesore segment of the North Fork of the Little River, a tributary of the Cumberland and Ohio Rivers, at its highly-visible location in downtown Hoptown.

The result is a 15 a. (6.1 ha.) park a half-mile long (.8 km) bordering the central business district (CBD), made up of riverwalks, a new public library in an old warehouse, new landscape plantings, street furniture and a public plaza where marriages take place and theater groups perform.

This new urban greenway, Little River Park, is the result of an unusual team effort involving the U.S. Soil Conservation Service (SCS), the city of Hopkinsville, and the landscape architectural firm of Miller, Wihry and Lee, Inc.

More than a decade of planning and strategizing went into the conception of the project. By 1968 the question was: what to do with a downtown quagmire lined with railroad tracks and a shabby warehouse district?

The answer grew out of earlier SCS flood control work upstream in the same watershed. Lakes Blythe, Morris, Boxley and Tandy, completed north of the city in 1967, had been designated "Watershed of the

Year" by the National Watershed Congress.

Little River Park, of course, was not the first urban geographic setting for SCS. Since it was established in 1935, SCS had keyed 1.3 billion a. (526 million ha.) in cities and counties across the land to a nationwide soil classification system, assessing soil properties for farming and sites for housing developments, highways and other urbanization features.

And, since 1954, the Small Watershed program (P.L. 566) had offered flood protection to downstream farmland, and small towns and cities as well, by means of small-scale earth dams and reservoirs. Stream channelization through urban areas had come to mean landscape stabilization and water-based recreation.

In some respects, the Hopkinsville project resembles the much grander-scale River Walk in downtown San Antonio, Texas. In fact, San Antonio's River Walk was a source of inspiration for Little River Park when Hopkinsville banker William Deatherage saw it on a business trip, and brought the design concept back to Hoptown.

Like San Antonio's River Walk, Little River Park's riverwalks run below street level, establishing intimacy with the river. The Hopkinsville development forms a long, U-shaped green space in the urban fabric. Unlike the San Antonio improvement, this was a recreation project from the start, facilitated by a unique SCS program with broader objectives than traditional conservation programs. Even the Tennessee Valley Authority got into the act, providing planning assistance in the early stages. This was accomplished through "Operation Townlift," a program normally intended for small cities with populations up to 10,000, but widened to accept Hopkinsville's 25,000.

The RC&D program, by which Little River Park came into being, was instituted by the U.S. Food and Agricultural Act of 1962 (P.L. 703). Local communities use it to launch projects for their economic and environmental betterment, through wise use and development of natural resources. RC&D money is available to match local funds. The program has helped fund an assortment of urban and rural improvement projects

throughout the U.S., dealing with erosion control, flood prevention, farm irrigation, land drainage, fish and wildlife recreation, agricultural pollution control and water quality management.

The Hopkinsville project dates back to 1964 when Christian County Conservation District members began discussing what to do with the North Fork, especially where it was in full view of the then spanking new city hall.

By 1968, district conservationist Ray Hutchens approached the Pennyrile Area Development District, the regional clearinghouse for federal programs, and with its director John Adams drafted a proposal seeking Land and Water Conservation Funds, administered by the Federal Bureau of Outdoor Recreation. (BOR funds, though, were not easy to come by.)

By 1970, during the administration of Mayor Alfred Naff, Hoptowners were astir over what to do with the river banks and how to improve local library facilities. The small three-story 1927 library was in desperate need of remodeling, according to the 1969 community facilities plan, which recommended either a new building or a new site.

In October 1970, more than 100 businessmen, professionals, officials and other citizens helped organize a non-profit corporation to get a new city-county library site. The parcel eyed most was the Ragland-Potter grocery warehouse overlooking the river bend. The property was bought as an ideal site for library parking, if the warehouse were removed.

Meanwhile, the Illinois Central-Gulf Railroad was site-seeking for a new freight terminal, while its former depot lay abandoned along the river downtown. A swap was then arranged. The city got five acres (two hectares) including the depot at the edge of the CBD.

A consensus emerged to build the library in conjunction with a riverside park, but the community was at a loss how to put it all together. They explored all sources of aid, including TVA, which had an "Operation Townlift" planning program. Townlift normally offers planning-and-design advice to communities of 10,000 and under in the TVA seven-state service area. Private firms are

Workmen install concrete casing for a smaller fountain mounted in the Little River.

retained to do final plans and drawings.

TVA's designers in 1972 finished a conceptual plan that would have provided an open-air fair or bazaar as part of a riverside park, library site and landscaped parking lots. Riverwalks were to lead from the library and bazaar area along the river, and even under a bridge.

Energetic George Atkins became mayor in 1972, and eventually appointed a Little River Project Committee. City planner George Farmer then noticed a proposal seeking city help in reclaiming the river from the local conservation district lying unheeded in city hall.

An "RC&D Measure Plan" was drafted, adhering to the original TVA concept, but the site was shifted downstream from the vicinity of City Hall. The project area of 15 a. (6.1 ha.) encompassed the former railroad property, a Ragland-Potter warehouse parcel and riverside easements — all directly west of the CBD.

Design firms were interviewed and the collaborative approach of Miller, Wihry & Lee and Louis & Henry, both Louisville architectural engineering and planning firms, was chosen.

The local project committee established an order of design priorities which helped integrate the proposed park with the CBD, the proposed library, and the needs of inner-city children and senior citizens in new housing nearby.

The final design had to be functional as well as attractive. A primary-focus fountain in a plaza/flagpole concourse was put on axis with Eighth Street, an important pedestrianway from the CBD. The fountain, with stone floor, surrounding sitting areas and a 15 ft. (4.5 m.) high cone of water, has proven perhaps the most effective feature of the project, according to Lee Runyan, Hopkinsville community development officer. She cited the fountain's popularity as a staging area. Project landscape architect Larry Wilson achieved a special nighttime shadow effect for the fountain, using varying thicknesses of stone for the floor and allowing floodlights to play patterns.

A river weir pools water at a depth of three feet along the length of the park for the safety of children fishing along the banks. The weir was notched to accentuate the cascade and to minimize the water's force upon riprapped shores downstream.

When architects Louis & Henry had difficulty arriving at a flood-proof library design within the budget, project architect Jeffrey Points suddenly asked: Couldn't the

Opposite, clockwise: neighborhood children inspect the large fountains in Hopkinsville's Little River Park; greenbelt winding along the riverbank to business district; redesigned West Side Park sports a new playsystem; a Hopkinsville youth steps cautiously across the Little River via the weir that dams water along the half-mile greenbelt recreational development; kindergartners demonstrate ease of crossing the river via concrete stepping stones spaced nine inches apart for safety's sake.

The Soil Conservation Service (SCS) is not the only federal agency which could coordinate a water-based recreational development such as Hopkinsville's. The Corps of Engineers was authorized by the U.S. Flood Control Act of 1944 to "construct, maintain, and operate public park and recreational facilities in reservoir areas." But the SCS also was mandated, by the Small Watershed Act of 1954 (P.L. 566), to develop and carry out watershed protection and flood prevention. The missions, thus, clearly overlap. The Corps' expanded multiple-use philosophy is the key here.

Generally, Corps projects are larger, in navigable streams, draining watersheds of 250,000 a. (101,000 ha.) or more, and usually requiring masonry and concrete spillways. The SCS, on the other hand, often deferring to the Corps, takes on smaller projects, under 250,000 a. in drainage area, more of the earthen dam type.

Jurisdictional conflicts have raged for years between the Corps and the SCS over flood-control projects. The matter was more or less resolved with a gentlemen's agreement in 1965, differentiating Corps projects as addressing major flood problems, offering protection downstream, and SCS projects as meeting minor flood problems, providing upstream protection.

But Resource, Conservation and Development projects (RC&D), generally smaller and not dedicated wholly to flood control, aren't covered by this guideline. Theoretically, the Corps could have been consulted for the Hopkinsville project.

But the RC&D course was taken as a logical outgrowth of the four flood control/water supply/recreation lakes constructed north of the city. Hopkinsville had prior experience and rapport with the SCS; cooperation had its own history.

W.B.

Ragland-Potter three-story warehouse be transformed into a library? It had enough space and it was six feet (1.8 m.) above the 100-year flood plain.

Some local people objected to putting the library in the abandoned warehouse, but the architects persevered, arguing to retain the basic walls, replacing interior wooden columns with glass and concrete, and using brick from the old third floor for a front entrance to interface with the park. They won out, and by September 1976, a recycled 24,000 ft. (2,230 m.) $1 million library was in place, integrated with and complementing a new riverside park.

Park and library have registered good effects in downtown Hopkinsville. More people come downtown; the library has had a 400% increase in readership. Park-side merchants have spruced up rear entrances and parking lots, and there is talk of a restaurant with outdoor seating on one of the stream banks. Public events are flourishing, inspired by a spring fashion show put on by a suburban department store. The maintenance program spurred interest in the park five-fold, and vandalism dropped.

Today, thanks to the concerted efforts of many individuals with an expanded vision of what "soil conservation" is all about, this dynamic new waterscape is no longer a dream.

FOOTNOTES

1. According to John Miner, Chief, Resource Development Division, Resource Conservation and Development Branch, U.S. Soil Conservation Service, Washington, D.C.

2. River Walk, unlike Little River Park, originatd as a flood prevention project after a 1921 flood took 51 lives; civic leaders thought they could lick floods by making the river a sewer and paving it over for a street. Resistance by a women's conservation group led to defeat of that plan. Instead, sharp bends were eliminated in the river and a cutoff channel constructed to bypass the horseshoe bend, and thus prevent it from flooding. Beautification of the horseshoe bend followed, with park-like construction in 1939 by the U.S. Works Progress Administration.

U.S. Runs Last Along the Waterfronts

By PAUL D. SPREIREGEN

RIVERS IN THE CITY, *by Roy Mann. New York: Praeger Publishers, 1973. Illus. 265 pp. $20.*

Rivers in the City is a fine piece of work, and merits much attention. Essentially it is a series of case studies, some 15 of them, of cities-on-rivers. Three are in the U.S., nine in Europe, three in Britain. Before saying more about the book, it seems obvious that the work could be expanded into a second volume, by the author or by someone else. Detroit, for example, has received some careful design and planning under Charles Blessing's skillful pencil. Copenhagen, Stockholm, Moscow — in fact all the major cities of the world — would well be portrayed in relation to their rivers. Some sort of systematic description of situation and prescription might add dimension.

Roy Mann presents the 15 cities from his point of view, quite an agreeable one. His choice of pictures, his text, his assertions, in short, his general approach to this subject stands up well.

His brief introduction makes its point: rivers are essential to nature's processes. Man and his cities must not destroy those processes. Both should and can coexist. The rest of the book is a discussion as to particular city-river relationships, particular problems in those relationships, and the solutions currently posed.

It is no surprise that those cities that have done the most to date — Zurich, Paris, Amsterdam — and have done it fairly continuously through their histories, promise the most for tomorrow. That leaves the United States running a distant last. Even the Boston park system (I grew up alongside it) which is a stream-park system, and certainly one of this country's great artistic heritages, has suffered severe intrusions, and there is no relief in sight.

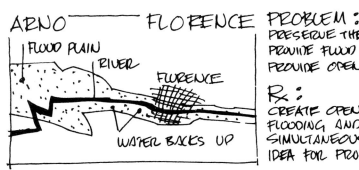

ARNO — FLORENCE

PROBLEM: PRESERVE THE OLD CITY; PROVIDE FLOOD PROTECTION; PROVIDE OPEN SPACE.

Rx: CREATE OPEN SPACE FOR FLOODING AND RECREATION SIMULTANEOUSLY — AN OLD IDEA FOR PROBLEM RIVERS.

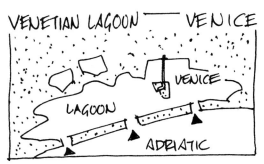

VENETIAN LAGOON — VENICE

PROBLEM: LAND FILLING, GROUND WATER LEVEL CHANGES, AND TIDES ARE UNDERMINING THE CITY.

Rx: A FAR-REACHING PUBLIC WORKS AND WATER MANAGEMENT SYSTEM

AMSTEL — AMSTERDAM

PROBLEM: ACCOMODATE GROWTH AND CHANGE WHILE PRESERVING THE HISTORIC CITY AND THE EXIGENCIES OF A FRAGILE LANDSCAPE.

Rx: A CORRIDOR URBAN PATTERN WITH OPEN SPACE WEDGES.

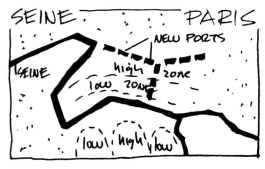

SEINE — PARIS

PROBLEM: EXCESSIVE PRESSURES ON THE CENTRAL CITY IN THE FORM OF BUILDING, TRAFFIC, AND CANAL SHIPPING.

Rx: NEW CANAL PORTS TO THE NORTH, DEVELOPMENT-INTENSITY ZONING, AND A REGIONAL PLAN.

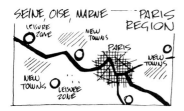

SEINE, OISE, MARNE — PARIS REGION

PROBLEM:
THE LONG EXISTING, BUT NOW ACCELERATED OVER GROWTH OF THE PARIS REGION.

Rx:
OBVIOUSLY, A PLAN FOR FRANCE AND THE PARIS REGION, WITH NEW TOWNS, OPEN SPACE, LEISURE ZONES, AND ALL THE REST.

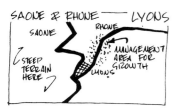

SAONE & RHONE — LYONS

PROBLEM:
PRESERVE THE OLD CITY, MANAGE THE RIVER, ALLOW FOR EXPANSION — ALL IN A CONSTRAINING TERRAIN.

Rx:
A DEVELOPMENT-INTENSITY ZONE FOR THE OLD CITY, PLUS SECTOR GROWTH UP THE RHONE.

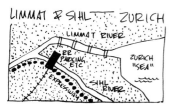

LIMMAT & SIHL — ZURICH

PROBLEM:
HOW DO YOU DESIGN A NEW EXPRESSWAY AND PARKING ALONG ONE OF THE CITY'S TWO RIVERS?

Rx:
BY EXPLORING AND EVALUATING THE EFFECTS OF MANY ALTERNATIVES.

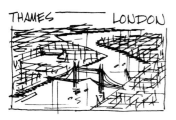

THAMES — LONDON

PROBLEM:
READJUST A HIGHLY DEVELOPED AND COMPLEX CITY RIVER SYSTEM TO A MYRIAD OF NEW USES.

Rx:
A COMPREHENSIVE AND SYSTEMATIC ANALYSIS TO START, THEN A FULL ARRAY OF BALANCED USES — COMBINING OLD WITH NEW.

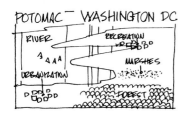

POTOMAC — WASHINGTON DC

PROBLEM:
MANAGEMENT OF A MAJOR RIVER BASIN IN THE FACE OF MASSIVE DEVELOPMENT PRESSURES.

Rx:
A LANDMARK PLAN BASED ON LANDSCAPE SUITABILITIES AND CAPABILITIES.... BUT THE TOOLS ????

LEA — LONDON

PROBLEM:
HANDLING A RIVER ENVIRONMENT WHICH HAS A VERY DELICATE SCALE.

Rx:
VELVET GLOVES.

RUHR — RUHR REGION

PROBLEM:
AN OBVIOUSLY ENORMOUS IMPACTION, COMPETITION FOR LAND, AND WITH ALL THAT MANAGE THE RIVER SYSTEMS.

Rx:
COMPREHENSIVE MANAGEMENT AND REGIONAL & LOCAL OPEN SPACE.

RHINE MEUSE — ROTTERDAM

PROBLEM:
DEVELOP ROTTERDAM INTO A EUROPORT, SIMULTANEOUSLY CLOSING OFF THE DELTA WATERS TO STORMS AND FLOODS.

Rx:
DO IT AND DO IT WELL. IT MEANS A VAST TRANSFORMATION OF "NATURE".

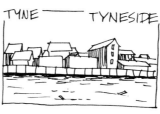

TYNE — TYNESIDE

PROBLEM:
THIS ONE IS ABOUT AS DEPRESSING AN INDUSTRIAL RIVER-SCAPE AS YOU COULD FIND. IT HAS A LINEAR CONFIGURATION.

Rx:
VERY CAREFUL ANALYSIS OF FORM — THEN VERY CAREFUL DESIGN.

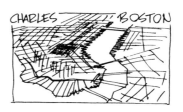

CHARLES — BOSTON

PROBLEM:
BOSTON HAS A GREAT STREAM PARK SYSTEM, ONE OF THE BEST IN AMERICA, BUT THE CITY HAS NOT DONE A GOOD JOB OF TAKING CARE OF IT.

Rx:
GET SMART, FAST.

HUDSON — NEW YORK

PROBLEM:
OBVIOUSLY OVER-IMPACTION AND NOW DEVELOPMENT PRESSURE ON THE SHORELINES.

Rx:
START BY TAKING ANOTHER LOOK AT THE WRIGHT-STEIN PLAN FOR N.Y. STATE. (1926).

Manhattan, all the fancy-pants shore-line designs aside, is still over-impacted to no real purpose or advantage. Its solution — and the Hudson's — still lies in the scopeful regional plan for New York State and its whole river systems as posed by Henry Wright and Clarence Stein in their classic plan of 1926.

The outstanding flaws in any hopes for effective river design for American cities are our lack of responsible and effective land-ownership policies, our lack of regional development mechanisms, and our competitive municipalities — not to mention the competition between agencies. As designers, we still talk through our hats.

I would like to think that the enormous accomplishments of Rotterdam's Euraport or the remaking of the Paris region and its rivers would be enough to at least cause us to take a serious look at our own inertia. I will continue to think so, because the alternative is un-thinkable.

Meanwhile, kudos and thanks to Mr. Mann for his illuminating opus. And we hope he is not fretting excessively over the map of the Hudson River Basin which was erroneously printed both backwards and upside down. Overall he came out well ahead.

3
Low-Lying Land Development

'The New Reclamation'

Our society has a well-developed penchant for dumping things it doesn't want or like into low spots — holes, gulleys, ditches, valleys, marshes, swamps — places accurately described as sinks. We have a long history of using such locational backwaters as dumps into which we shove waste, trash, garbage, servants, minorities and children.

Low-lying lands, in short, are traditional disposal-grounds and we describe all such lands as being "available for development." Thus some of the most beautiful and valuable marshlands in America have been filled in as building sites during the last century.

This age of indiscrimination is not yet over, but the new techniques of landscape analysis now make it possible to be discriminating in the entire process of developing large areas of land, water, marsh swamp and all their variations.

In North America this has been demonstrated with great clarity in the careful development of several large coastal resorts where fragile environments are worth millions of dollars as magnets for tourists and vacationers and new-town residents. At Woodlands, Texas; Cabin Bluff on the Georgia coast; in the Carolina Tidewater country; and at Amelia Island, Florida, careful landscape analyses made clear the need to set a limit to population and land use intensity. In each case, the salt marshes were to be protected from development.

Perhaps more telling of the shift in public sentiment in the 1970s, there have occurred several instances of landfills being *removed,* or new swamps *created* in order to bring back the former wetlands. In San Francisco Bay, the noted "Conservation and Development Act" has brought about the removal of landfill from a key tract of shore. And in Minnesota, old bogs once foolishly drained to make poor farms are now being rewatered in a three-year scheme to reclaim the land for wildfowl. This process of keeping or returning waters to their natural place in the landscape should rightfully be called "the new reclamation."

The Editor

Self-Imposed Limits to Development in the Carolina Tidewater

By HAL McNEELY

Planned destruction is not planning; conservation does not consist of aggregating greenbelts and buffer zones. Ecology is not tokenism or the waving of slogans by planners and developers to placate an aroused public.

The foregoing is all too apparent along the southeastern U.S. coast, noted for its vast and lovely tidal marshes, its unique mix of historic rice plantations (now attracting equal crops of game birds and tourists), and great stretches of quiet green stretching off to the horizons.

Too often, where there has been little development for generations, any proposal to subdivide land and bring in new settlers has been welcomed without discrimination.

We have watched the process with sinking hearts, "we" being a firm of landscape architects practicing out of Raleigh, North Carolina. The coast has a special magic for highlanders. And it was with special concern that we took on a proposal for the long-range development of 600 a. Litchfield Plantation, halfway between Myrtle Beach and Georgetown, South Carolina.

Litchfield Plantation represents an unusual example of self-imposed priorities. It puts a number of planning concepts on the line; although it represents a relatively small segment of the market, we expect it to serve as a local barometer for the new awareness in the environment.

The owner-developer is Young M. Smith, a 26-year-old lawyer, who, with his wife, inherited the property jointly with a third person whom they bought out. He has put his trust in careful investigation, conservation priorities, ecological consideration and the demand that they control

development, and no compromise. The developer has said he is determined to avoid "the Hilton Head effect" caused by continued development to the point of high density and eroded pleasure.

With such backing, we had no choice but to put everything possible into the planning process. This unique property, with its heritage and almost defiant character, represented an opportunity to prove other developers wrong. It stood for the things that others had not valued; it demanded a conscience, a

special sensitivity and grateful appreciation as to what it was and what it must be.

To the surprise of many, the plantation yielded submissively to the careful plans, and at times seemed to be cooperating with every difficult task that had to be performed. Methods that were untried proved successful; innovation worked every time. It was as if the plantation had been waiting all these years for someone to appreciate the ultimate worth and put it to use.

Litchfield Plantation is part of a

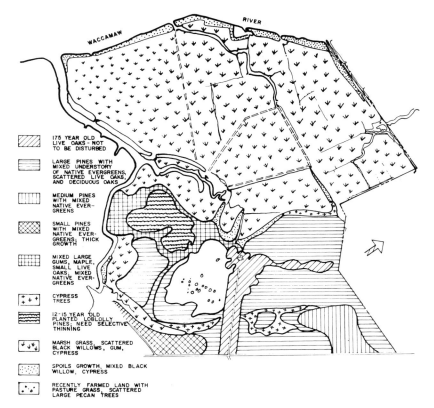

175 YEAR OLD LIVE OAKS - NOT TO BE DISTURBED

LARGE PINES WITH MIXED UNDERSTORY OF NATIVE EVERGREENS, SCATTERED LIVE OAKS, AND DECIDUOUS OAKS

MEDIUM PINES WITH MIXED NATIVE EVERGREENS

SMALL PINES WITH MIXED NATIVE EVERGREENS; THICK GROWTH

MIXED LARGE GUMS, MAPLE, SMALL LIVE OAKS, MIXED NATIVE EVERGREENS

CYPRESS TREES

12-15 YEAR OLD PLANTED LOBLOLLY PINES; NEED SELECTIVE THINNING

MARSH GRASS, SCATTERED BLACK WILLOWS, GUM, CYPRESS

SPOILS GROWTH, MIXED BLACK WILLOW, CYPRESS

RECENTLY FARMED LAND WITH PASTURE GRASS, SCATTERED LARGE PECAN TREES

DENDROLOGICAL EVALUATION STUDY

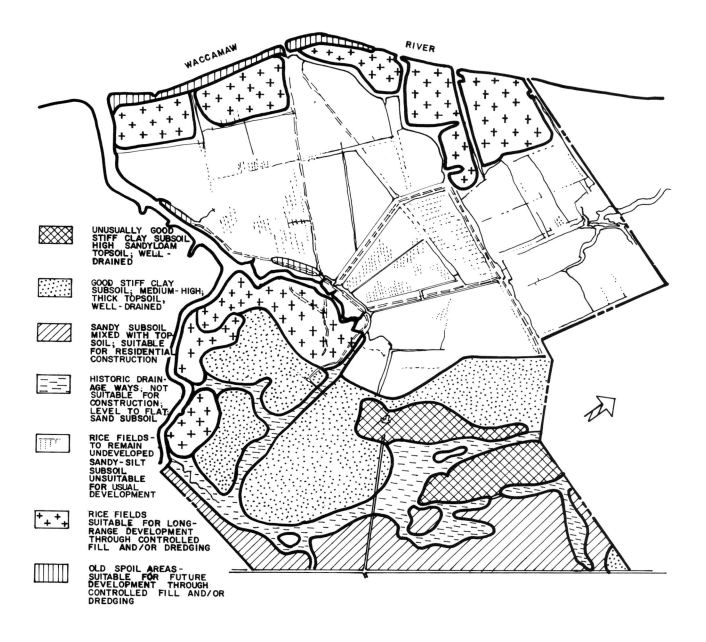

WACCAMAW RIVER

UNUSUALLY GOOD STIFF CLAY SUBSOIL HIGH SANDYLOAM TOPSOIL; WELL-DRAINED

GOOD STIFF CLAY SUBSOIL; MEDIUM-HIGH; THICK TOPSOIL, WELL-DRAINED

SANDY SUBSOIL MIXED WITH TOP-SOIL; SUITABLE FOR RESIDENTIAL CONSTRUCTION

HISTORIC DRAIN-AGE WAYS; NOT SUITABLE FOR CONSTRUCTION; LEVEL TO FLAT; SAND SUBSOIL

RICE FIELDS-TO REMAIN UNDEVELOPED SANDY-SILT SUBSOIL UNSUITABLE FOR USUAL DEVELOPMENT

RICE FIELDS SUITABLE FOR LONG-RANGE DEVELOPMENT THROUGH CONTROLLED FILL AND/OR DREDGING

OLD SPOIL AREAS-SUITABLE FOR FUTURE DEVELOPMENT THROUGH CONTROLLED FILL AND/OR DREDGING

LAND & SUBSOIL EVALUATION STUDY

historic river community comprised of old rice plantations along the Waccamaw, Black and other rivers, all meeting at Georgetown, South Carolina, where they empty into the Atlantic. All are tidal, but the plantations are far enough inland so that the rivers are fresh water. Thus these plantations flourished two hundred years ago when long-grain Carolina rice sold at a premium on the world market. A system of dikes and control gates accurately controlled water levels in the fields.

The 600 a. "heart"of the original 1200 a. plantation comprised of the

rice fields and the old planter's home was bought by the developer who felt it to be one of the most pleasant areas in the U.S. in which to live with a temperate climate, outdoor activities, resort areas and second homes. Yet so-called quality development in the coastal Carolina has been practically non-existent. Most development has been brutal, and this developer felt he might show a new format: sensitivity and conservation.

We decided that most of the rice fields would be restricted from development and kept for esthetic

and conservation purposes. This meant that less than half of the property would be developed, with a large portion of this utilized for community purposes. The 175-year-old plantation house and gardens and the 1/4 mi. avenue of equally old live oaks leading to it were made community property. The house is restored and on the annual spring tour of plantation houses in Georgetown County. Buffer zones and lakes were made community land and a new community building was designed without interfering with the old plantation house.

Additional acres were purchased off-site to accommodate community residents' recreational needs: beach house, stable, and pastures. The project was planned for conservation and a quality environment with a mere 150 available lots and 150 condominium sites, a result of the overall plan rather than the usual developer's concepts or rules of thumb.

Naturally, when the number of saleable items is reduced and the quality of the amenities rises, the cost of these items for sale goes up. The planners and the developer are confident that there are those who are sensitive to the integrity of the development and shall want to live at Litchfield Plantation.

Usually in this region, soil evaluation, topography, ground water evaluation, drainage and flooding considerations, and worthwhile existing tree locations establish a rather well defined pattern for the planner to use as a design base. The existing conditions are so restrictive and critical that they must become the first order of study. It's too easy to overlook the ingenuity of the 18th century planters, thinking they developed these great rice plantations on a trial-and-error basis, with hand labor and primitive tools.

This was brought home when we attempted to solve drainage problems in a 20th century manner with modern equipment and methods. Utilizing the low areas as lakes to handle the storm water, aerial topography and ground surveying were employed; the lake shapes were carefully staked in the field and then adjusted to the worthwhile trees.

Initially we had to cut ditches through the property to drain these low areas sufficiently to work in them; these ditches were mostly on a level line traversing the entire site, and were the approximate center-lines of our lakes. After working some months in these areas, we discovered we were right on top of hand-dug ditches laid out by the initial developer, the first planter. The ditches had been obscured by collected leaves, undergrowth and sheer time . . . but our studied route was identical. The original "developer" had to avoid large trees as he did not have the modern equipment that allowed us to move through the woods as we wished, but he had solved these same problems, leaving reminders for us to ponder 200 years later.

This was our cue, and this was our lesson; development wisdom was not invented by the first bulldozer operator with a conscience. It comes from a knowledge of local ecological history, a willingness to avoid the fast buck, and work consistently for long-term value.

The Rice Marsh as a Non-Development Unit

The rice marsh as a "non-development unit" is a new element in U.S. resort community design. Back when tidewater rice brought premium prices on the world market, the marshes sold at $1000 per acre. Today at Pawley's Island 320 of these acres have been set aside via restrictive covenants by developers of Litchfield Plantation, untouched by a plan that uses the remaining 300 a. for a luxury community.

The rice fields will stay as they are, since to create any large lakes where they exist would destroy the overall character of the property and create many problems. With their old ditches and dikes rebuilt (to repair the damage by otters, muskrats, and an occasional alligator) the rich fields offer canals for small-boating and fishing. Bicycles and horses can negotiate most of the dikes, and limited duck-hunting continues.

Generally, however, the marshes' values in visual and conservation quality have been the major consideration. All 95 single-family and 100-plus condominium sites of the completed Phase I (190 a., June '70) are located up from the fields on heavily wooded grounds. The word "lake" used on some of the plans is an indication of a completely diked area where the water level is controlled to encourage ducks and geese to stop. At the edge of the fields a marina on the Waccamaw River occupies the site of an old flailing house. You can still travel by boat into Georgetown to tie up on Main Street, or to visit other plantations, or out into the Atlantic.
H.M.

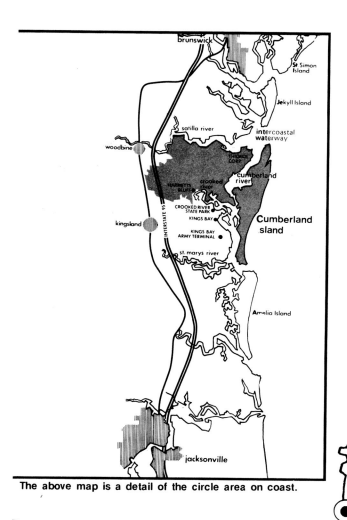

The above map is a detail of the circle area on coast.

Cabin Bluff Project

By THEODORE J. WIRTH

The creation of Cumberland Island National Seashore presents an unusual planning and development relationship for Cabin Bluff, a 50,000 a. pinewood plantation on the Georgia coast.

In 1972, Congress authorized Cumberland Island National Seashore, located among Georgia's Golden Isles 30 mi. north of Jacksonville, Florida. In addition to the island itself, the National Seashore plans include a 12 mi. parkway and a mainland reception center, both to be located on the Cabin Bluff property, the gateway to the seashore.

For 32 years Brunswick Pulp and Paper Company has managed Cabin Bluff's 50,000 a. as a pinewood plantation in such a way as to preserve the natural values of the area. Thus, the site has retained an unusually stable harmonious setting of upland hummocks, swampland, wildlife habitat and natural buffers to salt spray and coastal winds.

What would be the effect of thousands of visitors crossing Cabin

Bluff? This and other questions prompted the company to reexamine their property in terms of impact and options for development.

The company will continue the property as a pinewood plantation, retaining its environmental integrity while not denying obvious advantageous land-use options made possible by the National Seashore, and soon-to-be-completed I-95 on the west edge of the property.

Brunswick Pulp and Paper contracted our firm, Wirth Associates, to develop the comprehensive land-use plan and a 20-year development strategy for Cabin Bluff. Our planning process featured close coordination between client, participating consultants and the National Park Service.

This coordination represents a relationship which became increasingly clear in the planning: the Seashore would enhance Cabin Bluff and vice versa. For example, the scenic drive to the National Seashore through Cabin Bluff can provide a transition for the visitor from I-95 to the relatively undisturbed natural setting of Cumberland Island.

This differs radically from many national parks where nature begins only where commercial interests leave off at the park boundary. Likewise, Cabin Bluff can benefit from the influx of people drawn by the Cumberland Island Seashore, opening up recreational and residential development potential.

The planning sequence turned to nature first. We inventoried, evaluated, and interpreted the ecologic zones, hydrology, topographic relief, and soils suitability of the site from a development aspect. Fortunately, as part of a continuing management plan, Brunswick Pulp and Paper had developed over the years detailed soil survey maps and vegetative inventories. This shortened the time required for our resource specialists and landscape architects to evaluate the site.

We found the 50,547 Cabin Bluff acres divisible into five ecologic zones: bottom land hardwoods, pine flatlands (roughly 75% of the total and acreage), upland hardwoods, cypress ponds, and salt marsh. Since the bottom land hardwoods, cypress ponds, and salt marshes are highly productive wildlife habitat and have a low tolerance to development, we recommended that these areas not be developed.

After plotting the existing watercourses, watersheds, and the 100-year flood-prone areas, we found the upland areas most suitable for road construction and future housing, as can be seen from the accompanying maps.

Upon completion of the physical inventory, we developed a comparison matrix, establishing numerical values for each ecologic

Upland Hardwoods

cumberland island

upland hardwood

and soils category based on degree of suitability and constraint. Mylar overlays for each component gave us a composite land capabilities map. An evaluation of this map supplemented by the inventory maps defined five land capability categories for development.

Type	Total Land Percentages Acreage	of Total
Prime	1,772	4.5%
Good	3,817	9.7%
Fair	4,217	10.7%
Marginal	8,321	21.2%
Unsuitable	21,200	53.9%
Total	**39,327**	**100.0%**

Only 14.5% of 5600 a. were recommended for development. These are generally located on peripheral uplands, but isolated from one another by large sections of lowland.

We then took these development limitations and the aesthetic characteristics of the natural setting and applied them to findings of the market study. The market study focused on evaluating access and comparing similar existing land developments and markets along the Atlantic Coast from North Carolina to Florida, including the impact of Disney World.

Salt Marsh

ATLANTIC
OCEAN

salt marsh

CUMBERLAND
RIVER

We found primary home sites and industrial park developments have little market potential here, but a second-home market does exist within the two-day travel time market area created by the interstate system.

Out of this grew the development strategy and plan: a two-phase development program to be extended over a 20-year period in accordance with market potential, road completion dates, and National Seashore visitation. The program proposes development of mostly residential-resort communities and some tourist-transient facilities.

Each development is designed to be compatible with its natural setting. For example, Lake Village which is intended to capitalize on an existing duck pond area will be quite different in character from Black Point Recreational Community which takes advantage of its high overlook and scenic view of Cumberland Island.

Because the residential areas are planned to be of low density (one-acre lots) to medium density (six condominiums an acre) and are separated by large areas of natural habitat, the environmental and plantation integrity of Cabin Bluff will be maintained.

Phase I development planned for 1975-1985 includes five sites:
Black Point
Recreational Community	1,004 a.
Cumberland Village	140 a.
Cabin Bluff Lodge	200 a.
Shellbine Harbor	750 a.
Grover Island	430 a.

These sites comprise seasonal and retirement communities organized around a complete range of recreational and support facilities. Initial

Pine Flatwoods

Cypress Ponds

sales will offer both individual lots and the increasingly popular villas offered as condominiums.

We proposed Black Point as the logical location for the initial second-home resort development, since it already has access and is close to the Intercoastal Waterway and the proposed National Seashore ferry to Cumberland Island. In addition it enjoys a scenic view of Cumberland Island through its protective upland hardwoods. Waterfront lots, cluster condominiums, and an 18-hole PGA championship golf course and clubhouse on the upland promontory constitute the Black Point Site Plan.

Cumberland Village is to be located adjacent to the mainland reception center. This village will be a hub of activity, providing necessary services for the National Park Service headquarters and visitor center as well as for the second home-resort populace.

Phase II development proposes continued expansion of Cumberland Village, Cabin Bluff Lodge, and Shellbine Harbor to their full development potentials. Added development includes three residential-resort communities and a travel center:
Ceylon Bluffs	1200 a.
Lake Village	230 a.
Satilla Point	
Recreational Community	920 a.
Woodbine Travel Center	

The proposed parkway and road joining these communities create a loop system from the I-95 Woodbine

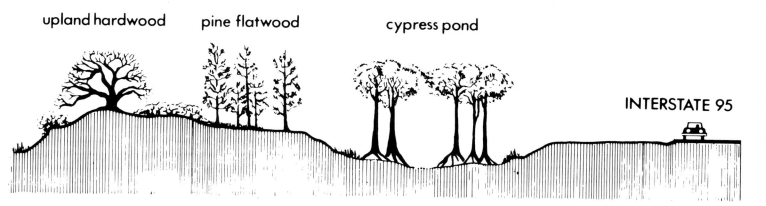

cabin bluff

upland hardwood   pine flatwood   cypress pond

INTERSTATE 95

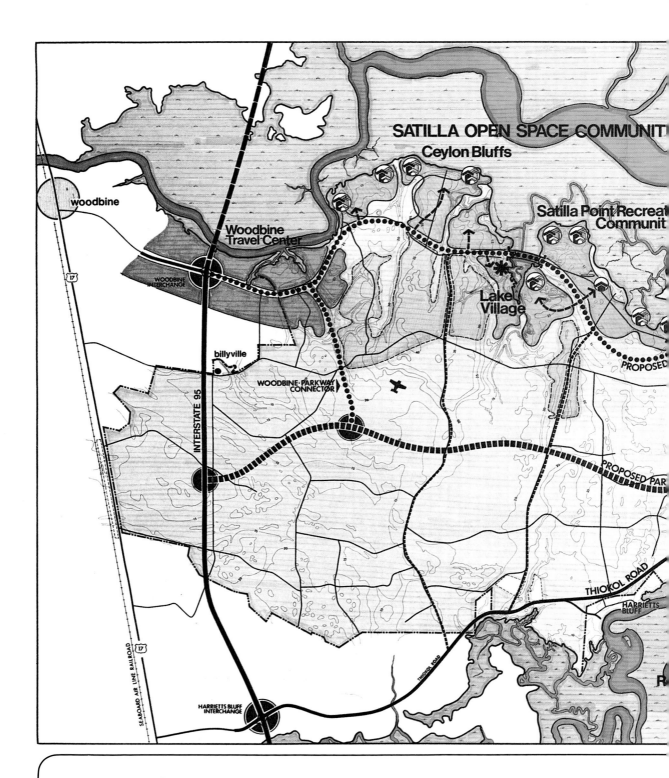

SATILLA OPEN SPACE COMMUNITY
Ceylon Bluffs
Satilla Point Recreation Community

woodbine

Woodbine Travel Center

WOODBINE INTERCHANGE

17

billyville

WOODBINE PARKWAY CONNECTOR

Lake Village

PROPOSED

PROPOSED PAR

INTERSTATE 95

SEABOARD AIR LINE RAILROAD

17

HARRIETTS BLUFF INTERCHANGE

THIOKOL ROAD

HARRIETTS BLUFF

THIOKOL ROAD

R

a land use plan
CABIN BLUFF PROJECT

prepared
SOUT

70

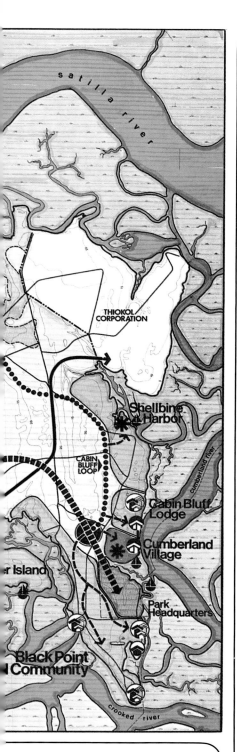

LAND USE PLAN

circulation

▬▬ PROPOSED PARKWAY

●●● PROPOSED ARTERIAL

▪▪▪▪▪ POTENTIAL FUTURE ARTERIAL

--➔ PROPOSED COLLECTOR

⊕ INTERCHANGE

✈ AIRPORT

commercial

✳ VILLAGE CENTER

⌂ LODGE FACILITIES

▦ POTENTIAL TRAVEL CENTER AREA

residential

▨ LOW DENSITY (AVERAGE 1/2 ACRE LOTS)

◉ MEDIUM DENSITY (CONDOMINIUMS 6/ACRE)

recreation

◠ COUNTRY CLUB

⚓ GOLF COURSE

⛵ MARINA

▢ CONSERVATION AREA

other land uses

▤ LAND WITH POTENTIAL FOR DEVELOPMENT

☐ SURROUNDING LAND USES

▤ TIDAL MARSH (TO BE PRESERVED)

prepared by

THEODORE J. WIRTH AND **ASSOCIATES**
billings, montana
chevy chase, maryland

0   2   4   10
        thousand feet

T REALTY COMPANY
brunswick, georgia

Interchange. The parkway will exclude commercial traffic and provide a scenic route through Cabin Bluff, offering the opportunity for an interpretive program of the plantation and natural setting along the drive. Except for the parkway right-of-way, the pine plantations will remain almost totally intact as part of a conservation area.

Woodbine Travel Center is proposed as a response to the demands created by the projected 50,000 vehicles; and overnight lodging will be needed in the vicinity of Harriett's Bluff and Woodbine interchanges of I-95. The Woodbine Center is to be a mutual effort with adjoining landowners.

We found the scenic qualities of Cabin Bluff comparable if not superior in many ways to quality resort projects on the market. Most similar coastal resorts have direct access to the ocean. Cabin Bluff does not, although the National Park Service's proposed ferry gives access to Cumberland Island's beaches and will attract visitors in itself.

Our strategy to offset this disadvantage was to develop a superior recreational package and a price range oriented to the broader middle income market not solicited by other resorts. The lower price range is feasible for Cabin Bluff because of the comparatively low land-holding costs.

The land-use plan and development strategy for Cabin Bluff, if certainly not the final answer for future development, is the first step in a continuing program of planning and design refinement. The plan serves as a beginning framework that can assure a compatible relationship between the existing setting and man's future use of Cabin Bluff.

Cabin Bluff

Ecological Plumbing for the Texas Coastal Plain

The Woodlands New Town Experiment

By IAN L. McHARG and JONATHAN SUTTON

In 28 sq. mi. of forest, north of Houston, a new city — Woodlands, Texas — is taking shape. It is a unique experiment. The plan of the new city is based on a comprehensive ecological study; indeed, it is the first city plan produced by ecological planning. Yet, its uniqueness will not be immediately visible. The housing groups contain pleasant and decorous homes set in the forest. The only exceptional fact is that the trees and shrubs will be so close to homes. Although not immediately apparent, the unique qualities of the Woodlands are pervasive and they derive from its ecological plan.

The planning process for Woodlands presented a novel experience for Wallace, McHarg, Roberts and Todd since the initiation of work in 1971 as part of a team of consultants planning an 18,000 a. new town for the Mitchell Energy and Development Corporation. It consisted of a four-year relationship beginning with a study of the region, selection of the new town site and the development of principles applicable to a single house or lot. The Woodlands job presents a planning method, developed during the project which is overt, explicit and replicable.

Having accumulated and interpreted the biophysical data describing the region and the 18,000 a. site, a method was developed which insured that anyone who employed the data and the method would reach the same conclusions. Moreover, the data and method were printed in four technical reports, describing the ecological inventory and interpretation as well as the ecological plans and consequential principles to be employed in land and site planning. Thus any engineer, architect, landscape ar-

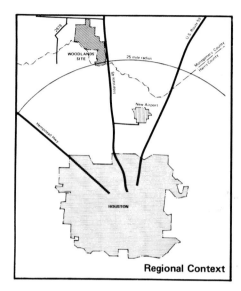

Regional Context

chitect, developer, and the client himself were bound by the data and the method.

Because of its comprehensive analysis from the region to the residential setting, the Woodlands project represents a generic study with broad application to the entire physiographic region of the coastal plain from Long Island, New York, to Florida and Texas. In this region there is a wide commonality of geophysical and biological phenomena.

Challenges of the Woodlands Site

The Woodlands site presented many problems. First, it is almost entirely forest — at once attractive, but also a difficult environment in which to build. Secondly, it is flat, indeed, so flat that local wisdom holds that you cannot predict where water will run unless you know which way the wind is blowing. Next, a high percentage of the soils are poorly drained. And finally, the site's streams are characterized by very low base flow and very high peak flows causing ex-

cessively broad and shallow floodplains in the flat topography. Nearly one-third of the site is within the 100-year floodplains of Panther, Bear and Spring Creeks.

A crucial ecological concern was how to preserve the woodland environment while draining the land for the new community. Orthodox drainage would have required destruction of the forest in order to lay drain tiles.

As most landscape architects and planners know, engineering principles related to storm drainage throughout the United States were largely developed in the northeastern cities and were appropriate to conditions of the crystalline Piedmont on which these cities were located. These principles emphasize accelerating runoff and disposal of this runoff in piped systems. An elaborate vocabulary of equipment and techniques composes this drainage technology.

The Coastal Plain, a great ground water resource, requires the opposite approach often inviting retardation of runoff to maximize recharge. Ecological planning for the Coastal Plain suggests solutions contrary to the orthodoxy of engineering. This was dramatically true of the Woodlands. It therefore became necessary to create, not only an ecological planning method appropriate to this unique and difficult region but to demonstrate its efficacy and economy to dubious engineers. Its effectiveness has now been clearly demonstrated. The elimination of a piped storm water drainage system as anti-ecological and excessively expensive was an important factor in the engineers' conversion to ecological planning. The development of an inexpensive natural drainage system was a necessary corollary.

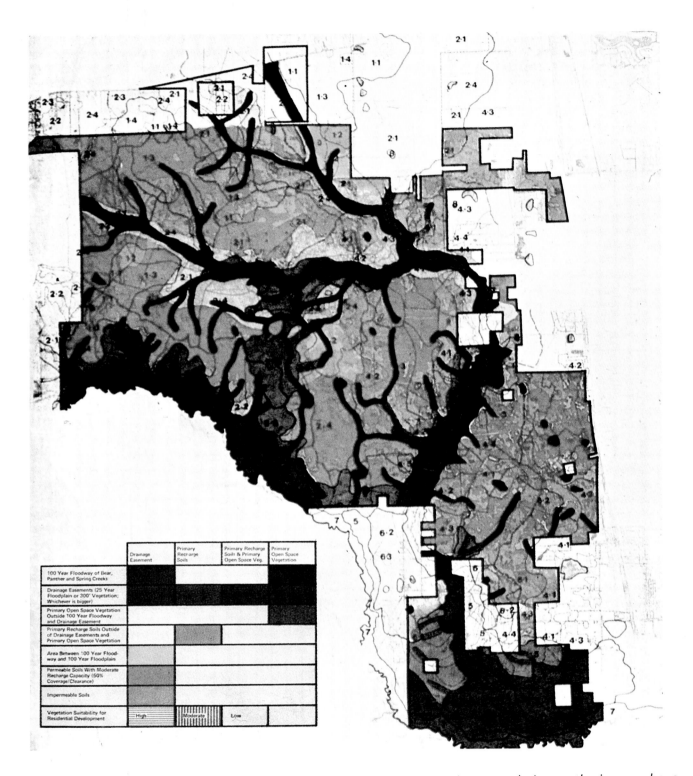

	Drainage Easement	Primary Recharge Soils	Primary Recharge Soils & Primary Open Space Veg.	Primary Open Space Vegetation
100 Year Floodway of Bear, Panther and Spring Creeks				
Drainage Easements (25 Year Floodplain or 300' Vegetation; Whichever is bigger)				
Primary Open Space Vegetation Outside 100 Year Floodway and Drainage Easement				
Primary Recharge Soils Outside of Drainage Easements and Primary Open Space Vegetation				
Area Between 100 Year Floodway and 100 Year Floodplain				
Permeable Soils With Moderate Recharge Capacity (50% Coverage/Clearance)				
Impermeable Soils				
Vegetation Suitability for Residential Development	High	Moderate	Low	

Varying levels of "landscape tolerance" for man-made developments are shown on design synthesis map above. This map produced a broad open-space network and indicated thresholds which were recognized in the subsequent revision of the general plan.

Contrast between conventional drainage ditch in nearby development, above, and natural swale, inset, used throughout Woodlands for slowing down stormwaters.

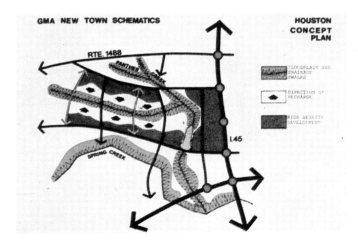

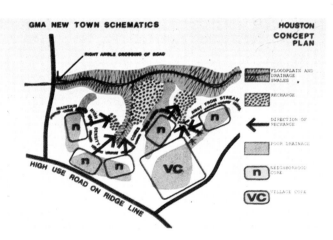

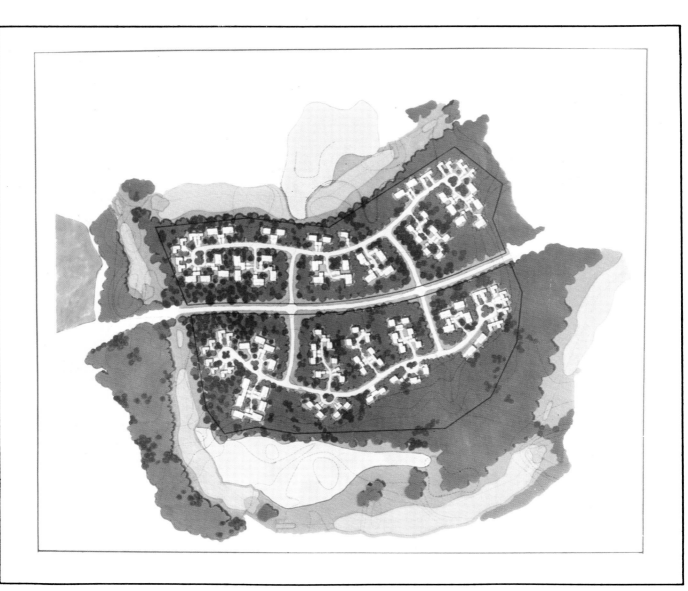

After guidelines were applied to two parcels of 48 a., the above site plan resulted. The drainage system has been designed (says WMRT) so that the roads perpendicular to the slope of (each) parcel intercept and direct runoff to points easily drained. Typical new town houses are at right.

The economic benefits of this approach were clearly demonstrated in the first engineering cost estimates for the storm drainage system of the new city. The costs of a natural drainage system were compared by the engineers with those of the conventional method of site drainage.* The construction cost calculations for the storm sewers required for the conventional system were $18,679,300 while the natural drainage system costs were $4,200,400, an impressive saving of $14,478,900. Such figures accelerate conversion to ecological principles. There is no better union than virtue and profit.

The First General Plan
In 1970 WMRT was retained to undertake an ecological study for Woodlands New Town. Gladstone Associates were retained to prepare market analyses. Richard Brown provided engineering studies and William L. Periera was responsible for land-use planning. Robert Hartsfield was the coordinating planner for the client. It is fair to say that the ecological studies were contracted less with a profound conviction of their necessity than as a concession to public environmental consciousness. The immediate objectives were three-fold: to ascertain market feasibility, to design a plan consonant with the market and environmental opportunities of the site and to apply for a HUD Title VII grant of $50 million.

The solution to these problems became so critical to the feasibility of the project that the ecological study moved from inconsequence to dominance. It determined the form of Woodlands. Moreover, the HUD review process concentrated upon environmental factors. The ecological study was conducted simultaneously as a planning and environmental impact analysis and this contributed largely to the award of $50 million in 1971.

All program allocation evolved from the ecological imperative that required maximizing recharge, protection of permeable soils, maintenance of water table, diminution of runoff, retardation of erosion and siltation, increase in base flow of streams, and the protection of natural vegetation and wildlife habitats. The satisfaction of these re-

quirements provided the major structure of the plan and became influential at the smallest scale of development.

In the General Plan, arterial and collector roads were sited on ridge lines away from drainage areas. Development density was generally most intense near major roads and intersections and decreased with distance from these locations. Intensive development was located on areas of impermeable soils (for example, the Metro Core). Minor residential streets were used as berms perpendicular to the slope of the site to impede flow over excessively permeable soils. Design solutions such as the installation of permeable paving were recommended to increase the storage of storm water. (An experimental parking lot with porous paving has been constructed at the Commercial Leisure Center — the village focus for Woodlands' First Phase — and is part of a monitoring program established by Rice University with grants from EPA and WDC.)

Phase I Planning
The next engagement of WMRT in Woodlands involved the first phase of development — an area of approximately 2000 a. which was called Grogan's Mill Village. Detailed soil and vegetation surveys were computerized, from both field surveys and false infra-red photography, and one-foot contour interval topographic maps were prepared.

At this point three members of WMRT refined the concept of natural drainage, their objective to develop a method utilizing the attributes of the existing drainage system — streams, swales, ponds, natural vegetation (with its litter layer), the storage capabilities of soils and to enhance this network by designing all infrastructure to satisfy water management objectives. Impoundments, settlement ponds and basins, berms to encourage recharge, golf course construction, highways, roads and streets were all considered as adaptive strategies to meet demands of a natural drainage system.

Having determined the structure's essential concept, it became necessary to quantify it. Elaborate studies were conducted to ascertain the contribution of each soil/vegetation type to the proposed water regimen. This investigation developed into the description of coverage/clearing ratios.

Determination of Landscape Tolerance as Established by Coverage/Clearing Ratios
Landscape tolerance is an index based on the requirements of the natural drainage system and the quality and adaptability of vegetation types. The measure of landscape tolerance is the percentage of a given soil and vegetation type which may be covered by imper-

---

*Turner, Collie and Braden, Inc., Houston.

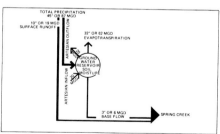

Woodlands Hydrologic Cycle

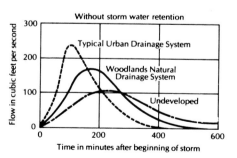

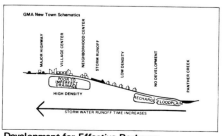

Development for Effective Recharge

New Town Storm Runoff Recharge

vious surfaces or cleared.

Permissible coverage is that fraction of an area which can be rendered impervious without affecting the ability of the remaining soil to absorb local runoff from high frequency storms (one inch in six hours). The amount of permissible coverage was derived from the excess storage capacity of each soil (down slope), which in turn was based on the depth of the upper pervious layer, its percolation rate and the height of the seasonal high water table and direction of slope.

Soil Groups A and B were termed "Recharge Soils" and depending on their location were recommended for protection. Permissible clearing for each vegetation type reflects its quality and landscape value, its importance as a wildlife food source, and its tolerance to compaction and development activities. Permissible clearing is expressed as a percentage of area which may be cleared. Since both permissible coverage and permissible clearing are expressed as percentages, they were readily combined on one chart which served as an index of landscape tolerance.

Determination of Land Use Impacts as Measured by Coverage/Clearing

Commercial uses, residential types and densities, golf courses and roads were examined for their landscape impacts. Each use was evaluated in terms of the amount of impervious surface and clearing involved. Expressed as a percentage of a given unit of land, this coverage/clearing ratio measured development impact.

A study of the areas of impervious coverage, five, 10, or 15 ft. around all building types (depending upon number of stories and construction technique for different densities) shows that coverage and clearing generally rise per unit area with higher densities. In order to check this conclusion against a wider sampling of developments, coverage and clearing as a percentage of total development area were taken from 22 representative site plans. The plans were published in various forms, and densities varied from one to 20 D.U./a. All schemes analyzed relied on at-grade parking.

Design Synthesis

In order to match landscape tolerance with development impact a design synthesis base was created to illustrate the distribution of landscape tolerance. In addition, this base kept the land-planning process up-to-date and made it site-specific. A base map was developed which included a composite of all the salient ecological data. The synthesis involved a method of adding ecological factors in stages so that the contribution of each stage could be properly understood. The data were added to the map in sequence: (1) Field topography (one foot contours); (2) Drainage pattern (watershed boundaries); (3) Soil types; (4) Vegetation types; and (5) Adaptive strategies.

Adaptive strategies include minimum open space corridors associated with the 25-year floodplain or the minimum of 300 ft. wide drainage easements and storm water storage areas, which for the most part take the form of Waller ponds. (Shallow ponds, predominantly open, occasionally forested, which are situated on the impermeable Waller soils.) Degrees of permissible coverage/clearing were established, based on the coincidence of soil types, vegetation types and drainage patterns. These ranged from preservation to nearly total modification.

The four steps leading to delineation of tolerance ranges in the Design Synthesis are: (1) Natural Drainage Systems; (2) Recharge Soils; (3) Prime Vegetation; and (4) Impermeable Soils, Flat Land Less than one percent and Permeable Soils and Sloping Land Greater than one percent (to be developed according to the percentages indicated on the Coverage/Clearing Chart).

Step four makes a distinction between land which is relatively well drained (because it has either permeable soils or slopes greater than one percent), and flat, poorly drained, impermeable areas. One percent slope was adopted as the limit for positive drainage in a forest with a litter layer. Therefore, impermeable soils on slopes less than one percent are considered poorly drained. The soil's ability to drain effects directly the permissible coverage/clearing percentages. The Design Synthesis Map shows the essential structure of Phase I on which the various program elements were subsequently tested.

Matching Development Impacts with Landscape Tolerance

The combination of landscape tolerance (permitted coverage/clearing) of given soil and vegetation types with land-use requirements (required coverage/clearing) yielded an allocation of development impacts in a gradient from complete protection to extensive modification. Development types having extensive coverage/clearing impacts were matched with soils of excess storage capacity for surface water and/or vegetation of high quality.

Each level of constraint required some additional development cost such as for increased drainage improvements, fill or landscaping. An opportunity implied a decreased or normal development cost. The costs were then compared with the anticipated value created by both natural and man-made amenities. The final synthesis revealed the least cost/greatest benefit solution on the basis of the existing landscape characteristics.

There were persuasive social or economic factors that modified the Design Synthesis — altering locations of roads, golf courses and shopping areas. Detailed vegetation studies caused us further to modify the plan. We calculated the acreage of each soil and vegetation type within each watershed to find its "development capacity" — i.e., the maximum area that should be covered and cleared. For example, the Grogan's Mill Village center was located directly upon impermeable soils — rather than over one of the absorptive recharge areas. We put all golf courses to a similar test — balancing development opportunities against costs to the environment.

Such were the steps leading to the land-use plan, which was derived from these structural elements: (1) drainage ways; (2) road net; (3) golf courses; and (4) community facilities and pedestrian paths.

This plan showed us those areas suitable to become development parcels. To each of these parcels we assigned a "program module" depending on their aggregated landscape tolerance, surrounding amenities, physical configuration, marketing potential and staging strategy. The exercise of matching "program modules" or density types with specific sites in Phase I (1,947 a.) suggested 4,350 dwelling units on 1,255 developable acres, including community facilities, a business park, and the commercial leisure center (note this reserved 692 a. as open space). In order to insure a sufficient pace and market response in Phase I much of the program called for single-family lots.

Plan for the Village of Grogan's Mill
The residential areas of The Village of Grogan's Mill are organized around the Community Leisure Center (CLC), which includes commercial and office facilities, community conference center, and sites for recreational activities. This large package of leisure facilities will give the CLC a catchment area well outside the Woodlands. It will supply the community focus and marketing impetus for Phase I.

The neighborhood in Zone I relates to the championship golf course, country club, tennis and conference center. The neighborhood in Zone 3 is focused on the Sawmill Community Center at the corner of Grogan's Mill and Sawmill Road. The public golf course, the existing Lamar Elementary School, with adjacent Tamina Mill Community Center and proposed park, provide neighborhood facilities and identity in Zone 4.

The three neighborhoods will be linked to the CLC by six miles of pathways for pedestrians and bicycles. The rights-of-way of the pedestrian system will provide at some future point the option of an alternative mode of vehicular transportation to the automobile. Grade-separated crossings of Grogan's Mill Road are planned at the CLC and at the Sawmill Community Center to reduce conflict between the pathways and the arterial road.

Guidelines for Site Planning
In order to carry out the actual "fitting" of development types to specific site conditions, a decision tree was devised. Using summary sheets for hydrology, limnology, soils, vegetation, wildlife, and climate, the method reviewed the critical site conditions revealed dur-

ing the ecological inventory. It also suggested the environmental objectives and physical adaptations related to each natural phenomenon. The main concern of the manual, though, is with the achievement of the natural drainage system and the preservation of the woodland environment. This is to be achieved through careful organization and communication of site planning information for each development parcel.

The key method was developed to identify specific site conditions and relate them to design strategies. Ecological data related to soils and vegetation has been organized in a form which can be readily utilized by planners and designers. A manual outlines the step-by-step process of applying selected criteria to a particular site. Given the criteria and the procedure, all consultants who employ the method can produce a variety of designs, all of which will satisfy the stated environmental objectives. The outcome of the process provides only the framework for the plan or design. The quality and character of the final product will still depend on the ingenuity of the individual site planner.

Site Design
The execution of a site plan for two parcels in Grogan's Mill Village illustrates how the key method of the Guidelines is employed. The parcels in question contain a total of 48 a., separated by a residential collector road and bounded by golf fairways and a primary drainage easement.

Taken together the sites were to form a sub-community of distinctive high and medium-priced detached homes. Of the total acreage all except the 50 ft. vegetation easements along Millrun Drive (to be assigned to the Community Association) and the land required for internal streets was to be converted to deeded home-sites. A preliminary scheme called for sites for a total of 113 units consisting of 43 single family detached high (SFD-H) and 70 single family detached medium high (SFD-MH). Up to 20% of this total could be planned as clustered patio-type units. The patio option was exercised to achieve the necessary match between program impact and permissible coverage/clearing ratios.

Dwelling Unit Prototypes
Several housing prototypes were recommended as a response to specific site conditions identified in the "Guidelines for Site Planning." Each site condition suggested a different design approach with respect to foundation type, setback requirements, access, parking, yard-space and housing configuration. A representative group of unit prototypes indicates the range of creative responses to specific site conditions.

General Plan Revisions
Since 1972, changes in the first General Plan have been made as more detailed ecological, marketing, transportation, and design studies have been completed and the 1,947 a. first construction phase begun. In

COVERAGE DISTURBANCE PERCENTAGES			
Soil Group	Soil Types	Capacity	% of Area that can be made Impermeable
A	Lakeland, Eustis	High	90%
B	Boy, Albany	Medium	75%
C	Fuquay, Lucy, Leefield, Bruno, Wicksburg	Low	50%
D	Angie, Crowley, Segno, Sorter, Splendora, Susquehanna, Waller	None	100% (effectively impermeable under present conditions)

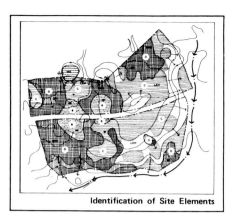
Identification of Site Elements

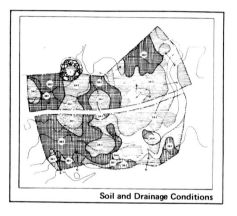
Soil and Drainage Conditions

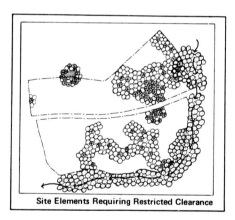
Site Elements Requiring Restricted Clearance

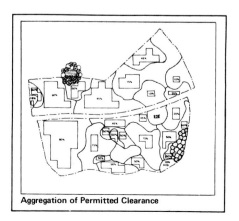
Aggregation of Permitted Clearance

1973, the following consultant team was assembled to prepare a Revised General Plan. In addition to WMRT, Land Design Research was responsible for land-use planning; LWFW for marketing, Turner Collie and Braden for engineering; Green Associates for transportation; and Espey and Winslow for hydrology.

The methods that had been developed in Phase I were used in revising the General Plan. A design synthesis base was established for the whole new city, indicating degrees of permissible coverage clearing, ranging from protection to nearly total modification. Levels of landscape tolerance are shown on the map by a range of colors. The map also gives an indication of the broad, open-space, framework and the distribution landscape thresholds which structure the Revised General Plan. Three major zones, each with a range of appropriate land uses, are defined by the map.

Primary Open Space — At the Townwide Scale
Primary natural open space for the whole town of Woodlands is conceived of as a conservation zone incorporating the ecologically valuable areas with respect to hydrology, wildlife and vegetation. These areas would include the 25, 50 and portions of the 100-year floodplains of existing streams as well as preserves of highly diverse vegetation suited for conservation, passive recreation, and wildlife food and cover.

Secondary Open Space — At the Development Zone Scale
Secondary Open Space includes components of the natural drainage system not included in Primary Open Space: secondary swales, storm water impoundment sites, and storm water recharge areas. The remaining wet-weather ponds, some of which may be impounded, are included as parts of the storm water control system and for their natural and aesthetic value. Wooded fringes outside of the Primary Open Space system are part of this category as are greenways, large stands of trees selected for preservation, and uncleared areas between development parcels.

Tertiary Open Space — At the Development Parcel Scale
Tertiary Open Space is important at the scale of the individual development parcel. Based on detailed vegetation mapping and analysis, this open space system is comprised of those areas of vegetation not cleared for development purposes; small natural green spaces among detached houses or in open areas in higher density development (vegetation buffers along roads or in traffic islands). The on-lot drainage system would also be incorporated into the uncleared areas which make up Tertiary Open Space.

The hierarchy of open spaces just described will provide a multi-purpose network integral to the maintenance of natural drainage, of the forested environment and of certain species of indigenous wildlife. High intensity recreation areas such as golf courses and playgrounds are situated to complement the basic structure of the Natural Open Space System but do not infringe upon it.

Test of Land Availability
In order to test how the development program could be adapted to the open space system, three alternatives of land availability were examined. Alternative A respected all elements of the Design Synthesis in terms of primary natural open space, and recreational open space. The acreage outside of the open space zone was divided into areas which could accept low, medium or high coverage in terms of development intensity, based on the coverage clearing guidelines of the Design Synthesis.

However, the available buildable acreage and the no proceeds open space of alternative A did not balance with the projections of the economic model. To achieve a larger buildable area, Alternative B developed certain areas of the Vegetation Preserve and 100-year floodplain. Alternative C increased the open space area over Alternative B in order to restore the balance between open space priorities and the need for an adequate economic return, while permitting selected recreational and low density uses within the Secondary Open Space System.

Alternative C formed the basis for the General Plan Revision, suggesting the overall capacity of the site for development, and establishing guidelines for land-use allocation. When an evaluation of coverage/clearing was applied to this alternative, the analysis suggested a "carrying capacity" of 33,000 dwelling units and 9,972 developable acres, given the assumptions of the economic model.

The primary objective of the Revised General Plan was to provide the direction for up-to-date development decisions that would be realistic as well as innovative. The plan will remain flexible in order to respond to changing conditions brought on by such concerns as the energy crisis or new market preferences. However, the site-specific basis of the plan will insure the attainment of certain fundamental environmental goals.

Community Structure
Once the open space network was established for the new city, the areas with highest priority for development were defined. The activity focus of these development zones and the business hub of the new community was the Metro Center. Residential villages of approximately 2000 a. each were organized around the Metro Center. The Village of Grogan's Mill was the first of these to be developed, and University Village will follow in the next phase.

The Revised General Plan intermixed employment, residential and community facilities at all scales. The higher density residential areas were related to the major roadways, to areas of maximum coverage/clearing, and to convenience shopping at the village center and Metro Center. The medium density residential areas (townhouses, quads, and patio units) were generally located near the major roads for easy access. These units allow for more flexibility in site planning, screening and orientation than do single family lots. The single family dwellings were generally related to the smaller scale streets, neighborhood collectors, loops and cul-de-sacs. Since about 60% of the proposed residential land is for single family detached

housing, the edges of major roads will be protected by vegetation easements, landscaping, and special fencing.

Lessons Still To Be Learned from the Woodlands
Much of the Woodlands story remains to be told. The opening day for the new city was October 17, 1974. However, the first three years of its development may be critical to the success of the new community. The ecological, social, and economic objectives of the new city will be greatly influenced by initial decisions and commitments. The objectives of the Woodlands Plan over the next 19 years are to minimize ecological and social costs while achieving economic goals. As each new area is considered for the next phase of development, the current benefits and costs as well as feasible alternatives will be considered.

Underlying such an evaluation is the continuing process of evolution in the ecological planning initiated over the last three years. It has established a set of analytical methods and vocabulary of adaptive form responsive to the hydrology, limnology, soils, vegetation, wildlife and climate of the coastal plain.

However, it is the quantitative capabilities of the method which deserve the greatest attention and refinement. While the data and the hypothesis employed in formulating the conclusions await testing, they represent a dimension of causality and quantification not heretofore accomplished in any projects by WMRT.

As the building of the new city is carefully monitored by the environmental planning staff of the Woodlands Development Corporation and several outside research groups, an in-depth understanding of this physiographic region will be gained. During the course of this research, the ecological planners' understanding of man's impact on the natural system of this area and of the manner in which these impacts can be mitigated will be greatly enhanced.

In fact, the construction of the first phases has already given testimony of the effectiveness of the natural drainage system. James

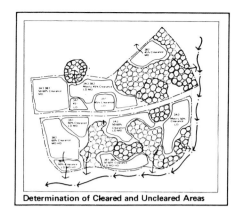

Determination of Cleared and Uncleared Areas

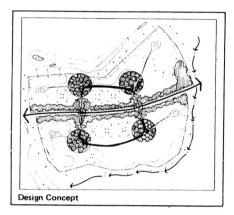

Design Concept

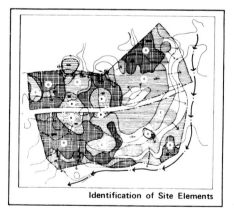

Identification of Site Elements

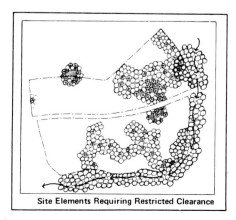

Site Elements Requiring Restricted Clearance

Veltman, Director of Environmental Planning for the Woodlands, reports, "that despite 13 in. of rain in three days, and four inches of rain in one hour, there was no surface water within six hours and that during this period there was effective operation of detention ponds which filled when it rained and reverted to their normal level within six hours."

The results of this planning and such observations should be immediately communicated to the Woodlands residents. They should understand the drainage function of wet-weather ponds and temporarily wet lawns. They should realize that the presence of water in their yards is critical to the survival of the woodlands themselves. They should be aware of the special characteristics of their environment, their community, and the exciting experiment of which they are a part.

If such a level of environmental awareness was reached in a new community, it would be unique. During the period when Reston and Columbia were being planned, environmental issues had hardly been voiced and ecological planning was at a rudimentary stage. It would be fair to say that no ecological planning, as it is now understood, was employed in the initial design of either of these new towns. The planning of Woodlands occurred in a much different social climate during a peak of environmental sensitivity and in a particularly intolerant landscape. Moreover, the environmental impact analysis composed a major requirement for the HUD title VII application.

The effort to achieve increased public (not just professional) awareness of the generic qualities and resources of the Coastal Plain landscape is one of many new direc-

tions in the ecological planning work for the Woodlands. These new directions are the logical extensions of what has already been achieved. The next steps in the planning process are as follows: monitoring the developing of a new city; understanding social processes in the Woodlands; energy conservation as a community design determinant; transportation as a design determinant; and adaptive architecture in the Woodlands. All these new directions, if vigorously and carefully pursued, will lead to an increasingly successful adaptation of the man-made to the natural environment.

Epilogue
The Woodlands site is a mute record of ancient seas and the deposition of clays and sands which underlie the forest. The seasons of the year, the hydrologic cycle and the recycling of vital nutrients continue. Hurricanes sweep over from the Gulf and produce intense storms. Incident precipitation enters the ground and in time replenishes the stream flow. Vegetation holds the sandy erodible soil in place and provides food and cover for wildlife. It is critical to recognize the dynamism of these physical and biological processes, for they affect man and are affected by his intervention.

As projects such as the Woodlands are planned, built and monitored throughout the country, many lessons will be learned from each, thereby increasing the collective knowledge of the profession. Such knowledge of each physiographic region should be thoroughly documented and understood. This resource, if exploited with creativity and imagination, will usher in a new era of environmental design.

Crazy-Quilting the Jersey Meadows

By KEN NELSON

The future of the Hackensack Meadowlands has generated much controversy and long debates. Located in northeastern New Jersey, the Meadowlands can be generally described as a severely disrupted tidal marsh/estuary of 19,600 a. surrounded by a vast urban complex that includes Newark, Paterson, Passaic, Jersey City, Hackensack and New York City.

Now a state commission created by the New Jersey legislature has completed two major beginning efforts in its study and direction of the Meadowlands' future: (1) a comprehensive land-use plan; and (2) a zoning ordinance/map.

For centuries the Meadowlands was able to resist any intensive development and the fact that large sections of this area remain vacant today attests to those resistive powers. Two principal factors, the low elevation of the land which induces tidal flooding, and the instability of the existing soil structure which requires the use of sophisticated engineering techniques, combined until quite recently to make any large-scale development projects within the Meadowlands too costly and in some instances impossible.

This is not to say that the Meadowlands has not been subjected to and affected by a variety of disruptive influences. Beginning with the early Dutch settlers in the 17th century, man has attempted over the years to leave his mark on the land. Some succeeded, many others failed; in the process more than 7000 a. were committed to various forms of development

In 1969 the Hackensack Meadowlands' 19,600 a. (partially shown in airview) were under the jurisdiction of 14 municipalities; now one commission is responsible for planning.

Vestiges of the natural marsh remain in spite of disruptive influences (diking, ditching, pollution, dumping, dredging, etc.).

New York City's skyline is a familiar backdrop to Hackensack, New Jersey, Meadowlands which early Dutch settlers 300 years ago first tried to exploit.

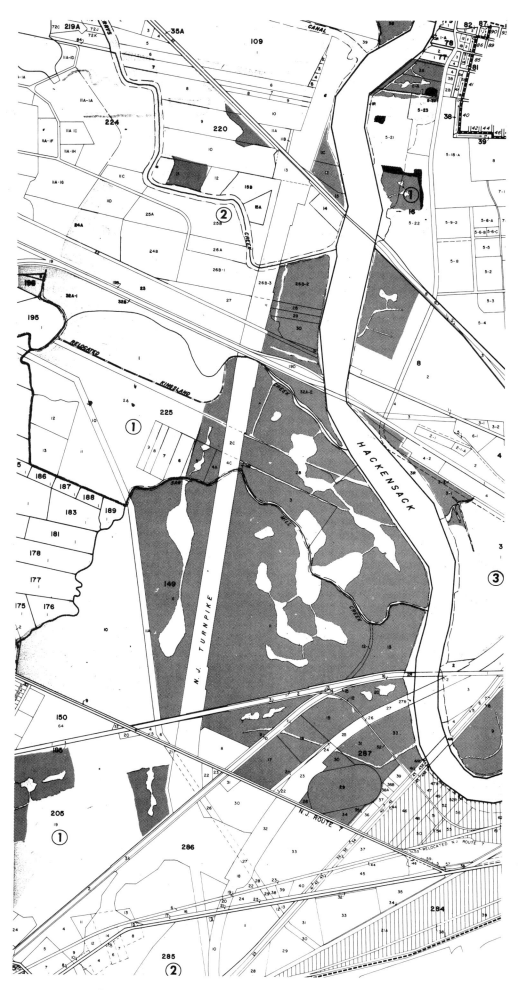

resulting in an existing land-use pattern of an extremely haphazard nature.

And all this severe disruption of the Hackensack River estuary, its formation having begun 20,000 years ago with the retreat of the Wisconsin Glacier, has occurred within the relatively short time of 300 years. Disruptions include ditching, diking, use of insecticides to control mosquitos, industrial pollution, road and rail building, dumping, filling, dredging, as well as the construction of industrial and commercial facilities.

The present condition of the marsh, then, is not surprising in view of this massive intervention. What is surprising is that vestiges of the natural marsh and the life it sustains are still present.

In 1969 New Jersey's legislature realized that the potential of the Hackensack Meadowlands was being lost. Noting that the 19,600 a. were under the jurisdiction of 14 separate municipalities, the legislature saw the need to place the Meadowlands under one governmental unit, the Hackensack Meadowlands Development Commission. This was made responsible for the orderly, comprehensive development of the new Meadowlands district "in order to provide more space for industrial, commercial, residential, public recreational and other uses," and at the same time concern itself with preservation of the delicate balance of nature.

The legislature has given the commission broad planning and implementation powers: (1) to prepare, adopt and enforce a master plan and corresponding zoning ordinance (the zoning powers of the 14 municipal governments that formerly held jurisdiction over this area are in effect superseded by the commission's powers); (2) to establish a tax-sharing program aimed at sharing among 14 municipalities school costs associated with new residential development within the district; (3) to create special districts for the express purpose of raising revenue by

Open-space map shows part of 6000 undeveloped acres within the district, proposed as permanent open space. Another 6000 a. will accommodate housing for 100,000, plus other uses.

direct assessment of a given area; (4) acquire or hold land by any legal means including eminent domain; (5) undertake development projects; and (6) review and regulate all subdivisions within the district. These form the basis of effective regional planning.

The size of the Meadowlands district can scarcely allow it to be called a region, but for the first time in New Jersey's history the theology of local control has been reformed under the obvious need for more effective and comprehensive planning.

The question now arises: what has the commission accomplished so far? First, and most importantly, it established a solid foundation by retaining two consultants known for excellence and innovation in their respective fields. Dan Coleman and Associates of San Francisco prepared a comprehensive land use plan for the district (released in November 1970), and the legal firm of Ross, Hardies, O'Keefe, Babcock, McDugald and Parsons of Chicago developed a zoning ordinance expertly tailored to fit regional needs. The zoning ordinance and official zoning map translating the Coleman plan into a legal document were adopted on November 8, 1972.

The comprehensive land-use plan is addressed to the problem of determining how much of the district should be retained as permanent open space. Should that open space consist primarily of wetland areas preserved in their natural stage and which wetland areas should be preserved and which developed? Unfortunately, the commission, partly because of its legislative mandate and partly because of the fair market value of Meadowlands real estate could not develop a master plan based solely on environmental criteria. (In recent months land sales within the district have in some cases exceeded $100,000 per acre.) As a result several prime wetland areas must be sacrificed to development if the plan as a whole is to succeed. This fact, together with other decisions, has caused many environmental groups to attack the commission.

Briefly, the master plan proposes that 6000 of the remaining 12,000 undeveloped acres within the district be set aside as permanent open space. The 6000 a. to be developed will accommodate housing for 100,000 people, a major regional shopping center, a sports complex (football stadium and racetrack),

several transportation centers, and additional industrial development. The racetrack and stadium are being constructed, 600 water-oriented housing units are on the drawing boards, and industrial construction continues. Each proposed new development receives exhaustive engineering and planning review; the commission's powers have been legally upheld; and research is underway to find a new method of disposal for 50,000 tons of solid waste per week.

The administration of the open space program is the responsibility of the Environmental Programs and Planning Section. The engineering and legal sections of the commission also play a key role in the day-to-day decisions which affect the operation of this program. In addition, other activities carried on within the environmental programs and planning section such as water-quality monitoring and estuarine research help reevaluate the open space priorities that have been established.

The open space plan, in existence since 1971, calls for a complex network of waterways, active and passive park areas, tidal wetlands, school sites, and waterfront recrea-

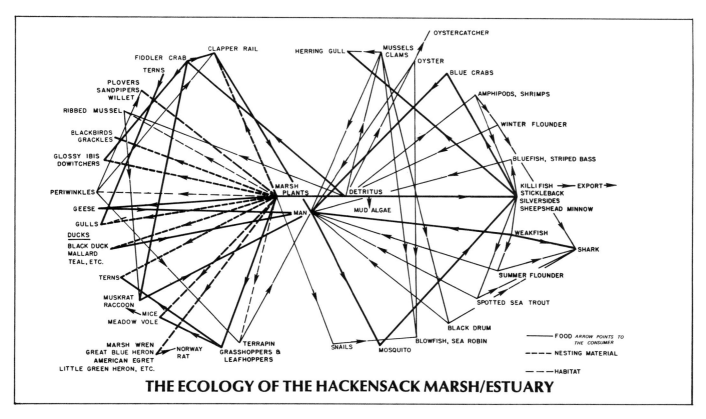

THE ECOLOGY OF THE HACKENSACK MARSH/ESTUARY

tion areas. The Hackensack River will serve as a major focal point and the river's tributaries are visualized as connecting devices. The waterways, wetland areas and waterway buffer strips are intended to be the heart and lifeblood of the open space system. Together they will comprise nearly 75% of the entire network. Park sites, schools and waterfront recreation areas will serve as satellite focal points utilizing natural upland features, inactive landfill sites and prime waterfront locations.

Hackensack Meadowlands leave an extremely false impression. For many years it was considered "dead" — incapable of supporting life except for the Norway rats and herring gulls living off garbage dumps. But a surprising amount of life does exist within this distressed ecosystem. Hunters and trappers have watched the wildlife decline over the years, but by no means can this area be considered dead. Flounder, bluefish and striped bass are gone because the lower part of this estuarine system is so severely stressed (lack of oxygen, thermal and industrial pollution) that the migration of these fish into the open sea and back again becomes impossible. The blue claw crab, however, has returned in recent years and fiddler crabs, grass shrimp, killfish and a species of mussel known as Congeria leutopata now exist in abundance. In fact, steps have been taken, with the planting of oysters, mussels, and clams, to expand the number of marine species.

Sections of the Meadowlands also serve as resting and breeding areas for a variety of songbirds, shorebirds, waterfowl, birds of prey, and marsh birds. More than 200 species have been observed within the district from time to time; some are quite rare, such as the glossy ibis and others, such as the snowy egret, can be found in surprisingly large numbers. A partial listing of some of the birds that utilize the Meadowlands follows:

Spotted Sandpiper
Killdeer
Common Tern
Red-winged Blackbird
Marsh Wren
Black Duck
Canvasback

Blue-Winged Teal
Green-Winged Teal
Pintail
Mallard
Rough-Legged Hawks
Marsh Hawks
Screech Owl
Short-Eared Owl
Great Blue Heron
Green Heron
Black-Crowned Night Heron
Least Bittern

Each open-space site has its own biological characteristics, thereby determining what type of life can be supported. The disruptive activities mentioned earlier have created dozens of microenvironments, each with a distinctive vegetative pattern, each accommodating varying degrees of tidal inundation, and each subjected to developmental intrusions — some extensively, others to a lesser degree. The result is a crazy-quilt pattern — areas of unbelievable beauty existing within close proximity to environmental disasters.

The proposed open-space sites range in size from 10 to 800 a ; as mentioned previously, they will all be legally interconnected in some way at some future point in time. Certain sites provide great vistas, especially old landfill areas which are elevated 30 ft. to 40 ft. above the surrounding terrain. One site in particular, the proposed Losen Slote Creek Park, provides an interesting transition from wetland through lower field and upper field to a lowland forest. Another site, the Kingsland/Sawmill marsh, is a lovely piece of wetland which is considered the key element of the open space plan. Consisting of more than 800 a , it rivals, in terms of beauty and productivity, other wetland areas along the East Coast which exist under less stressed conditions.

A description of the open space preservation techniques which the commission hopes to employ is a complex topic. Basically, the commission is attempting to utilize a variety of techniques which will preserve the maximum amount of open space for the least amount of money. This, of course, is the goal of any open space planner; however, in this particular case, considering the fair market value of the land, it is imperative that techniques be used

which will minimize the preservation costs.

Briefly, the commission has used its zoning powers to announce its intention to preserve certain areas. This has been done in two ways. First, certain areas have been designated as Marshland Preservation sites and others have been placed in a Park and Recreation category. This places a temporary hold on a piece of ground until a more permanent technique can be applied. The second zoning power which the commission expects to utilize is known as the Specially Planned Area concept. An SPA, which is similar to a PUD, has an open space requirement attached to it. For example, in an Island Residential SPA the developer must set aside 50% of the area as permanent wetland open space. In addition, certain design, developmental and operational controls are imposed to insure that the integrity of the open space is not jeopardized. The developer, in effect, pays for the open space that is set aside within the SPAs, thus leaving the commission to concentrate on how to "pay" for the open space sites that have been designated on the zoning map as Marshland Preservation and Park and Recreation areas.

As mentioned in the preceding paragraph, zoning a piece of ground for open space usage provides only a temporary hold. Obviously, our legal system prevents zoning land for open space purposes unless the owner of record agrees to that zoning or is ultimately compensated in some way. The more permanent techniques that the commission will employ to reinforce its zoning decisions are:

1. Purchase of the fee simple title where the other less expensive techniques fail.

2. Purchase of scenic and conservation easements, based on the fair market value of the land, where the cost is not prohibitive.

3. The use of the commission's eminent domain powers where it is not possible to agree upon a proper reimbursement.

4. Acquisition of courtesy easements granted for a token fee. This becomes possible if the owner of record is another governmental unit or a quasi-public organization.

5. The use of the state of New Jersey's riparian claim which is a complicated issue that clouds the question of ownership to several thousands of acres within the district. Basically, the riparian rights doctrine states that any land flowed by the mean high tide belongs to the state. This doctrine dates back to colonial times, unfortunately; however, the state did not actively pursue this doctrine until quite recently. The courts will ultimately decide the ownership question and where the state is judged to be the owner, the land will be set aside as permanent open space.

6. Donation of the fee simple title. This is expected to be a rare occurrence.

7. The use of some form of the public trust doctrine, as defined in a recent Wisconsin legal decision, may be applicable to a select number of sites. In that decision, known as the Just case, the court declared that where a public harm will be prevented by restricting development, the state is only utilizing its police powers; therefore, a taking is not involved and compensation is not required.

The commission's strategy is to apply as many of the preceding techniques to as many of the sites as possible. Where we find a site protected by only one technique, we consider that site to be endangered.

A final note involves the problem of finding funds which will allow the commission to purchase easements and other fee interests where it is deemed necessary. The shortage of open space funds is undeniably acute; the commission is relying on those remaining monies from New Jersey's Green Acres bond issue, any federal funds that are available, donations from private sources and the general public. The commission also has the capability of establishing a revenue producing recreation facility, such as a golf course, which might supply a limited source of funds for additional acquisitions.

The commission is actively involved with at least a dozen projects each employing one or more of the preservation techniques previously listed. A partial listing of the projects includes:
— The dedication of 85 a. of prime wetland along the Hackensack River by the New Jersey Turnpike Authority. The Turnpike will also construct boardwalks through this wetland area as a means of providing controlled public access.
— The Hartz Mountain Realty Company has agreed to donate a combined wetland/upland area as a nature park. Federal funds are being sought which will make it possible to provide the necessary improvments that a nature park requires.
— The New Jersey Sports and Exposition Authority has agreed to preserve and restore 135 a. of wetland located along Berrys Creek. An environmental education center will be constructed adjacent to this site which will be of value to school children in the immediate area.
— The city of Jersey City has agreed to grant a trail easement to the commission along a portion of the Jersey City Aqueduct which traverses the district. This trail will be used as a means of access to a wetland site that the commission envisions as an outdoor biological laboratory.
— Several boat launching and boat landing sites are in the process of being established. These sites are a necessary ingredient in the commission's plan to see the river and its tributaries serve as a recreational resource.

In all of the aforementioned projects, the role that each site is expected to play within the total open space system has been studied. While there is a need for active recreational facilities, there is an equal need to determine where in this ecosystem people should not be allowed, or allowed only under careful supervision. The commission has had to determine what types of key estuarine habitat need protection from the curious. But simple prohibition is not the complete answer. Procedures must be devised which will encourage and reward the curious, not simply banish them from areas that are susceptible to disruption.

The next 10 or 20 years will see either the success or failure of the commission's plans. The tools are certainly available and the goals are certainly commendable. Only time can judge, however, whether or not the commission will be successful in its endeavors.

Postscript 1978 by Ken Nelson
This account of four years ago touched on the planning efforts that had been undertaken. Quite frankly, however, at that time there was much doubt about the viability of the master plan that had been prepared and adopted. It called for a number of things that the skeptics felt could not be accomplished — i.e. preservation of open space, the introduction of housing into an area that had not been considered suitable for residential use. Happily the skeptics have been proven wrong — at least so far.

A great deal has been accomplished in the last four years. A sports complex has been constructed consisting of a football stadium and racetrack. This facility has become the focal point of the Meadowlands District. In addition, a large-scale town house project and industrial growth has continued despite the general slowdown in the economy of the Northeast.

Development oriented projects have received much publicity, but so has the commission's open space preservation program. Several thousand acres of the delicate marsh ecosystem have been set aside for the enjoyment of future generations.

It appears the Meadowlands master plan is a viable one. It is not without its problems, however, and future decisions by the commission will be as critical as many of the earlier decisions. The integrity of the master plan is being challenged by some developers as well as by a number of vocal citizen groups. It may require periodic refinement but such refinement should be objective and based on valid planning grounds.

Union Bay Reaches Inland to Shape an Arboretum

By PETER M. HARVARD, GRANT R. JONES and PHILIP N. OSBORN

A stranger site for an arboretum can hardly be envisioned, but the University of Washington (Seattle) Advisory Committee on Arboreta had little choice in 1971 when they designated it to be the potential administrative, teaching, and research core of the university's expanding arboretum program.

As late as 1915 the site on Lake Washington had been open water, — shallow, reedy Union Bay — covering the deepest peat deposit in the state. Lowering the lake's level the next year to accommodate a lock connection with Puget Sound created an extensive marsh. Through the years, landfilling occurred in random response to the expansion of the city and university. By 1960, sophisticated engineering techniques utilizing floating "dikes" allowed filling to extend rapidly over the marsh, compressing the peat below. Rubble and refuse were extending into open water in 1965 when landfill opera-

tions ceased, and succeeding years saw attempts to cap, sculpt and seed the quaking landfill.

After 1972 the site was left undisturbed, to find its own repose, and the committee found themselves in a position likened to a gypsy palmist struggling to divine the lifeline in a mutilated hand. Grassy and windswept, actively subsiding at rates in excess of one foot per year, generating methane and sulfur dioxide that burned in surface cracks, the former "Montlake Dump" was a unique, dynamic anthropic site.

Without traditional environmental inventory data available, the basic planning question of siting the buildings and collections had to be deferred until the future extent of the subsidence was determined and it was known whether flooding would result.

If the area was to be inundated, it was necessary to know what factors were most influential in the continu-

ing settlement in order to determine how much of the site would eventually be reclaimed by the lake. To the best of our knowledge, no similar documented studies of any length have been attempted. Although we used careful, scientific methods of data collection and rigorously tried to portray their importance accurately, a certain subjectivity has undoubtedly crept into the analysis, through the need to derive a final map — however conservative. This is probably unavoidable, as intuitive reasoning usually plays a part in any scientific study.

Numerical settlement data for the 115 a. Union Bay site were available for 1967-1971, although these were difficult to interpret since regrading for improved surface drainage had substantially altered the surface topography. We resurveyed the site and, through new photogrammetry, were able to extend this data to

The 72-year history of arboretum site, in maps, on this and following pages.

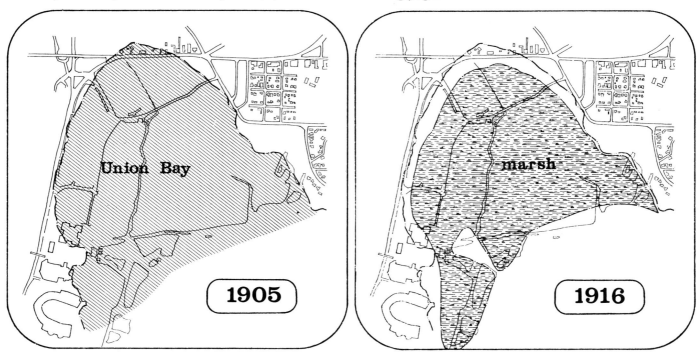

1905   1916

March 1975. Data for 1971-1975 were considered most accurate since no regrading of the site occurred after 1971.

Recognizing that certain relationships exist within the geology/soils/hydrology ecomass, and that these relationships determine the unique characteristics of the site, we first tried to identify the major causes of settlement. These elements were: depth to groundwater table; relative permeabilities; thickness of overburden covering the fill; thickness and extent of refuse fill; and placement of dikes surrounding the site. This list was later expanded to include: the height of ground water (measured above an artificial horizon to eliminate bottom slope effects); the thickness of saturated refuse (as compared to the total thickness of refuse); and movement of ground water through the fill.

Field studies were undertaken from March through June 1975 to determine the primary or triggering factors in the settlement rate. Data collected were: soil type and permeability; thickness of the overburden (depth to refuse); depth to water, subsurface and surface soil temperatures; quality of water (both surface and groundwater); and chemical composition of emitted gasses.

All data collected were compiled

and plotted on standard base maps (1" = 100'). Where possible, isometric lines were used to contour and extrapolate from the data. Overlay maps were then prepared, enabling the individual data elements to be compared and contrasted, as we attempted to visualize any correlations and to reach some conclusions about the interaction of natural processes on unnatural elements.

This process of "overlay and compare" was supplemented with cross-sections of representative areas and graphs of the numerical subsidence data. Several of the basic data maps were used in composite to prepare second generation maps. For example, a topographic contour map and a depth to water plot were combined to form a contour map of the water surface elevation.

Although several interacting factors were found to influence the subsidence rate, the primary identifiable ones were the total thickness of saturated refuse and the progressive northwest to southeast movement of the mounded water table causing a change in the relative height of saturated refuse. These factors were portrayed in conjunction with past settlement records and a subsidence potential map was drawn to show the areas

where greatest, moderate and least subsidence can be expected to occur. The subsidence records were then used to draw a series of projected settlement curves for these various areas. These curves were applied to the subsidence potential map and the result was a series of maps showing the presumed land form in future years.

Knowing the future shape of the land — assuming no new intervention by man — was the key. Design is a synthetic act giving form to meaning in the landscape. We held secure with nature, in this case the real designer, in order to draw our plan. On this site, "working with the landscape" took on a new meaning, and the plan reflects a total commitment to allowing the site to find its own internal angles of repose.

Narrowly considered in terms of fostering basic research and teaching in the plant sciences, the site was quite adequate. But its unique combination of characteristics makes it suitable for a broader effort in reclaiming "urban wilderness"; plant survival under stress from toxic gas, acid water and constant dynamism; rejuvenation of urban anthropic soils; landfill dynamics, leachate mitigation; habitat creation and enhancement — a host of problems

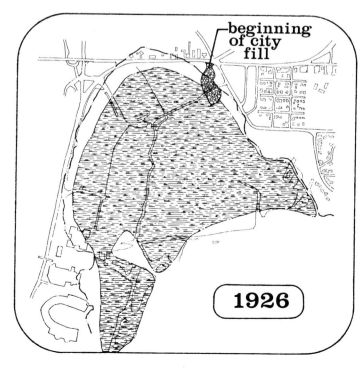

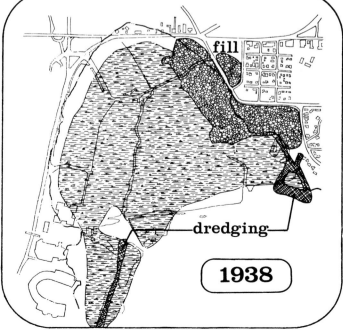

Ultimate shape of settled site reveals new water bodies, the whole arboretum overlooked by offices and library at upper right. Scale model by Jones & Jones.

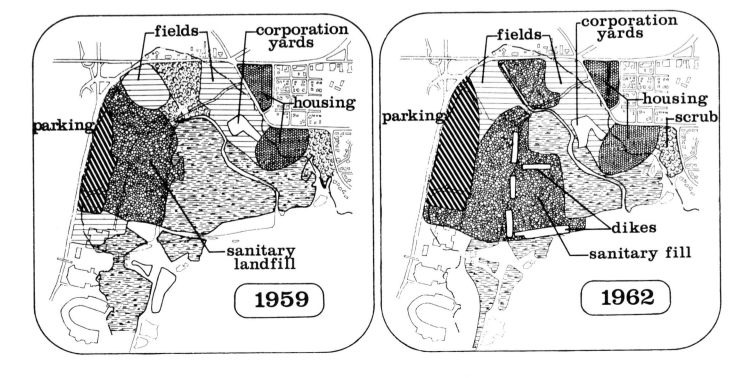

we are forced to meet head-on everywhere.

The Arboretum functions pivot around the core building complex, designed to house the administrative offices of the University of Washington Arboretum and provide office space to horticultural support groups. Classrooms and meeting rooms would be flexible to service a wide range of users. The library and herbarium would be accessible to scholars and visitors. Greenhouses would be connected to the laboratory portion of the building and serve both propagation and research functions, while the labs would be suitable for a range of research activities. The building would be energy conserving, utilizing solar panels and a low profile,

History writ vertically in this soil profile.

View across present landfill toward University of Washington.

Exhaust vent for flared methane gas on western edge of site.

Sudden hailstorm interrupts machine-aided digging of soil samples.

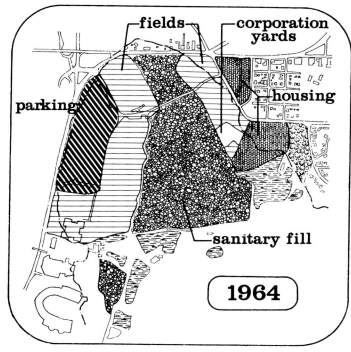

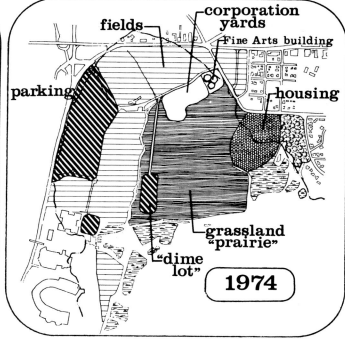

and be oriented for maximum insolation and minimum visual impact.

The nursery is securely located in the sheltered lee of the original remnant marsh/shoreline vegetation and the plan distributes more permanent collections and facilities around the periphery on land made stable by complete compaction or — in the case of the teaching collections along the canal — by timber diking.

Basic support of this facility would come from the state legislature as university capital improvement funds and/or regular academic funding which supports the rest of the University of Washington's ongoing arboretum program. Of the three other sites currently in use, the Arboretum in Seattle's Washington Park (to the south immediately across Union Bay) is best known. This facility, designed in 1936 by the Olmsted Brothers, Brookline, Massachusetts, is a magnificent display and public service effort enjoying great public support. Active lay horticultural and botanical groups in the region have provided considerable financial assistance in the past (the Olmsted Plan in 1936, and this effort in 1975) and maintain an active interest in the overall program.

Left unchecked, the eventual inundation of the interior of the site will eliminate the ephemeral pond edge habitat critical to shorebirds rarely seen in the heart of the city, as well as the passive grassland cherished by walkers. Theoretically, some potential exists to modify the extent of the inundation and future research and observation will provide the necessary guidance for that decision.

This strange, anomalous landscape was created through ignorance and expedience. Through patience and concern we may ease its journey toward a more valid, reposeful state, learning its lessons and adding new meaning to the word "reclamation" when the water has the final say.

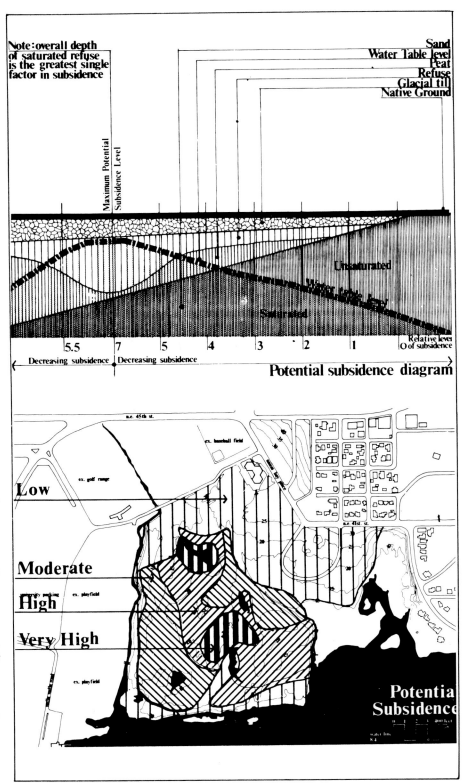

Detailed analysis of underground layers and water levels at last revealed the future landscape. Its future ponds, formed after final subsidence, are shown in "very high" subsidence areas on lower map.

Seeking the Right Environmental Fit for a New Resort Community at Amelia Island, Florida

By WILLIAM H. ROBERTS and JONATHAN SUTTON

Thanks to the ending of the Korean War, a lovely North Florida island with ancient forests, extensive salt marshes, and spectacular dunes was never strip-mined for its minerals, but eventually sold for an unusual resort community now being developed.

The whole southern end of Amelia Island, including four miles of ocean frontage, 1,642 a. of high ground, and 1000 a. of outstanding tidal marshland, had been acquired in 1970 from Union Carbide Company by the Sea Pines Company of Hilton Head Island, South Carolina.

In January 1971 the firm of Wallace, McHarg, Roberts and Todd contracted with the owners to conduct an ecological planning and land-use study which would establish the guidelines for development of a large new recreational community on Amelia, 25 mi. northeast of Jacksonville.

The objective set by Sea Pines Company was ambitious: to find the optimum fit between man's requirements in a new resort and the existing animal and plant ecology, and special natural features of this barrier island, southernmost in a golden string along the Georgia and Carolina coasts.

Under the authors' direction the firm chose to fulfill this objective by developing a design approach which could synthesize information from a wide range of professional disciplines, and re-focus it into a program and plan. The exceptional beauty and fragile nature of the site demanded a detail of natural science data not usually associated with land planning studies.

The planning process for the Amelia Island Project was complex but rewarding. Months of study, coordination, interchange, and review was undertaken by the com-

pany's professional staff and by a diverse range of outside consultants (planners, natural scientists, engineers, market analysts, and golf course architects).[1] This environmental design team was counseled by an Environmental Planning Advisory Council comprised of nationally known experts in planning and design, as well as leaders of local citizens' groups familiar with regional conservation and planning problems.[2]

The consultant group was fortunate in that its client was thoroughly committed to high standards of development and had as a consequence enjoyed considerable success and admiration for Sea Pines Plantation at Hilton Head Island, South Carolina. Furthermore, in addition to the energetic leadership of Charles Fraser, president of the company, an outstanding in-house professional staff added its perspective to the entire planning process.

In evolving a planning method we looked at the environment as a series of "to whom it may concern messages."[3] Our objective was to discern as many relevant messages as possible in making decisions which had environmental impact. Some messages are more obvious than others. A hurricane surge of four-year frequency will positively determine locations to be unsuitable for house sites, whereas it is more difficult to decipher the relevance of other messages, such as the relation of various wildlife species to development locations and conservation practices. The planning method employed to decode these environmental signals had the following sequence.

Data Assembly

In many respects Amelia Island exists in a geographic no-man's land,

being generically but not politically linked to the Golden Isles to the north. We found that coastal studies of natural scientists had generally overlooked the island, therefore much-needed scientific information on the geology, soils, plants, and animals of the island had to be developed in the field by the team of natural scientists.

To initiate this investigation, WMRT sub-contracted with Jack McCormick Associates of Devon, Pennsylvania, for the detailed vegetation mapping and the selection and coordination of other natural scientists for field work. Recognized authorities in climatology, oceanography, geology, limnology, soils, beach erosion, dune restoration, salt marshes, ornithology, herpetology, mammalogy and anthropology contributed specific data and interpretation to this phase of the study.[4]

Spatial Description of the Data

In a project of this scale it was necessary to create a comprehensive frame of reference to record each environmental message by transforming all the information into spatial data. For example, each vegetation type, soil association, or wildlife habitat defined a certain area on the site. In some cases these were very specific areas; in others they were approximate. All were mapped at a common scale and in a manner which allowed comparison and testing for coincidence of phenomena.

Many sophisticated techniques have been developed for recording and interpreting spatial data, including the use of computer graphics and other cell systems with code indices. For reasons of cost, legibility, accuracy, and utility during preliminary phases, we decided in this case to map all data in tonal ranges on translucent sheets and thereafter make additional maps of areas of coincidence and conflict.

No static descriptive maps can accurately convey the dynamics of natural phenomena or man's ever-changing awareness of them. A series of interpretive maps, suggesting the processes of each natural phenomenon over time, was derived from the descriptive data. By recording rates of erosion or relative heights of tides or temperature gradients, such information was categorized and then reconstituted into locational values.

Creation of Locational Values

Certain costs attach to modifying the existing landscape. These may be direct, such as construction costs or service costs (flood protection, provision of sewers, roads, and water supply). There may also be indirect costs in terms of resources lost with respect to maintaining wildlife habitats, natural water supply, and visual amenity. To find the development areas of least cost (both direct and indirect) was the goal of determining locational values. These values were defined by a series of three "nested" matrices. These matrices matched every natural phenomenon with each prospective land use to discover whether it was suitable, moderately suitable, or unsuitable with respect to the physical characteristics of the particular environmental factor. For example, a depth to water table in the range of 0-1.5 ft. (a characteristic of soils) is revealed as unsuitable for residential development because of the hazard to the particular use and the high cost of overcoming the constraint.

This process involved interpreting the base data provided by the natural scientist and then the preparation of a series of maps ranking the attributes of each natural phenomenon for the location of all prospective land uses. For example, the maps of locational value related to vegetation included the following: relative abundance of types, marsh quality, foredune quality, sand/soil stabilizers, and tolerance to disturbance. We matched the locational criteria to the physical characteristics of the site by increasing the refinement of the analysis as we

Matrix 2: Environmental Evaluation Matrix for Residential Land Uses on Amelia Island

Vegetation

Physical Characteristics	Sub-classification Characteristics	Single Family Detached	Bartoli	Pavilion & Pools	Patio	Villas	Town-houses	Dune Houses	Garden Apart-ments	Planning, Design and Management Guidelines
Tolerance to Disturbance	1. sea oats grassland	U	U	U	U	U	U	U	U	no residential uses
	2. sea oats savanna	U	U	U	U	U	U	L	U	
	3. wind-pruned scrub	U	U	U	U	U	U	U	U	no residential uses
	4. wind-pruned woodland	M	S	U	S	U	U	S	M	siting in the field with minimum clearance
	5. broadleaf forest	S	S	S	S	S	S	U	S	
Tree Size	1. over 10" dbh	S	M	M	S	S	S	S	S	selective clearing
	2.									
	3. 6"–10" dbh	M	S	S	M	S	M	S	M	minimum trimming of lower branches
	4.									
	5. under 6" dbh	L	L	L	L	L	L	L	L	
Height of Tree Canopy	1. 0'–6'	U	U	U	U	U	U	U	U	
	2. 6'–12'	L	U	L	U	L	U	U	U	
	3. 12'–25'	M	M	M	M	M	L	M	U	minimum trimming of lower branches
	4. 25'–50'	S	S	S	S	S	S	S	M	preserve canopy
	5. 50'–70'	S	L	L	M	M	S	U	S	
Understory Type	1. wax myrtle	M	S	L	S	L	S	U	M	minimum clearance
	2. slash pine	S	U	U	U	M	S	U	M	incorporate into landscape plan
	3. berry thickets	U	S	U	U	U	U	U	U	
	4. mixed	S	S	S	S	S	S	S	S	
	5. saw palmetto	S	S	S	S	S	S	S	S	incorporate handsome stands into landscape design

□ = Unsuitable   ⊟ = Low Suitability   ▣ = Moderate Suitability   ■ = Suitable

(In the table above: U = Unsuitable, L = Low Suitability, M = Moderate Suitability, S = Suitable)

Environmental Evaluation Matrices for Land Use on Amelia Island (The Site Selection Process)

Matrix 1 Generalized Land Uses		Matrix 2 Land Use by Sub Types	Matrix 3 Sub Type by Site Conditions
			Marsh Related
			Lagoon Related
			Ocean Related
Conservation	C	Single Family ———	Quayside
Passive Recreation	PR	Bartoli	Fairway
Active Recreation	AR	Pavilion & Pools	Interior
All Residential Uses	D1	Patio	
All Commercial and		Villas	
Institutional Uses	D2	Townhouses	
Traffic	T	Dune Houses	
		Garden Apartments	

moved from matrix 1 to matrix 3.

At this juncture the generalized land uses were to serve as broad guidelines for program options and did not identify precise densities and quantities of housing for each area. The residential development mix was based on studies by the Sea Pines Company which indicated that a diversity of dwelling types should be planned to allow for the full complement of recreational and retirement housing demands and site conditions. The particular choice of a dwelling type, site planning, and design would be in specific response to the attributes or constraints of the chosen locations.

Besides the recreational component, the recreational program included 45 golf holes, a marina, yacht club, tennis center, three inn sites, as well as a commercial center for shops, offices and company headquarters.

Economic and social considerations such as the relative real estate demand for different frontages* or the relative accessibility of development zones were spatially displayed. The distribution of these phenomena would obviously influence the settlement pattern and cause certain trade-offs to be made within the range of options suggested from ecological analysis.

---

*A marked preference for marsh lots became apparent. Two lots with both marsh and fairway overlooks later sold for $103,000.

Determination of Suitabilities

Having already mapped each environmental factor in one of several tonal values on transparent maps that represent a range of most-to-least conditions on the site, the next step was to assemble the maps relevant to the suitable location of each prospective land use and superimpose them. The darkest area indicated the maximum coincidence of all positive factors and the fewest constraints on the location for land uses in the general development program.

Still there were unresolved problems. The preceding series of suitability maps did not mediate between the demands of two conflicting land uses for the same site area, even though both might be suitably located according to their own criteria. This required a synthesis process which again depended greatly on mapping as the agent of discovery.

The final synthesis map required graphic innovation. Instead of grouping all the similar values together and assigning a sum value to them, our intent was to show the areas of interaction of locational values. To display this information, two densities of dot screen were chosen to represent conservation value, while two densities of straight line screen were selected to symbolize development value.

Some areas of the site exhibited only one suitability, for conservation or for development. They were less of a problem than areas where suitabilities conflicted. For example, when highest conservation value

coincided with moderate development value, we proposed conservation as the highest and best land use. In the reverse situation, development in such an area might be acceptable provided that it conformed to a set of ecological management guidelines. The final synthesis map determined the trade-offs which had to be made between conservation and development on a comprehensive basis and was modified by the socio-economic parameters of frontage and access referred to earlier.

The Master Plan

Admittedly we built certain biases into the trade-off decisions leading to a master plan. Sizeable areas of each characteristic vegetation type on the property — such as a remarkable cabbage palm swamp — were preserved in their natural state regardless of their relative abundance or importance as a wildlife habitat. This was done to maintain prime examples of the rich diversity of the island landscape.

The pattern of conserved areas suggested the relationship of residential clusters to shared community facilities, so clusters were then linked to the centers by an open-space system of golf cart, bicycle, and pedestrian pathways. Although the master plan shows the distribution of all land uses for the entire site, we made specific locational decisions only for the initial stages of development where more refined data could be employed.

Total Area	2693 a.
Marshbank	968 a.
Additional conservancy areas	364 a.
Resort recreation areas	646 a.
Hy. A1A right-of-way	84 a.
Net developed area	630 a.
Residential area	498 a.
Non-residential support uses	132 a.
Total Dwelling Units	2900

Refinement of the Master Plan

Previous analysis had revealed that the northern end of the site offered the most promising areas for the initial development phase on account of access and diversity of site conditions.

Detailed field surveys provided greater precision in determining constraints on the location of component parts of the residential pro-

Master Plan

Master Land Use Plan

e Master Land Use Plan and Program is the
sult of the combination of the foregoing
udies with the information supplied by the
a Pines Company's market research. Several
eas of the site permitted great flexibility of
oice of residential mix and density whereas
her areas explicitly limited choice. In all
ses, however, standards for site development

and management were necessary to achieve
compatibility.

Gross acreage	2693 acres
Tidal marshland	968.0 ac.
Conservation areas	364.0 ac.
Resort recreation (incl. 45 golf fairways)	643.8 ac.

A.1.A. R.O.W.	84.0 ac.
Roads and utilities	99.0 ac.
Total conservation and open areas	2158.8 ac.
Residential and resort land uses	534.2 ac.
Total dwellings on 498 acres	2900 D.U.
Commercial and resort lodging	36.2 ac.

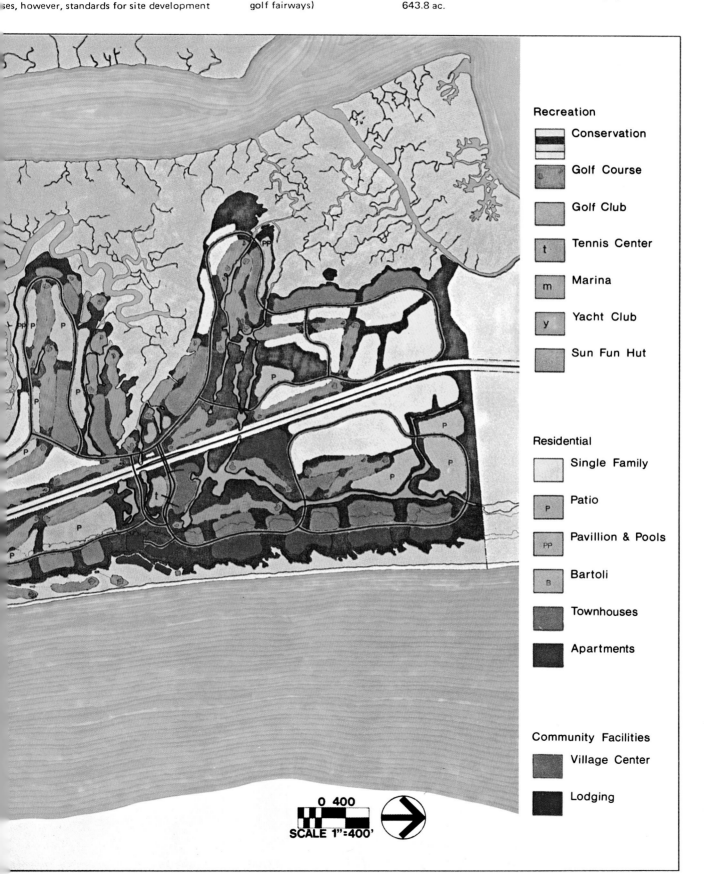

Recreation

Conservation

Golf Course

Golf Club

t Tennis Center

m Marina

y Yacht Club

Sun Fun Hut

Residential

Single Family

P Patio

PP Pavillion & Pools

B Bartoli

Townhouses

Apartments

Community Facilities

Village Center

Lodging

0 400
SCALE 1"=400'

gram. We related various types and densities of residential uses to ranges of elevation.

Vegetation data for zones 1 and 2 was also refined with additional field work.[6] By walking the surveyor's lines, maps were made of particular vegetation characteristics with implications for the structure of residential habitats — tree type, size, canopy height, and understory type.

Distribution of these characteristics had a significant influence on the recommendations for size, density, and location of buildings. Given a choice, for example, between saving a group of larger trees, with diameter at breast height over 10 in. and a high canopy, or a stand of small trees (dbh more than six inches) of lower canopy, the latter would be judged less valuable in terms of ecological value and potential for accommodating various residential types.

The ability to make value judgments at a more detailed site-planning level inspired several specific design studies, and we were fortunate to bring these insights to the particular problem of routing golf course fairways.

Although golf courses are considered as open space in recreational terms, in ecological terms their construction modifies an area far more drastically than any residential layout. Almost 80 a. of clearance is required for 27 holes and a totally new environment of open, irrigated grassland is introduced.

In routing the fairways we worked with the golf course architect Pete Dye to determine least-cost corridors, in the following sequence: first, locating areas of critical ecological value to be conserved and avoiding fairways near these; second, areas with low real estate amenity or other building constraints were mapped as opportunities for fairways as highest and best use. These two maps were then compared with another set showing areas where least environmental damage would occur through fairway clearance.

Once all these maps were combined, the darkest tone revealed distinct corridors on a synthesis map which were refined into an alignment (above). Then we were able to

relate residential uses to the fairways as well as to other valuable site features. Each site's value could now be established by its proximity to natural amenities such as beaches, marshes, lagoons, or to man-made amenities such as golf fairways.

A chart was then prepared to show the acreage of each separate development parcel, its elevation and edge amenity conditions, as well as the types and number of dwellings that could be accommodated. This option chart and map provided an innovative solution to the developer's need to evaluate the various housing mix options and their prospective yield as sales inventory, thereby testing the financial return from many prospective solutions.

In the first development zones 1 and 2, we established a set of design and management guidelines for subdivision and site planning that suggested which particular housing types were most suited to the various climatic conditions, vegetation and elevation of the sites. Some were exposed to ocean gusts, others deeply sheltered within live oak forests, and others were sited amid fragile dunes needing special protection from footprints as well as buildings.

Since completion of the plan in 1971 and its publication, the company has interpreted and supplemented it as development proceeds. Other planners and architects have assisted the company in implementing the principles of the master plan in a highly successful first phase. To have a record of those principles the company published the "Report on the Master Planning Process for a New Recreational Community." The accompanying insert includes 20 of the 68 illustrations from the report.[7]

A master plan must necessarily be a dynamic one, adapting to change like the processes of nature and the human society it is intended to serve. What must not change is the commitment that ensures that man's expansion into such areas takes account of the ecological and human balance his presence is affecting. This particular study offered a unique opportunity to promote that commitment.

1. Planners — WRMT
Natural scientists — see footnote 4
Civil engineers — Bessent, Hammack, & Ruckman, Inc.
Soil Engineers — Ardaman and Associates
Market analysis — Sea Pines Company
Golf course architect — Peter Dye
2. Environmental Planning Advisory Council:
Prof. Patrick Horsbrugh, Professor of Environmental Design and Planning, University of Notre Dame
Grady Clay, Editor, LANDSCAPE ARCHITECTURE
Prof. Vernon J. Henry, Ph.D., University of Georgia, Marine Institute, Sapelo Island, Georgia
Mrs. Helen Bird, President, Southeastern Environmental Council
Marvin Hill, executive director, Jacksonville/Duvall County Area Planning Board
3. From Norbert Weiner's "Design for a Brain."
4. Natural science consultants to WMRT:
Coordinator, Jack McCormick, Ph.D.
Vegetation, Jack McCormick, Ph.D., Richard Squiers
Climatology, Donald Bunting, M.S.
Geology, Vernon J. Henry, M.S.
Limnology, Richard Franz, M.S.
Soils, Ronald B. Hanawalt, Ph.D.
Dune restoration, W.W. Woodhouse. Jr., Ph.D.
Salt marshes, Robert J. Reimold, Ph.D.
Ornithology, David W. Johnston, Ph.D.
Herpetology, Howard W. Campbell, Ph.D.
Mammology, James N. Layne, Ph.D.
Consultants to Sea Pines Company:
Oceanography, Herb Windom, Ph.D.
Oceanography, P. Braun, Ph.D.
Anthropology, Charles Fairbanks, Ph.D.
5. Definitions of general land use categories:
Conservation and preservation: represent areas that should not be developed, because of hazard to life and health, or possess important social values that are ecological, scientific, educational or historic.
Passive recreation: represents activities with low levels of exertion that require low intensity of developed facilities and have minor impact upon the ecosystem; for example, walking, sunbathing, and nature observation.
Active recreation: represents activities of moderate to high levels of exertion with a greater intensity of developed facilities, such as golf courses and tennis courts.
Development density 1: represents all residential uses — single family, detached, bartoli, pavilion and pools, patio, dune houses, villas, townhouses and garden apartments.
Development density 2: represents all commercial and institutional uses, such as village facilities, churches and schools.
Traffic: represents all paths of intensive movement — pedestrian and vehicular.
6. Jack McCormick, Richard Squiers, Edward Boyer
7. All diagrams and maps included in this article have been excerpted from "A Report on the Master Planning Process for a New Recreational Community, Amelia Island, Florida." Copies are available from the Amelia Island Company, Fernandina Beach, Amelia Island, Florida, 32034, or WMRT, 1737 Chestnut St., Philadelphia, Pa. 19103, ($10 per copy).

Minnesota Restores Marshes for Sherburne Wildlife

By THE EDITOR

The nation-wide mania for draining marshes to create farmland in the 19th century continued well into the 20th century, leaving in its wake millions of acres of "reclaimed" farmland — some of it hardly worth longterm farming. In seven states* from 1850 to 1971, there was a 46% reduction in wetlands.

In the process, one of North America's great wildlife regions of bogs, marshes and high water tables in Minnesota was drastically altered in the early 1900s by drainage schemes. Much land was converted to crops and pasture, but many schemes were unsuccessful, thousands of acres reverting to sedge-meadow. Many drainage ditches succeeded only in lowering the water table and increasing spring flooding by accelerating runoff.

Typical of such regions — one noted as a remarkable wildlife hunting ground — was the St. Francis River area 45 mi. northwest of Minnesota's Twin Cities where old glacial remnants — ponds, swamps, moraines, eskers, kames and occasional exposed sand dunes — formerly teemed with wildfowl. By the 1950s, however, it had become clear that the highest and best use of this land was for wildlife, not for farming. The St. Francis River region lies on major flyways for ducks, Canada geese (including a flock of Giant Canadas), snow and blue geese and whistling swans.

It was a grassroots effort in 1950 that pushed the idea to develop Sherburne Refuge in this area. Local sportsmen and conservation organizations recognized the latent wildlife potential and became interested in possible restoration of the damaged lands. Asking for assistance from the Minnesota Department of Conservation, these local groups demonstrated that the

---

*Arkansas, California, Florida, Illinois, Indiana, Iowa and Missouri.

PROPOSED IMPOUNDMENT SYSTEM

WATER DEPTH
0 - 6 in.
6 in. - 3 ft.
3 - 5 ft.
over 5 ft.

SHERBURNE
NATIONAL WILDLIFE REFUGE

BATHER, RINGROSE, WOLSFELD INC.   612/831-2300
7101 YORK AVENUE SOUTH   EDINA, MINNESOTA 55435

0   1 mi   2 mi

The use of a specialized computer program assisted Sherburne's planners in the placement of some 30 impoundments.

area still held great potential for wildlife.

State biologists and others found the area to be excellent for habitat reestablishment. Once completed, the refuge can produce 10,000 waterfowl per year and provide refuge for 100,000 duck and coot and 30,000 Canada geese. In 1961, with the concurrence of local conservation groups, the state referred the project to the Fish and Wildlife Service. In 1965, plans to begin acquisition of Sherburne National Wildlife Refuge were realized.

As land acquisition proceeded — by 1966, 7,272 a. were bought in 65 tracts — it was possible to begin management of Sherburne Refuge to accomplish some preliminary goals of wildlife reestablishment. In a few years of operation, careful management of the area's resources has

brought a good wildlife response.

In 1974 the firm of Bather, Ringrose and Wolsfeld Inc. of Edina, Minnesota, was retained to undertake the development of a master plan and management plan for the refuge's eventual 30,500 acres. A team of landscape architects assisted by ecologists, biologists, hydrologists, computer technicians, fish and wildlife planners and managers were assembled to undertake the project. The team was aided in its planning efforts by a computer utilizing the environmental planning and programming language (EPPL) developed by the University of Minnesota Landscape Architecture Program and currently in use by Minnesota state agencies and private firms for resource planning.

One key to the political success of the plan is the fact that revenue-

sharing legislation returns to Sherburne County about $20,000 per year for schools and roads.

Already the region had many small lakes and bogs which previous ditchers-and-drainers found unprofitable to dry out. Even wild hay off the marshes had turned unprofitable. Among the existing elements of the area to be re-watered are: 4000 a. of sedge-blue joint meadow, a large, low-lying wild hay meadow being invaded by willow brush; 1500 a. of closed marsh with about a foot of water year-round; Lake Josephine of 300 a.; some 600 a. of river channel marshes, many with old beaver dams.

High prices for beaver pelts during World War II just about wiped out beavers from the entire basin. A former lake, Rice Lake, was once a noted source of wild rice, heavily used by local Indians who made their last harvest in 1961. A final blow to the wildlife ecology was an invasion by carp in the 1940s.

Planners and wildlife managers estimated in the 1960s that the region had a potential for creating 30 impoundments totaling 10,300 surface a. Most of these are to be realized in the current master plan. Depths vary down to 11 ft., but only 5% of the lakes/pools will be deeper than 4½ ft. The plan also calls for about 100 semi-permanent or perma-

nent pot-holes dug to provide waterfowl breeding sites. The 50 mi. boundary of the 30,479 a. refuge is to be fenced, and carp barriers installed at the Rice Lake outlet.

All land necessary for the giant refuge has been bought by the U.S. Fish and Wildlife Service, with land acquisition so far coming to $3,275,500. Construction contracts are to be let in the summer of 1978, covering the first of eight major and 30 minor water-control structures (dams and dikes).

This article incorporates material supplied by Guy R. Johns, and by the Twin Cities, Minn., office of the U.S. Fish and Wildlife Service.

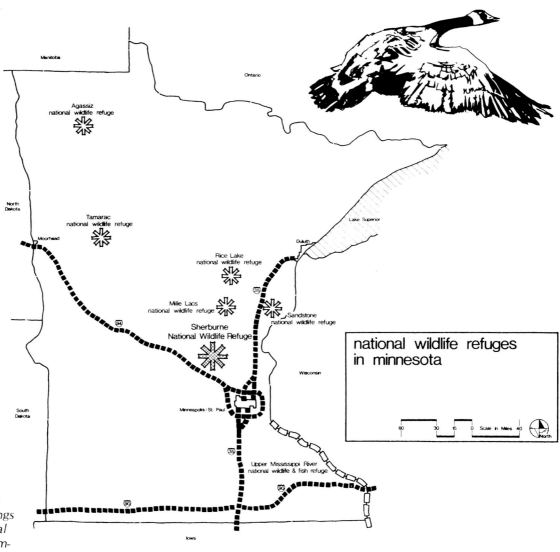

national wildlife refuges
in minnesota

Master plan, opposite, is result of computer findings placing some 46 potential activities in the most compatible areas with least possible conflict; opposite below, aerial view of the wildlife refuge.

4
Hazards

On Knowing Where *Not* To Build

You'd think a well educated people would know better than to build their homes precisely where they will be flooded, earthquaked, tsunami'd and covered with land-slide. And yet the population of that notoriously expensively schooled nation the United States of America notoriously persists in building, investing, speculating and attempting to carry out full life functions in hazardous locations. If there's a seismic fault where land can be marketed, developers will hire more prestigious experts than the local government can produce — as the City of Los Angeles has learned to its chagrin — and at the public hearings, any restrictions on new buildings in old fault zones will be ridiculed as "over-protection of the public."

How long have we watched this process? To know that Pompeians had been warned about Vesuvius' dangers is to know that foolishness is endemic and long-lived. To know that North Americans are moving steadily toward the oceanic shores is to know that they are moving steadily toward high risk locations.

All the more reason, then, to undertake detailed studies of all such risk-ridden places so that when we build there — if we must — we have cut our risks to the minimum; so that when we move there — if we must — it will have been for the better.

Beyond all such considerations, there is something very special about the finished design of a place, for example, that is made-to-be-flooded. It works differently from other places; it usually therefore looks different from other places; and if designers attempt to disguise it, so much the worse for the public. A riverside park that gets flooded every spring should have a special configuration: no thick rows of trees perpendicular to the floodwaters, for example. For such rows snare and collect debris that is ruinously expensive to remove after the flood is gone. At Nag's Head, North Carolina, oldtime vacationers long ago learned to build their cottages high on sturdy piers so hurricanes could sweep *through* the structure without ripping it apart.

In the end all landscape dangers must be confronted and meticulously examined for frequency, intensity and duration. In learning where we *can* build, we also learn where *not* to build. The differences will be endlessly debated, the costs and penalties forever in dispute. Of course it is foolish to flatly condemn all locations that are occasionally subject to some hazard; and it is worse than foolish to disregard expert warnings merely because the art of flood-quake-hurricane prediction is less than perfect. We live at risk; why make it worse by building in hazardous places?

The Editor

On a Rampage
Through a Suburb

By MICHAEL G. BYRNE and JAMES Y. UEDA

The Indian Bend Wash floodway project in Scottsdale and Tempe, Arizona, is an impressive, coordinated answer, offered by a group of firms, agencies and communities, to the problems of reducing flood damage and providing needed recreational areas.

Indian Bend Wash is usually a low-lying, dry floodway feeding the Salt River, with a history of severe flooding — 15 floods between 1921 and 1975 — generally flash floods of increasing damage as the area has increased in population.

People moved into the Indian Bend flood plain area without realizing the hazards. As the holding capacity of the natural channel was inadequate to carry maximum floods prior to development, the increased runoff from streets, housing and parking areas simply compounded the problem.

As the population in the Phoenix area increased, so did the demand for recreational and green open space. Within the Phoenix metropolitan area, of which Scottsdale and Tempe are a part, the demand for recreation is expected to jump from 32 million recreational days (one person/one day of recreation) in passive activities to 48 million recreational days in 1985. In 1973 the metropolitan area lacked some 38,000 a. of space for water-oriented activities, 2800 picnic units and 1000 multi-use courts.

During 1972, Scottsdale's greenway turned brown with flashflood waters, here viewed toward south.

As early as 1963 floods prompted Maricopa County to request the U.S. Army Corps of Engineers to supervise the development of an overall concept of flood control; in 1965 Congress authorized a seven-mile, concrete-lined channel for Indian Bend Wash — the standard solution of the time. However, public opposition to channelization plus the rise in demand for recreational space caused the city of Scottsdale to join with the Corps to develop a system to satisfy the demands for both flood control and recreation. The authorized plan was reformulated in 1973 and approved in 1974. This plan is currently being carried out with results visible during every flood.

Basic to the entire plan was a set of hydraulic parameters: anything proposed to go into the floodway must not obstruct floodwater flow. If it did, the channel would have to be deepened to accommodate the decrease in channel capacity. The water surface for the 100-year flood was calculated by using a roughness coefficient determined by past experiments and experience. This roughness coefficient was put into the Manning hydraulic flow formula to determine the water surface. This was a part of a prolonged process of compromise between the various agencies and groups to arrive at the final design of Indian Bend Wash.

A low-flow channel is under construction along portions of the floodway to accommodate nuisance runoff water so that the recreational areas will not be inundated every time someone overwaters his lawn. This channel will carry 4000 cfs. while the main channel will accommodate up to 30,000 cfs., the 100-year flood. Zoning restrictions ensure that the floodway will remain open.

The area north of the interceptor channel known as McCormick Ranch was planned by Victor Gruen and Associates and developed during the early 1970s by the Kaiser/Aetna Corporation from a desert into a planned community with greenways and golf courses doubling as floodways. The greenway spaces direct floodwaters to the interceptor and inlet channels at Indian Bend Road. The interceptor channel will carry water from east of the Kaiser/Aetna development to the inlet channel location. A 100 ft.-wide corridor between the interceptor channel and the Arizona Canal is planned as a wildlife and bird sanctuary. Designed by the Corps of Engineers, this area will be hydroseeded with native seeds and scatterings of palo verde and mesquite trees for people to observe nature but not exploit the area. The design of the interceptor channel allows a maximum of about 7000 cfs. to be carried to the inlet channel.

The inlet channel will extend from Indian Bend Road southward to McDonald Drive, with a base width ranging from 480 to 1,050 ft. and a depth of seven to 10 ft. Portions of the inlet channel and adjoining areas will be developed into a golf course by the city of Scottsdale with the clubhouse and a few greens protected from the 100-year flood. The area immediately south of Indian Bend Road, straddling the west side of the inlet channel, will be a hotel complex to be developed by Revelis Corporation and designed by a team

The actual greened floodway is six miles long and was developed jointly by the city of Scottsdale, Maricopa County Flood Control District, the U.S. Army Corps of Engineers and private developers. This urban greenbelt floodway which to date is over 70% complete contains recreational facilities such as parks, golf courses, lakes and a trail system, all compatible with flood control requirements.

These hydraulic parameters were used as a basis for their master plans by landscape architects Royston, Hanamoto, Beck and Abey at Chaparral Park; and by landscape architects Ribera and Sue at Vista del Camino Park. Their use resulted in the aquatic and community centers being located on high ground or built on pads above the 100-year flood elevation. Open field sports are located in the floodway minimizing the blockage of floodwater flow. Both parks were co-sponsored by the city of Scottsdale, BOR and HUD.

Existing developments such as golf courses have not created problems because of their nature. A compatible land use, most golf courses have been developed within the greenway, principally by private interests. Another golf course is being designed between Indian School Road and Thomas Road by a team of consultants: a hydraulic engineering firm, Water Resources Associates; two engineering firms, Ellis, Murphy, Houlgate, and Johnson Engineering and American Engineering, and a golf course designer, Jeff D. Hardin, Associates.

Between flash floods, public parks, along Indian Bend Wash get heavy use by Scottsdale residents.

The first open-space project in Arizona, El Dorado Park was designed by Art Barton and Ribera and Sue, landscape architects. In 1972 El Dorado Park successfully tested the greenway theory during heavy flooding.

The Corps of Engineers and the city of Scottsdale are co-sponsoring the development of Indian School Park, a visitors center, and an exhibition plaza. The proposed Indian School Park will help satisfy the community demand for active and passive recreational activities. Facilities planned for the passive areas include horseshoe pits, shuffleboard courts, promenades, sitting areas, picnic tables and barbecues.

The active area will occupy 15 a. for paved court activities such as volleyball, tennis, basketball, handball and croquet.

To inform visitors of the purpose of the greenway, an information center is planned next to the lake in Indian School Park. Known as El Pasadero de la Tira Verdosa (Host of the Greenbelt), the structure will be built above the 100-year flood elevation. Indian School Park, the lake and the information center were designed by Cella, Barr, Evans and Associates, landscape architects and engineers, with guidance from the Corps of Engineers.

An exhibit festival plaza was designed by Schoenberger, Straub,

Indian Bend Wash

1. Proposed Golf Course
2. Villa Monterey Golf Course
3. Proposed Golf Course
4. Mountain View Golf Course
5. Vista Del Camino Park
6. El Dorado Park
7. Chaparral Park
8. Existing Bikeways
9. Open Grass Area
10. Proposed Thomas Road Rest Area

11. Lake Area of Indian School Park
12. Proposed Open Field Sports
    of Indian School Park
13. Scotts Park Golf and Tennis Club
14. Proposed Court Center
    of Indian School Park
15. Proposed McKellips Fishing Lake
16. Proposed Mitigation Strip
17. Bike Paths
18. Pedestrian and Bike Bridge
19. Proposed Public Use Park

20. Exhibit Festival Plaza
21. Open Field Sports
    of Indian School Park
22. Proposed Golf Course
23. Information Center
24. Neighborhood Square
25. Neighborhood Park and Center
26. Neighborhood Center
27. Civic Center, Zocalo and Old Town
28. Neighborhood Park
29. Neighborhood Facility

Indian School Park (see No. 11 in airview on preceding page) will have a
floodable lake, parking areas, courts
and sports fields. (Design by Cella,
Barr, Evans & Associates, Tucson,
Arizona.)

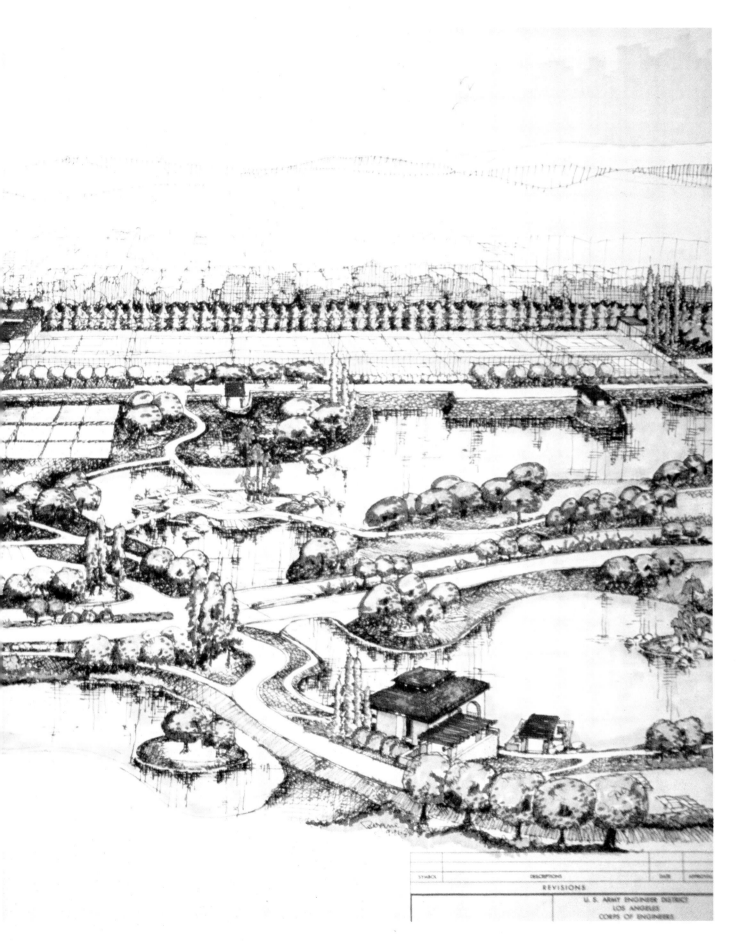

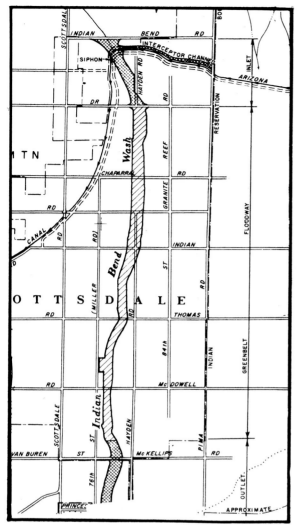

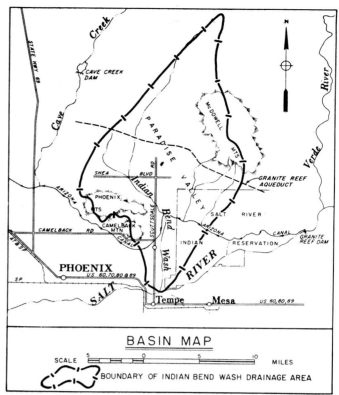

BASIN MAP

SCALE [5 0 5 10] MILES

BOUNDARY OF INDIAN BEND WASH DRAINAGE AREA

The 206 sq. mi. drainage area of Indian Bend Wash is 24% mountainous, a watershed subject to extensive flash-flooding. At Indian Bend Road (top of map, left) the vital Arizona (irrigation) Canal which now crosses the Wash will be put into a siphon under the Wash. During future floods the junction of the Wash and Indian Bend Road will become a highly visible testing ground for the plan's effectiveness.

Florence and Associates, architects, following Corps of Engineers' criteria under and immediately north of the McDowell Street bridge. Designed to specific flood-control standards, the facility will be used throughout the year with activities scheduled every week, such as art shows, craft classes, animal shows and instructional classes.

The greenway trail system is continuous from Arizona State University to the intersection of Maricopa County's Sun Circle Trail on the Arizona Canal. The backbone from which lateral trails will branch, the major trail is designed not to conflict with vehicular traffic. A trail headquarters area will be developed at Thomas Road to link up all portions of the greenway.

At McKellips Road the Indian Bend Wash channel narrows, drops in elevation and turns southeastward. To prevent scouring and

VICINITY MAP

SCALE [50 0 50 100 150 200] MILES

BOUNDARY OF GILA RIVER DRAINAGE AREA

AREA COVERED BY MAP

erosion of the channel bottom and the levee sides and to also alter the direction of the floodwaters from southeastern to south, a six-acre lake

is proposed. As the primary recreational purpose for developing the lake is to allow fishing for children, the Arizona Game and Fish Department will stock the lake with bass, catfish and sunfish.

A recreational development in the outlet channel is sponsored by the city of Tempe and is conceived as retaining the native character of the site, complete with native vegetation.

The Indian Bend Wash project is considered to be an outstanding engineering achievement and was selected by the National Society of Professional Engineers as one of the 10 outstanding engineering achievements for 1974. This is because of a channel design for flood control which maintains the highest standards, simultaneously incorporating environmental considerations, aesthetic considerations, social impact and recreational opportunities.

Planning for Hazards
In Everyday Landscapes

By ROBERT W. KATES

A river's rise, a crustal fracture, a reduction in soil moisture, an increase in windspeed — all are acts of nature, God, or gods; but floods, earthquakes, droughts or storms are acts of men. This is one central finding after 15 years of intensive geographical research on natural hazards, their geophysical dimensions, human impact and social response. While reminiscent of the somewhat sophomoric question, "if a tree falls in the wilderness and no one hears it, is it sound?," this finding is nonetheless significant. *There are no floods unless there are people, buildings or livestock to be damaged; there is no drought unless crops wither and water supplies dry up.* The responsibility falls where it should, on those who use and inhabit the large areas of the earth subject to high recurrent natural hazards, and even more directly on us who plan land use and design habitations.

If nature is neutral, human occupance is not accidental. People encounter hazard in their search for the useful. The 50 million Americans at major risk from hurricanes, the 20 million at major risk from earthquakes, the 35 million at major risk from floods, are not at risk by chance. Mankind has always chosen the intersections of land and water as desirable sites for settlement, for they provide multiple opportunities for ecological access. Thus, where mountains and marsh meet the sea, where hillslope gives way to rich valley plain, where hilltop offers view for protection or pleasure, where narrow valley provides gaps in mountain massives — all are ideal places to use or inhabit. They are also ideal places for earthquake, hurricane, flood or landslide.

Thus, while the hazardous is useful, it is also costly. It includes not only the toll of life and property destroyed in natural disaster, but also the everyday expenditures designed to reduce or prevent such disaster. The costs usually are heaviest on those least able to pay, at least on a global scale. Floods in Sri Lanka (Ceylon) cost that small nation between one percent and two percent of the GNP; in the U.S. it was perhaps 1/10 that amount. For a comparably-sized earthquake in Managua, Nicaragua, and San Fernando, California, the death toll in Managua was 70-100 times greater. Overall, the global pattern is high death rates and proportionately high loss rates in developing countries, and rising absolute losses and declining deaths in industrialized countries.

In the U.S. losses from all geophysical hazards are on the rise, approaching $5 billion annually, with perhaps half as much again spent on preventive action. Deaths, on the other hand, have remained low — less than 1000 out of 100,000 accidental deaths per year are attributable to natural hazards.

Hazard Events
The pattern of costs, losses, deaths and injuries is much affected by the specific characteristics of the hazard-producing events: their source, frequency, magnitude, duration, area affected and suddenness of onset. I can demonstrate this with five major U.S. hazards — urban drought, flood, hurricane, earthquake and tornado. For each I assumed a major hypothetical event that poses potential disaster for human populations and estimated the frequency of its recurrence, the

relative magnitude of the event in terms of energy release or dissipation (measured by the solar constant), the areal extent or pathway covered by the event and its duration in time. In essence, for each of five major hazards for an imaginary place with a record of recurrent events, I ask the questions: how often? (frequency); how powerful? (magnitude); how widespread? (areal extent); and how long? (duration).

We can identify a pattern in these events' characteristics. A frequent event like drought lasts a long time and covers a large area, but is low in per unit energy release in contrast to tornadoes and earthquakes, which are rare, release enormous amounts of energy in short periods, and affect relatively small areas. We have called drought-like geo-physical events pervasive and the high-energy events intensive; in medical language, it might be the distinction between the chronic and the acute. Hurricanes and floods have characteristics of both, and all of the characteristics are important for social response.

Social Response
The pervasive events are most readily responded to by society because they are frequent, provide time for an adequate response, and the low unit energy can be dealt with easily. Drought, fog, frost, soil creep and expansive soils are contained, so to speak, by long-term investments in preventive measures.

Consider, for example, urban drought where the population at risk is that half of the population of the U.S. which draws water from publicly-owned surface water systems. To ensure a steady flow of water, they spend some $200 million

Characteristics of Major U.S. Hazard Events

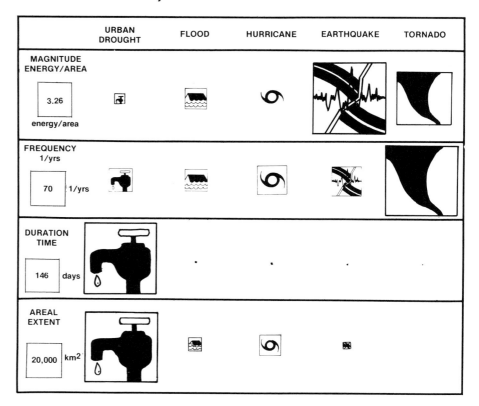

	URBAN DROUGHT	FLOOD	HURRICANE	EARTHQUAKE	TORNADO
MAGNITUDE ENERGY/AREA 3.26 energy/area					
FREQUENCY 1/yrs 70 1/yrs					
DURATION TIME 146 days		.	.	.	.
AREAL EXTENT 20,000 km²					

per year for storage structures to ease the normal fluctuation of precipitation. Perhaps once in 30 years, precipitation shortfalls, cumulative over several years, lead to shortages and subsequent losses. But considering the risk to such a large population and high recurrence, these losses are surprisingly small for at least three reasons: the substantial investment in damage-reducing adjustments (dams, reservoirs, etc.), the considerable over-capacity provided in such structures, and the slowness of onset so that the creeping character of drought can be matched by modest reductions in consumption.

In contrast, tornadoes threaten some 40 million persons on the Great Plains, Midwest and Florida. The point recurrence for a tornado is extremely rare despite their large number per year (650) because the average path is quite small. Besides warning facilities (and these are limited), improved response to warning and storm cellars, little is or can be done to reduce the burden of hazard. Thus, while the death rates have diminished, they are still relatively high. The costs per capita for both tornadoes and droughts are of similar order, but the pattern of expenditure is reversed and the loss of life is fundamentally different. Drought, a pervasive hazard — frequent, low energy, and slow of onset — leads to development of high levels of preventive adjustment. Tor-

nadoes — rare with high energy output, highly localized and of sudden onset — discourage prevention and lead to higher levels of death and relative damage. Earthquakes are similar to tornadoes.

In between these extremes, floods and hurricanes exhibit characteristics of both classes of events. Flash floods in small mountainous watersheds approach the high-energy, localized effects of the intensive events. Floods on the main stream of a great river rise slowly and cover large areas at much lowered velocities of flow. Similarly, hurricanes differ widely in their impact — between the narrow coastal strip where they move on to land which is subject to high winds, massive rain and wave action and storm surge, and more interior areas. But it seems this combination of characteristics makes these the most costly hazards.

To a degree, society's response is a function of the hazard itself, but it is also a function of available wealth, social organization and pattern of settlement. For example, the high per capita losses per person in flood plains is not only an expres-

sion of the frequency of major floods, but of the historic strategic function of riverine sites as places of commerce, industry, residence, agriculture and water transport. Traditionally, a substantial portion of society's wealth and productive activity has been concentrated along both riverine and oceanic shores. In the face of hazard, the basic modes of response are similar: men can adapt themselves to the hazard, seek to modify the natural events or adjust their livelihood systems. In rare cases, they may make fundamental changes in their location or mode of existence. But application of these potential actions, the favored mix of social response, differs seemingly by wealth and social organization.

In folk society, ritual or myth softens the expectation of nature; extended families and clans share in the vicissitudes of nature, and many small adjustments are built into everyday life. For example, in the case of drought, oral histories are often dated by the occurrence of great droughts. Rainmaking powers and ceremonies are common, kinship relationships provide emergency

Societal Impacts of Major U.S. Hazards

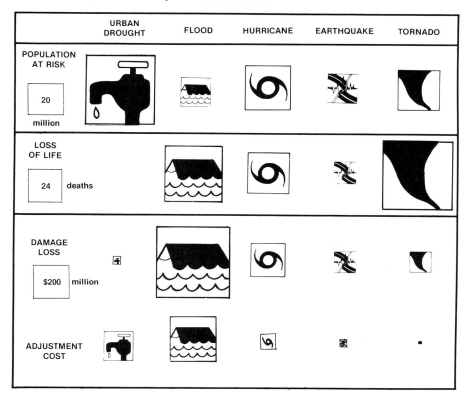

	URBAN DROUGHT	FLOOD	HURRICANE	EARTHQUAKE	TORNADO
POPULATION AT RISK 20 million					
LOSS OF LIFE 24 deaths					
DAMAGE LOSS $200 million					
ADJUSTMENT COST					

access to multiple resource areas and occupations, and a surplus to allow for bad years is the rule in all subsistence societies. The response to hazard is both flexible and (in a group survival sense) successful, albeit burdened by occasional heavy losses of life when the system is overwhelmed by enormously powerful events, such as the recent drought in sub-Saharan Africa.

In contrast, industrial society narrows the range of response with increasing efficacy of technological power. Industrial man resorts less to prayer, seasonal movement, multiple occupation and careful selection of micro-landscape and topography. Natural events are met head-on, so to speak. Complex irrigation facilities are constructed to mitigate drought, dams are built to prevent floods, sea walls are constructed to block hurricane surges, steel frames are erected to resist earthquakes. This resort to the technological fix, while effective within a range, still has limits — costly ones to developed countries and tragic ones to developing countries.

In developed countries like our own, the resort to high capital inten-

sive adjustments may prove counterproductive. Partial protection of flood plains may actually encourage flood plain development. Sea walls may destroy the very amenity that encourages a seaward location. Irrigation may result in waterlogging and increased salinity. Seismic-resistant construction may provide buildings that maintain their form by avoiding collapse but lose their initial functionality. Indeed, while many adjustments may reduce the frequency of loss, catastrophic potential seems on the increase. Major tragedies appear very much in America's future; only their timing, location and magnitude are in doubt.

A major challenge is posed, therefore, to planners and designers to assist in the development of more flexible technical and social responses to landscape hazard. Can we broaden the range of technique and behavior in the face of hazard? Can we retain some of the flexibility and sensitivity to nature of the folk society, but translate such efforts into meaningful terms for our complex society and its economic-technical capability?

There is some evidence that this is indeed possible, and in selected areas we are moving in this direction. At the land management level, we are moving toward a minimal "design with nature,"* first in selected states and eventually everywhere by future national land management standards. Wetlands, flood plains, steep slopes, dunes and beach will have severely restricted permitted uses. To complement this trend, there is need at the site design level for new ways of providing access to hillside and shore without imperiling structure, occupants or environment; to make safe the second and mobile home; to build for the exceptional as well as the everyday. But planning for a hazardous future, either on the site or at the regional level, is not the everyday practice of any broad professional group. Learning how to do so is probably our most immediate need.

*From the title of the seminal book by Ian L. McHarg

The research reported on in this chapter was supported by the National Science Foundation grant #GS 3184 and involved the close collaboration of Ian Burton, of the University of Toronto, Gilbert F. White, of the University of Colorado, and the many members of the International Geographical Union's Commission on Man and Environment.

The Rush to the Shore
How to Live With Coastal Erosion

By J.K. MITCHELL

Coastal areas throughout the world are experiencing strong pressures for increased residential, industrial and recreational development. In the United States more bulk cargo terminals, nuclear power stations and offshore drilling sites are contemplated for an already burdened littoral zone. Resorts, marinas and lagoon homesites have also spread to previously unoccupied sections of coast. These trends have stimulated a variety of actions to limit the modification of undeveloped maritime landscapes and to bar specific classes of land use from the shore zone.[1] Despite these decisions, continued investment in shorefront homes and other facilities appears likely. Over one-third of the nation's population now lives in coastal counties and human occupance within one mile of the shore has been increasing at more than three times the national growth rate.[2]

Depending upon their location and the nature of coastal landforms, shorefront residents must come to terms with a number of serious physical problems. In addition to coastal erosion these include wind damage, flooding, tsunamis, landslips and surface instability, fragile vegetation associations, high levels of soil and atmospheric salinity, salt water encroachment into aquifers or brackish lagoons and readily polluted substrata. The interplay of so many risks adds to the complexity of designing appropriate adjustments for any specific coastal hazard.

Excluding Alaska, 43% (15,400 mi.) of the U.S. oceanic and Great Lakes shore is experiencing significant coastal erosion.[3] Direct economic costs of subsequent damages have been conservatively estimated at $150 million per year. Densely populated reaches of the Atlantic coast are worst affected, although serious problems also exist in California and along the shores of the Gulf of Mexico and the Great Lakes. Low-lying sandy coasts are most susceptible to erosion but other landforms are not immune to damage. Permanent shoreline retreat is primarily a function of severe storms and of human interference with normal longshore transport of beach sand supplies. Rates of recession commonly range from a few inches to more than 20 ft. annually. Larger rates have been recorded in the lee of jetties, groynes and other barriers to longshore drift. Neighboring properties may experience quite different conditions because erosion intensity fluctuates widely within relatively short distances. Likewise, many years of shoreline retreat may be followed by an apparently inexplicable return to conditions of stability or progradation.

In the United States, beach cottages, second homes, hotel boardwalks, shorefront parks, navigation facilities, transportation routes and utility lines are the premier casualties of erosion. A large number of adjustments is available to counter such losses. Unfortunately, only a minority of these are currently used by affected individuals or communities. Federal, state and local agencies have traditionally been enthusiastic proponents of groynes, beach nourishment and sophisticated structural devices such as seawalls and revetments. Where they did not simply bear erosion losses, private residents have favored constructing wooden bulkheads, installing pilings under exposed structures and similar small scale engineering practices. Growing awareness of the undesirable consequences of misapplied industrial technology has begun in recent years to popularize dune grass planting and coastal zone protection programs.

This concentration upon a relatively narrow range of adjustments has arisen in part because some alternative methods of protection, such as storm track modification and beach nourishment, are expensive or experimental in nature. More often, neglect of other adjustments stems from unawareness of the existence or specific nature of alternative techniques, misperceptions of the erosion process and biases toward certain long established practices favored by the conventional wisdom of coastal protection agencies. Moreover, present practices are often unsuccessful in halting erosion losses. Outflanked bulkheads, undermined seawalls, decayed pilings and vanishing beaches testify to the technical ineffectiveness of many popular engineering devices. Such expensive structures as sand bypassing plants, groynes and concrete revetments may also be incompatible with existing ecological relationships and jarring to the aesthetic sensibilities of local populations.

As participants in the field of coastal planning and design, landscape architects can play an important role in offsetting many of the deficiencies of current protection practice. Some have already been active in this general area.[4] They are well qualified by training and professional outlook to emphasize the use of several adjustments which have been comparatively neglected in the past. These include landform modification and stabilization practices on individual properties, the layout of coastal access routes, public facilities and open spaces at the local community level, and the

establishment of coastal reserves and special use zones on a regional basis. It should be emphasized that, by themselves or in combination, these types of adjustments do not necessarily constitute foolproof responses to erosion. This point has been most forcefully demonstrated in the Cape Hatteras National Seashore. Here, well-intentioned schemes for the stabilization of eroding dunes have deprived adjacent beaches of sand supplies, producing unexpected reductions in beach width and consequent increases in population pressure on the remaining resource base.[5] This circumstance underscores both the complexity of erosion problems and the need for comprehensive, coordinated responses on the part of different shore management specialists. When judiciously applied, biological, social and engineering techniques can be mutually reinforcing.

A conservative strategy toward the modification of coastal environments seems highly desirable. Widespread settlement on exposed oceanfront shores is largely a post-World War II phenomenon and we know little about the long term environmental effects of extensive building construction and coastal protection programs. Available evidence for short term trends underscores the dynamism and fragility of maritime landforms.

Wherever possible, human occupance of erosion susceptible shorefronts is best avoided. Sand spits, narrow barrier islands and headlands composed of poorly consolidated material are the least suitable sites for building construction. Such locations are subject to rapid configurational changes, frequent breaching and concentrated wave action. Parks, recreational facilities and wildlife preserves might

occupy these areas. Cliff edges, steep slopes, fore and main dune lines are also susceptible to rapid undercutting. Back dunes, raised beaches or other natural platforms and rearward depressions on cliff tops are most suited for building sites.

Retention of eroding areas in open space uses has been accomplished — at great cost in time and money — through public purchase of vulnerable areas. Spectacular examples of erosion are now incorporated within national and state parks, recreation facilities and other special reserves. Unfortunately, most backshore property adjacent to eroding areas in the United States is privately owned. Where such land is presently unoccupied or in low density uses, it is still possible to effect some control over future development without resorting to outright public acquisition. Though usually

Adjustments to the Hazard of Coastal Erosion

Adjustments to Loss	Modifications of Loss Potential	Modifications of Erosion Hazard	Adjustments Affecting Hazard Cause
Loss bearing	Storm warning and evacuation systems	Regulations against destruction of dune vegetation	Prohibition of beach excavation and harbor dredging
Public assistance	Public purchase of eroding land	Emergency filling and grading	Reduction in soil conservation activities
Insurance	Condemnation	Beach nourishment	Storm track modification
	Zoning for open space and low density uses	Dune stabilization	Sand bypassing
	Planning maps	Grading slopes	Removal of dams on rivers
	Scenic easements	Bulkheads seawalls, and revetments	Biological control of erosion-causing fauna
	Subdivision regulations, building codes, orders and ordinances	Breakwaters, tetrapods, artificial seaweed, bubble breakwaters	
	Moving endangered structures	Groynes	
	Installing deep piling	Phraetophyte removal	
	Landfill		
	Planned Unit Developments		

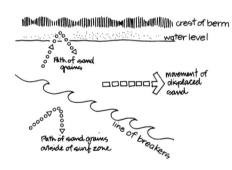

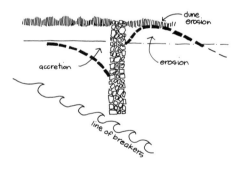

are maintenance and, where necessary, reinforcement of existing natural barriers to wave erosion, and minimization of other site modifications.

At the community or neighborhood scale of land planning for low sandy coasts or friable cliffs, widely-spaced access roads at right angles to the waterfront are preferable to fine networks of streets or longitudinal marine drives. If major public and commercial facilities are subsequently located well back from the shoreline, taking care to avoid wetlands or other sensitive bayside areas, the dominant pattern of movement to and from the shorefront is reinforced. This subjects less of the vulnerable dune systems and cliff tops to human use except at a handful of strategically protected access points. Judicious siting of public parking spaces is also an effective method for channeling pedestrian traffic along selected access routes.

Individual structures can be protected by locating them on the rearward margins of lots and retaining the maximum amount of seaward open space. Application of the planned unit development concept, whereby relatively high population densities are achieved by building intensively on small fractions of tracts and leaving the remainder open, can aid in attaining this goal.

During development of shorefront lots there are further opportunities for introducing measures to reduce erosion losses. These affect three phases of site occupancy: (1) preparation; (2) construction; and (3) management. Site preparation is frequently preceded by wholesale destruction of existing vegetation cover. Tightly knit swards of native holly trees, beach plum, bayberries and greenbriers or dense stands of sub-tropical hammock vegetation do

expensive, scenic easements which prohibit significant alteration of existing coastal vistas, and purchase of development rights are sometimes feasible tools. Discount bonds and leaseback arrangements can also be utilized. Setback lines and ordinances against construction in vulnerable dune, clifftop or wetland areas may be employed to prohibit or to remove structures from the zone of immediate erosion hazard. Coastal development plans, zoning and permits to eliminate high densi-

ty occupancy and specific land uses are increasingly popular devices.

Most of the preceding adjustments can be incorporated into any coastal management plan and are not the exclusive preserve of landscape architects. In contrast, where construction or other development is contemplated close to the shore, landscape architects involved in master planning and specific site plans have greater opportunities to affect directly the future course of erosion losses. Keys to this process

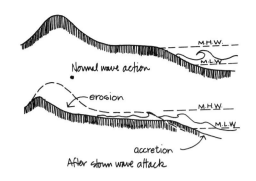

Normal wave action

M.H.W.
M.L.W.

erosion

M.H.W.
M.L.W.

accretion

After storm wave attack

not facilitate the active recreational pursuits which many property owners appear to favor. The exotic nature of such vegetation is also often at odds with prevailing social norms for dooryard gardens, lawns and cultivated plants. These comparatively minor deficiencies must be set against the admirable beach vegetation, the protection which it offers against sand and salt laden winds, and the diverse habitats which it provides for animal life.

Levelling and grading tend to reduce the height of protective dunes and permit overtopping during storms. Wrongly placed fill may intercept littoral drift and promote leeside erosion. Unless carefully protected during the construction phase, and subsequently refilled, excavations on barrier islands provide instant weak points which can easily be breached by rising flood water.

Once construction has begun, the nature and siting of buildings and

ancillary facilities require close supervision. On sandy coasts, lightweight, flexible and easily moved houses, resting on deep pilings are preferable to massive, permanently sited buildings. Cantilevered cliff top residences are likewise inadvisable. Where seawalls or bulkheads are required for the protection of especially valuable structures, these can be tied in to stable portions of adjacent property to prevent outflanking.

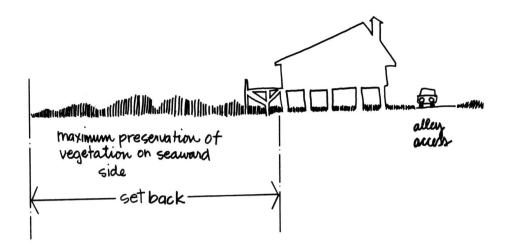

maximum preservation of vegetation on seaward side

set back

alley access

Care must be taken to facilitate drainage upon coastal properties. Impervious surfaces such as black top parking lots can accelerate runoff and initiate cliff top or back dune erosion. In contrast, gravel paths and loose cobble driveways permit ready infiltration. Water should also not be permitted to accumulate in pockets behind bulkheads, protective walls or cliff tops since seepage can weaken their foundations.

After major structural modifications have been completed, landscape architects and other involved designers can initiate sound management practices which should later be continued by site occupants. Chief among these are the placement of sand fences, new vegetation cover for stabilization or shelter, and the selection of modes and routes for shore access which minimize subsequent erosion losses.

The U.S. Army Corps of Engineers, state experiment stations and private sources have prepared detailed tables of vegetation species which are suitable for planting in different coastal environments.[6] Although exotic plants can be successfully employed, the sometimes unfortunate consequences of introducing unaccustomed biological material into new environments give pause for caution.

American beach grass (Ammophila breviligulata) has been widely used as a pioneer plant in outer dunes along northern latitude coasts in the United States. Sea oats (Uniola paniculata) is a favored species on South Atlantic, Florida and Gulf coasts. These and other grasses may be planted through holes in plastic sheets if a totally bare sand surface is being stabilized. Clover, peas, lupines and dune sunflowers form useful ground cover in many areas of low relief. Alpine plants or dwarf shrubs can be utilized on steep slopes. Hardy species of myrtle, willow, holly, rose and cherry have been successfully maintained for back dune stabilization on northern coasts. Cabbage plants (Sabal palmetto), wax myrtle (Myrica cerifera), and various types of pines thrive in similar Florida sites. Depending upon the species being utilized, optimum planting times vary throughout the year. Costs of installation may amount to several hundred dollars per acre.

As previously noted, this paper is not a comprehensive survey of human adjustments to coastal erosion. It also reflects the author's predominant experience wth problems of erosion on the Atlantic and Gulf coasts of the United States. Nor does it do justice to the full range of potential adjustments which landscape architects are capable of putting into practice. Nevertheless, most of the measures discussed are basic constituents of informed management programs for eroding shorelines and deserve careful evaluation by persons engaged coastal modification activities.

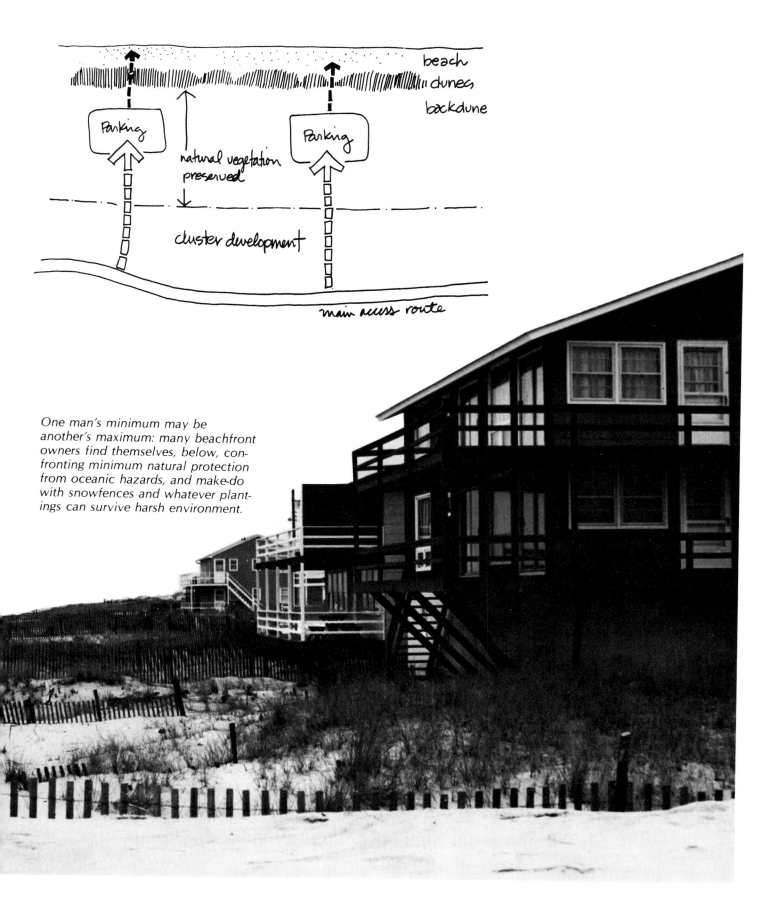

beach
dunes
backdune

Parking

Parking

natural vegetation
preserved

cluster development

main access route

One man's minimum may be
another's maximum: many beachfront
owners find themselves, below, confronting minimum natural protection
from oceanic hazards, and make-do
with snowfences and whatever plantings can survive harsh environment.

Riprapping the beach — as well as raising the roofline, left, and floor level, below, are familiar devices for capturing the value, as well as attempting to moderate the risks of moving close to the ocean's edge.

FOOTNOTES

1. The state of Delaware has recently moved to ban heavy industry from its coastal zone. New Jersey has imposed a moratorium on wetlands construction. California is the latest state to enact a comprehensive coastal protection bill. Among others, Washington, Oregon, Texas, Michigan, Massachusetts and Florida possess similar legislation.

2. Water Resources Council, *The Nation's Water Resources.* The First National Assessment of the Water Resources Council, Washington, D.C., 1968.

3. U.S. Army Corps of Engineers, *National Shorelines Study.* Washington, D.C., 1971. See Regional Inventory Reports, Shore Protection Guidelines, Shore Management Guidelines and Final Report.

U.S. Department of the Interior, Fish and Wildlife Service, *National Estuary Study* (7 vols.), Washington, D.C., 1970.

4. Albert Fein, ed., *Landscape into Cityscape: Frederick Law Olmsted's Plans for a Greater New York City,* Ithaca, New York: Cornell University Press, 1968.

Ian L. McHarg, *Design with Nature,* New York: Doubleday and Co., Inc., 1969.

5. Robert Dolan, "Barrier Dune System Along the Outer Banks of N. Carolina: A Reappraisal," *Science,* 176 (April 21, 1972). 286-88.

6. U.S. Army Corps of Engineers, *Dune Formation and Stabilization by Vegetation and Plantings.* Beach Erosion Board Technical Memorandum No. 101, Washington, D.C., 1957.

John A. Jagschitz and R.S. Bell, *Restoration and Retention of Coastal Dunes with Fences and Vegetation,* Rhode Island University Agricultural Experiment Station Bulletin 382, Kingston, 1966.

Edwin A. Menninger, *Seaside Plants of the World: A Guide to Planning, Planting and Maintaining Self-Resistant Gardens,* New York: Hearthside Press, Inc., 1964.

V.J. Chapman, *Coastal Vegetation,* New York: The Macmillan Company, 1964.

'Graceful Retreat' from the Battering Ram of Hilo's Tsunamis

By WESLEY MARX

The battering force of the 1960 seismic sea wave (tsunami) wrecked Hilo's Liliuokalani Gardens.

Like most tourists, I came to the big island of Hawaii to see the Hawaii Volcanoes National Park. Yet, with all due respect to the natural majesty of the volcanoes, the most impressive sight was the bayfront of Hilo. Unlike other urban waterfronts, no high rise monoliths, commercial strip, and NO TRESPASSING signs exist to sever Hilo from its shore. Instead, the shore is predominantly green and open, bisected by a free-flowing river and fish pond. Fishermen and picnickers outnumber traffic police and condominium realtors. Set back in deferential fashion from this friendly uncongested waterfront is a clustered commercial complex and the homes of the 26,000 Hilo residents who can see as well as use their shorefront.

This open shore contrasted sharply with the one I had just visited. To truly see the Waikiki shore — or what remains of it — I had to take an ear-popping elevator ride to a hotel penthouse high enough to overlook the view-blocking bulk of other hotels. From this altitude, I could see the Waikiki Shore in all its slender hotel-shadowed glory, the beach shifting abruptly from brown to white to gray tones in deference to the many artificial sand sources tapped to maintain the eroding shore.

Unfortunately, the Waikiki shore is more the urban norm than the Hilo shore. Indeed, the uncommercial nature of the Hilo shore is as much a social wonder as the volcanoes are a natural wonder. I became curious. Had a legendary planner come forth to inspire, shame and cajole Hilo into conserving its

shorefront, as Daniel Hudson Burnham did for Chicago? Had an aroused citizens' group overcome high-rise variances to protect the shore from the same fate as Waikiki? Had the Sierra Club and Ralph Nader combined to enjoin subdivision of the shore and the sky above?

After questioning local officials, however, I learned that the Hilo shore was once just as cluttered, congested and nondescript as its urban counterparts. The change agent was not an aroused citizenry or environmental litigants but a seismic sea wave. The wave — or, to be scientifically accurate, train of waves — occurred one evening in 1960 and killed 61 people. Over $22 million worth of property was damaged, 288 structures were demolished, and the city's communication and transportation systems were severed. The scope of

damage reflected the fact that, for all intents and purposes, downtown Hilo was the shorefront.

Once the nature of the change agent was revealed, a new question came to mind. Time and time again, communities punished by floods, earthquakes, hurricanes and seismic sea waves rebuild in the flood plains, fault zone, and beach zone for a return engagement with disaster. This propensity for disaster may not reflect human wisdom, but it does reflect human nature. The opportunity to return to familiar surroundings, to be reunited with one's neighbors, and to begin together the busy task of rebuilding can act as therapy to the shock and disorientation of disaster. Relocation to unfamiliar surroundings, however safe, can compound the shock and disorientation of disaster. What possessed Hilo to get out of disaster's way?

In the wake of the disaster, Hawaii County established a Hawaii Redevelopment Agency and the State authorized a $2.5 million bond issue to cover the local share of a disaster renewal project to be funded largely by federal funds. Such financial machinery serves to get the community back into commission as soon as possible. Such funds normally go to restoring economic services, with only secondary attention devoted to minimizing exposure to future disaster. The assumption is made that structural works — flood storage dams, dikes, seawalls — can be built at a later date with federal assistance. Thus public policy reinforces human nature to discourage relocation to safer ground. Here Hilo departed from the norm.

Coastal or submarine earthquakes can displace sea bottom or shore, energizing waves that can wash ashore thousands of miles from point of origin. Globally, these seismic sea waves (also called tsunamis) are among the more rare disasters. Hawaii, however, happens to sit in the middle of the Pacific basin, which is rimmed by an active seismic belt. Since 1819, 42 seismic waves emanating from Alaska, Chile, and Japan have battered the Hawaiian shore. While imperceptible in the open ocean, these waves can turn into walls of water 50 or even 100 ft. high at the shore. They occur as a train of waves that may last for 30 minutes or more. The destructive energy is two-fold: the wave itself and the churning debris. The shorefront of Hilo literally turned against the residents, as buildings became battering rams.

Hilo has the uncertain distinction of being the most tsuami-prone of the island communities. Fringing reefs help reduce the energy of tsunamis along other island shores, including Oahu. The island of Hawaii, however, is geologically the youngest and such natural protective barriers have yet to evolve on any large scale. Most island communities, because of their shore configuration, are exposed to tsunamis from only one portion of the seismic belt, whether it be Japan, South America, North America or New Zealand. Hilo's crescent-shaped bayfront catches tsunamis from both

Alaska and South America. The one in 1960 came from Chile. Much of the demolished shorefront was only 15 years old, rebuilt after a 1946 tsunami that had come from Alaska and claimed 96 lives.

The Army Corps of Engineers, which has traditionally been willing to mitigate the consequences of poor land use with taller and taller seawalls and floodwalls, was prepared to extend this method to Hilo. But tsunami design specifications — 50 ft. of height — stretched cost and reliability to the point that even Congress could not be depended upon to finance this massive exercise in brute force engineering. Residents of Hilo themselves were not particularly agog over the specter of a "super seawall" that would excise bay views and put Hilo in the shadow of a concrete slab.

Another response to disaster doesn't require a single concrete pour: disaster forecasting and evacuation. Seismic sea waves can now be forecast. In contrast to the 1946 wave, Hilo had warning in 1960, yet still lost 61 people. Sole reliance on evacuation is often a fatal reliance on human temperament. Moreover, the tsunami warning system can only predict areas of possible landfalls, not the major determinant of damage, wave size. Another shortcoming is so self-evident that it is often overlooked. Unlike people, buildings can't heed evacuation warnings. Even so-called mobile home complexes have been immobilized by Atlantic and Gulf Coast hurricanes.

While willing to finance Hilo's recovery, state and federal agencies were not prepared to underwrite such an evident return engagement with a seismic sea wave. Hilo could qualify such critical financial assistance but only by implementing the traditional last resort to disaster mitigation: better, safer land use.

The Hawaiian land planning firm of Belt, Collins and Associates was retained to prepare a plan for redevelopment. Such a plan for redevelopment, however, takes time to be completed and approved by public agencies. In this critical interim, residents and businessmen tend to reoccupy unsafe areas, resume daily activities and resist relocation. Foreseeing this, public of-

ficials decided to acquire property within the damaged area for redevelopment once the plan was completed. This foresight meant the relocation of 228 family units and 83 businesses. The state owned public lands in Hilo and these lands were made available to expedite relocation.

Within a year, a redevelopment plan was completed and approved at local, state and federal levels. The project was called Kaiko'o, or "rough seas." However tragic the seismic sea wave was, the planners realized that now Hilo had a singular opportunity to completely redesign both its downtown and its shorefront. In taking advantage of this opportunity, the planners reversed the traditional pattern of urban land use at the shore. Of the 350 a. in the project area, 10 a. were allocated to limited industrial and commercial use, including a commercial fish market and dock. Set at the landward edge of the project site was a 40 a. commercial site raised 26 ft. above sea level to minimize tsunami exposure. The remaining 300 a. were placed in an open, landscaped safety zone. Thus the major portion of this urban waterfront would be undeveloped. The switch from sprawling commercial strip to a consolidated commercial district dominated by open vistas promised significant economic dividends in the form of consolidated public services — from streets to drainage — and integrated development controls, including landscaping, underground utilities and sign control.

This planning vision generated public support; but was it economically viable? Local businessmen did not have the financial resources to develop such a large commercial site. Outside financial investment would be required — perhaps from the mainland — and local businessmen were concerned about their ability to compete with a brand new retail center. At the same time, large investors don't rate disaster renewal projects as hot prospects, particularly one named Rough Seas.

The public found the capability to overcome such economic qualms. The county had earlier planned to build a $1.7 million headquarter complex at a nearby tree nursery,

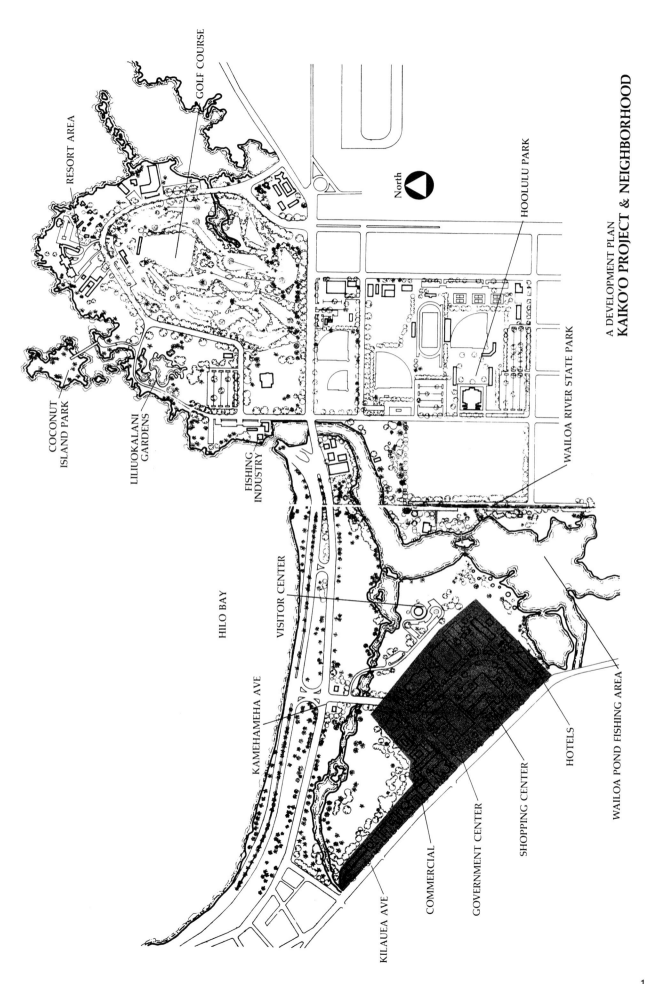

RESORT AREA

GOLF COURSE

COCONUT ISLAND PARK

LILIUOKALANI GARDENS

FISHING INDUSTRY

HILO BAY

VISITOR CENTER

North

HOOLULU PARK

WAILOA RIVER STATE PARK

A DEVELOPMENT PLAN
KAIKO'O PROJECT & NEIGHBORHOOD

KAMEHAMEHA AVE

KILAUEA AVE

COMMERCIAL

GOVERNMENT CENTER

SHOPPING CENTER

HOTELS

WAILOA POND FISHING AREA

but switched to the Kaiko'o site. The state then announced construction of a $2.5 million administrative complex next door.

This induced an Oahu developer to handle the private end of redevelopment and he attracted such major tenants as Kress and J.C. Penney. To provide local merchants with the same credit potential as major chains, the Small Business Administration provided lease payment guarantees to the landlord. Shiigi Drug and Margolis Fashions became neighbors of Penney and Kress.

Often, the private portion of a redevelopment project will succeed while the public open-space portion will subside into weeds due to lack of adequate provisions for maintenance. Variances for temporary commercial uses will be granted and gradually such variances will supplant paper plans for spacious park grounds. Kaiko'o has avoided this fate. Formerly, the project area contained Liliuokalani Gardens, an Edo-type Japanese Garden with ponds and picnic grounds, and this was restored. Coconut Island, a palm-fringed islet, was also restored as a picnic ground. Within the project area lies Hawaii's shortest river, the Wailoa, less than a half mile long. This spring-fed river became a State Park in 1954.

As Project Kaiko'o evolved, the State decided to expand its park to embrace the entire 300 a. safety zone. Seismic sea waves can travel up a river mouth, much like a tidal bore, and overflow the banks so such expansion provided additional safety benefits. Fishing and pleasure boating facilities, promenades, equestrian and bike paths and flower displays now occupy Hilo's former downtown district. Trees and landscaping materials were considered for their relative resistance to tsunamis. The 1960 tsunami moved 20-ton boulders hundreds of feet inland and the park people don't want their landscaping materials turned against Hilo by a future tsunami.

Observed Megumi Kon, Deputy Managing Director of the Hawaii Redevelopment Agency, in a letter to this writer, "In lieu of the plantings, the wide expanse of open space between the shoreline and the building areas was established. One

theory is that the open space would dissipate the energy of the tsunami in the same manner as a wide sand beach does to a large wave."

According to Kon, Hilo's recently completed community plan envisions restoration of a black sand beach that once existed along the bay and relocation of an existing bayfront highway to make room for a beach park. Sewage discharges which once polluted the bay have been eliminated.

With Hilo's bayfront reopened to view and to recreational use, significant tourist opportunities were present. Kaiko'o was able to attract another prominent commercial client, a resort hotel and convention center.

Hilo's more efficient use of shorefront property is not only safer and more attractive than the former conventional use but just as economically productive. Back in 1960 it would have been easier to peddle lava land subdivisions than tell local residents that tax income from Hilo's downtown could be doubled while turning most of it into a playground. Yet, in 1971, this is what had occurred. What with overall economic growth and Hilo's access to direct mainland air service, the former downtown would have prospered too. Yet Hilo would be without one of the most beautiful urban waterfronts in the nation.

The federal government invested more money in Hilo's renewal than the ordinary disaster relief project, some $6.68 million. But when another tsunami hits Hilo, the federal government will only be asked to help returf a park, not rebuild a downtown.

Can Hilo's graceful retreat from disaster be utilized elsewhere? Before discussing this, it would be best to stress the special factors which made Kaiko'o possible. Hilo's dramatic vulnerability to seismic sea waves and the community's lack of political clout at the national level strengthened the position of state and federal officials in encouraging relocation. Mainland urban areas often appeal successfully to Congress to overturn land-use restrictions that the executive branch may impose on disaster relief funds.

Many urban areas suffer from an acute land shortage, public or

private. Relocation to safer ground may mean relocation to another political jurisdiction. In Hilo availability of nearby undeveloped public lands assured success of relocation.

In the early '60s, financial and technical resources of the Department of Housing and Urban Development were available to expedite Kaiko'o as a disaster and urban renewal project. Today HUD's overall capability for urban renewal has been drastically downgraded. Few states or cities — even with revenue sharing — could now put together such a comprehensive package. It is even questionable if Kaiko'o would have materialized if the seismic sea wave had waited till 1970. Presently, use of federal relief funds is generally restricted to repair of damaged structures and services. Permanent improvement schemes — such as relocation and safety zones — tend to be discouraged by such a stipulation. The General Accounting Office criticized the Officer of Emergency Preparedness for spending $10.5 million to relocate Valdez, Alaska, after the 1964 Good Friday earthquake. The GAO claimed that Valdez was only entitled to $315,000 for emergency repairs. The GAO's strict interpretation of disaster relief legislation is probably correct. Yet, if this is the intended policy, Congress is literally keeping communities in disaster's way. Valdez was formerly sited on a glacial flood plain subject to earthquakes, subsidence, and seismic sea waves; it has been relocated five miles distant on a more stable site. The original site is now a recreation area.

Such policy constraints help explain why Hilo's response to natural disaster is far from being a universal response. To make such responses more common, federal policy should be reformed to make relocation to safer ground a more realistic alternative, even though the initial cost may exceed rehabilitation on site. In the long run, such a policy would remove, rather than prolong, exposure to disasters.

The Defense Civil Preparedness Agency presently encourages cities to develop standby emergency plans for natural disasters. This program might be expanded to include contingency plans for relocation to safer ground with potential sites identified and inventoried. (It should be noted that one difficult problem in relocation to private lands would be control of speculation: on the other hand, some very conducive sites — such as surplus military bases — might be utilized.)

A plan by itself, however imaginative, appealing and rational, will not assure a graceful retreat from hazardous sites. Immediately prior to the 1906 San Francisco earthquake and fire, Daniel Hudson Burnham completed a plan for the city that envisioned wider streets, plazas and considerable open space. But this plan was ignored and subsequent redevelopment fulfilled a 1907 prophesy of the U.S. Geological Survey: "It is very probable that the new San Francisco to rise on the ruins will be to a large extent a *duplicate* of the former city in defects of construction."

No matter how good the plan, resistance from the residential, and to a lesser degree the commercial, sector must be assumed and the

reasons for this resistance — cultural attachment to place, uncertainty over unfamiliar surroundings, separation from neighbors — recognized.

As one reflection of this concern for people problems, the Agency only had to go to a court trial for final determination to acquire three of the 388 parcels in the cleared area. Indicative of how sensitive relocation work can be is a souvenir retained by one Agency field office representative: a knife drawn on him by an elderly Chinese gentleman who didn't want to move.

The difficulties raised by disaster relocation emphasize the need to keep people and buildings out of disaster's way in the first place. The federal government has spent over $9 billion since 1936 on structural works for flood protection and yet the nation is more flood-prone than ever before. Instead of being the victim of its own disaster policies, the federal government should reserve for itself the power to prevent new development, particularly residential

development, in hazardous lands, possibly in the emerging national land-use legislation. The National Flood Insurance Program administered by HUD, which ties minimum land use and building controls to community eligibility for flood insurance, is a step in the right direction. Alternative uses of hazardous land — agriculture, horse stables, golf courses — can be required and property tax assessments modified to reflect such use. The federal government's power could extend to prohibition of grants for public support services — sewers, highways, housing — to hazardous lands.

Two centuries' experience with floods, earthquakes, seismic waves and hurricanes attest to the fact that we cannot build flood walls high enough, breakwaters strong enough, seawalls long enough to disaster-proof the United States. If the goal of disaster management is to conserve lives and public funds, Hilo's graceful retreat must become public policy.

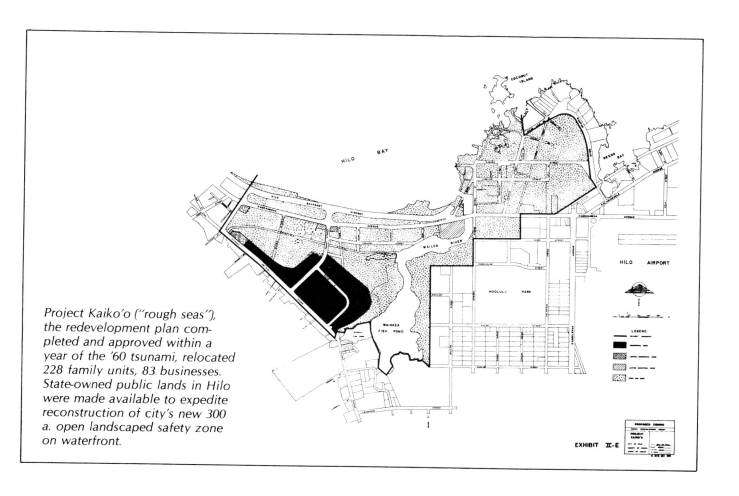

Project Kaiko'o ("rough seas"), the redevelopment plan completed and approved within a year of the '60 tsunami, relocated 228 family units, 83 businesses. State-owned public lands in Hilo were made available to expedite reconstruction of city's new 300 a. open landscaped safety zone on waterfront.

EXHIBIT II-E

Beyond the Water Mystique

By DAVID G. PITT

WATER AND LANDSCAPE: An Aesthetic Overview of the Role of Water in the Landscape, *by R. Burton Litton, Jr., Robert J. Tetlow, Jens Sorensen, and Russell A. Beatty. Port Washington, New York, Water Information Center, Inc., 1974. 314 pp. Photographs, drawings.*

Water has a magnetic attraction in the landscape that is unrivaled by other materials or elements. Regardless of its form, we almost automatically attach a highly complex but very special significance to the presence of water. Our initial response to water depends primarily upon the visual, auditory and tactile senses. The authors note that the information received from these senses is then processed by the individual observer in light of his own experiences, beliefs and current emotional states and in light of his context for observing the stimulus. The interplay of these three sets of variables (environmental stimulus, personal state of mind, and context of observation) result in an aesthetic experience, the nature of which is a function of all three sets of variables interacting.

Landscape architects have long appreciated the complexity of our response to water, but as the authors note, have avoided direct, forthright treatment of the subject. Generally, their reaction has been similar to the mystical statement offered at the outset, above, concerning the magnetic attraction of water. However, with the advent and political mandate for such concepts as multi-purpose landscape resource planning and environmental impact assessment, it has become increasingly important to approach this aesthetic response in a more systematic and objective manner.

Water and Landscape, a photographic reproduction of a report prepared for the National Water Commission, is a systematic investigation of the visual characteristics of the water-oriented landscape. Specifically, the authors state two objectives for their study: (1) to develop a visual classification system for fresh water streams and bodies, proposing descriptive categories showing interrelationships among water, landforms and vegetation; and (2) to consider how human use, man-made facilities and manipulations concerned with water can be characterized as enhancing, compatible with or degrading to the landscape.

The visual classification system examines water and landscape expression at the regional, setting and site scales. Within each scale, the landscape is divided into *units* or discrete entities having a distinct visual character. The units are limited; they can be singled out and identified. *Landscape units* are suggestive of a regional or geographic context for water. Water appears as a series of streams or lakes rather than as individual elements. Visibility of the entire unit is possible only over time, and air flights are usually needed to define the landscape unit. A *setting unit* consists of a water element and the landscape that is its surrounding container. It is a visible, distinct and defined land area and takes its form from the water and landscape elements the observer sees from a ground-level position. The setting unit is the most important of the three types of units as it contains tangible relationships between water and landscape. *Waterscape units* are defined as those combinations of water and landscape in which water is the key element and where there is a unity or continuity of a specific, identifiable visual character. They represent distinct areas of shore and water within a parent body which have their own visual identity. The text identifies and discusses in considerable detail the elements that create the visual image perceived within each of these three types of unit.

For evaluating the quality of the visual expression created within each of the three units, the authors propose three aesthetic criteria: *unity of water, variety* and *vividness*. Unity refers to water's capacity to be an element of continuity and cohesion within the landscape. Through its unity of material, color, movement and surface configuration, water helps pull together various elements in the landscape, creating a higher quality visual expression. *Variety* has several expressions in the water-oriented landscape. Movement, color, surface texture, surficial configuration, spatial configuration, stream alignment and associated vegetation are but a few examples. The authors suggest that the assembly of more and varied elements, particularly as they may be seen in an orderly fashion, helps to identify quality. *Vividness* is defined as that quality which gives distinction or produces a strong visual impression. It is primarily a function of contrast, the placing together of dissimilar elements. For each of the three criteria, a verbal benchmark statement is offered to describe typical high and low visual quality expressions of the various elements that define the visual image found in the landscape, the setting, and in waterscape units.

Depending upon their primary form of visual expression, man-made structures or alterations are organized into several groups: *linear elements, area elements, mass and enclosing elements, point elements,* and *color and texture*. Within the landscape, setting, and waterscape units, the authors discuss the primary visual characteristics and landscape relationships of each category of alteration. Five terms are proposed for evaluating the visual expression created by man-made structures in the water-oriented landscape: *unifying, focal, enclosing, organizing* and *enhancing*. Benchmark statements are again used verbally to describe high and low quality expressions of each criterion within the landscape, setting and waterscape units.

Finally, the authors recommend the adoption of two sets of policies: a specific definitive *aesthetic policy* for use in the appraisal of native landscape conditions and of development impacts created by man-made modifications; and a unified "policy on design guidelines" that would set broad standards of performance and give better coordination among federal and other agencies. The authors suggest that the classification and evaluation systems developed in the text might serve as the bases for such policies. They offer general planning guidelines for aesthetics in the water-oriented landscape and suggest areas for future research.

As is characteristic of other publications by Professor Litton (see *Forest Landscape Description and Inventories,* Berkeley, Calif., USDA Forest Service Research Paper PSW-49, 1968), excellent drawings and photographs are used extensively to illustrate many of the principles and concepts developed in the text. The text itself contains several typographical errors and inconsistencies in format which make reading somewhat difficult. However, the graphics more than compensate for these minor shortcomings, and the principle ideas are, for the most part, clearly expressed.

Water and Landscape is an important addition to the growing body of literature in landscape assessment primarily because it provides a framework for analyzing the visual characteristics of water-oriented landscapes and the man-made modifications that are introduced into these landscapes. Its recognition and treatment of landscape perception at three distinct geographic scales eliminates some of the problems encountered in comparing a grand vista to an intimate space. A major criticism of *Water and Landcape* is that the authors have not synthesized the quality assigned to individual landscape elements into an overall visual quality assessment of the total landscape. In perceiving landscape visual quality, we do not necessarily derive quality from distinct and independent elements in the landscape (such as those offered by the authors in their classification framework). Rather, we respond to a combination of elements which interact together to create an overall visual quality.

While the authors have done a very creditable job of identifying and describing these elements at various geographic scales, neither their classification nor their evaluation system provide any guidelines as to how the qualities derived from the individual elements relate to the overall quality ascribed to the total landscape we perceive. They have analyzed landscape visual quality in terms of the elements that evoke the visual response, but they have not synthesized the individual qualities derived from these various elements into a total visual quality response to landscape. In evaluating the visual quality of both native landscape and man-made modifications, the authors offer benchmark statements representing typical high and low quality expressions. Unless the people charged with implementing the evaluation model have a very clear understanding of the authors' meaning in these statements, problems may arise in test-retest validity among the model's users. If the visual values emanating from the model are to have any meaning for landscape planning, it is important that they be reproducible among the people using the model. Such assurances could be guaranteed only through preliminary training of the model users by the authors or through the development of a more objective evaluation device.

5
Resource Analysis and Management

What We See is What We'll Get

If I were George Perkins Marsh reincarnated, and had access to all of NASA's satellite pictures of the world, and to Dr. Eugene P. Odum's insights into contemporary ecological disruptions, and a red-hot team of AAS researchers run by Professor Howard T. Odum, it might be possible by the 1980s to publish a defensible judgment on the worldwide state of ecological disruption, giving chapter, verse and verification.

But such is not yet the case. Marsh is long dead; his great book, *Man and Nature; or, Physical Geography Modified by Human Action,* is more than a century old, living on in reprint and influence. The Odum brothers range, and are published, widely, adding to everyone's knowledge of landscape disruption and dereliction. A worldwide survey of the sort we envision is still a long way off. But we need not wait to make a case, and to exhibit the evidence as it has begun to accumulate in expanding volumes.

The Odums would, I think, agree that landscape disruption is old stuff, and was going on (via flood, drought, quake and fire) long before man became a worldwide destructive force. Marsh saw the possibilities, gathered the first worldwide evidence; the Odums explore and expose the risks; and on all sides, new teams of scholars, designers, and scientists are examining the state of the landscape and the waterscape.

Our world is sprinkled with landscapes beyond recall, ecological sytems unrecognizable, thresholds crossed long ago, points-of-no-return now far behind us. Who can bring back passenger pigeons; restore to forested beauty the infamous Ducktown Basin of Tennessee, now sulphur-fumed beyond redemption; or stop the desertification of northern Africa?

Short of such cataclysms we stand poised while varied ecodisasters hover overhead. On the following pages we begin a new kind of exploration — reports from the new age of environmental analysis, a booming field in academia as well as among designers, hardware salesmen and other hustlers.

Some of this exploration gains fuel from a pervasive sense of impending disaster which is loose in the world today. Some researchers seek merely to count the hours till Doomsday. But those represented on the following pages come from a newer tradition, in which the sense of potential disaster is muted by a keen sense that salvation may yet lie beyond the next environmental impact statement. Here are people who study a river *system*, and not merely A River; who seek the hidden order in a seemingly chaotic shoreline; measure audience reactions to famous or infamous coastal scenes, measure the "destruction value" of marshlands; or devise survival tactics for a desert, a damaged lake, a filled-in bay, or streams invaded by power plants.

Such are the followers of George Perkins Marsh today, penetrating with technical gaze the environmental maze, seeking clues to human survival among the man-made and man-damaged scenes of a diminishing world.

The Editor

Saving the Nooksack

How to Resist the Pressures on 'A Matchless Resource'

By GRANT JONES, BRIAN GRAY and MICHAEL SWEENEY

The Nooksack River Basin in Washington State faces increasing pressure for outdoor recreation from the population of a large area from greater Vancouver, British Columbia, south to Seattle. Rising in the North Central Cascades of Whatcom County, Washington, the Nooksack flows 96 mi. into Bellingham Bay on Puget Sound.

To save the basin from typical recreational exploitation, this study of the Nooksack seeks ways to protect and to maintain critical natural resources of the river basin by identifying those portions of the river best suited for preservation and for passive and active recreation; and to recommend acquisition and control priorities.

Studies for the Nooksack plan were prompted by public interest and by the Whatcom County Park Board's commitment to a river recreation system. Three members of the Seattle firm of Jones & Jones here outline its comprehensive study.

Approach

The Nooksack River is preeminently a river of incomparable esthetic value and potential for recreation use, due to the diverse and distinctive natural processes operating within the river basin. Both the processes and resultant forms must be understood before a plan can be developed for land use and management.

The river basin may be resolved into its various parts, with the characteristics and qualities inherent to each part recorded, classified and evaluated, to discover how to utilize the river resource as a whole while preserving its rare and fragile assets.

A river system is a matchless resource for recreation; the question is how to maximize its inherent esthetic qualities and consider recreation uses which are unique and oriented toward the river experience. Rather than attempting to identify scenic values or preferences, which often leads to ambiguity and confusion, we need only to discover the highest quality of river experience. The potential level of experience will depend on how strongly the river expresses itself; a function of the level or magnitude of intrinsic river characteristics operative at a given location. Areas possessing high esthetic quality may be assumed to be those which most strongly and distinctly express natural processes and form.

A simple quantitative level of landscape expression (supply), however, will not compose a complete picture, since the health of the environment affects the quality of the experience. One must judge the supply qualitatively by adding the dimension of health, since the quality of every landscape is enhanced or

---

River study map, below, delimits channel boundary, stream and floodplain as classified by zone, reach, run and unit.

Uniqueness

That quality which conveys the significance and distinctiveness of a characteristic relative to a given zone of the river.

Diversity

That quality which relates to the variety, complexity, activeness and eveness of physical and visual characteristics on the river and within the riverscape.

Fragility

A term describing that quality of durability, resiliency, resistance to change, or ability to survive environmental stress.

Seasonality

A quality which conveys a cyclical sense of time through changes of particular elements or processes within the riverscape.

Encroachment

A modifying human action which intrudes upon an element and/or process existing in an harmonious state, thereby promoting a condition of visual, physical and/or biological disequilibrium.

---

diminished by the presence of certain conditions which indicate health and determine overall landscape integrity. The study proceeded on the basis that *quality of experience* can be predicted and assigned a value based on the magnitude of natural landscape expression and its health, combining as "landscape integrity." Thus four propositions were established concerning the approach to this study:

1. Rivers are systemic and each constitutes a realm that can be identified, delimited, and classified into orders and/or regimes.

2. River channels are predictable in continuum and can be subdivided into distinct segments for analysis.

3. Each distinct river segment can be experienced and the array of natural, cultural, and esthetic characteristics which locally contribute to the experience can be quantitatively recorded to establish basic supply or magnitude or characteristics assignable to each of these river segments.

4. Each river segment's basic supply can be evaluated qualitatively

according to indicators of health and an assessment of the overall landscape integrity assignable to each segment can be made.

Defining the Study Area

A river system is considerably more than water flowing in a channel. Recognition of the river as a natural, complete, interrelated system within which continuous river processes and drainage systems occur must override artificial, man-made boundaries. Over-all considerations of a study area boundary include both the physical territory of the watershed and the visual domain of the river or viewshed. Both the watershed and the viewshed can be mapped spatially, and together constitute the river realm.

The realm can be further classified into smaller drainage basins and related to stream order. Initially that land area which predictably will be inundated by the river at least once every 50 or 100 years, the floodplain, must be identified. Within the floodplain lies the natural boundary of the streamway, or

"stream-dependent" corridor defined by Bauer (1972) as "that . . . corridor of single or multiple wet or dry channel or channels within which the usual seasonal or storm water runoff peaks are contained, and within which environment the flora, fauna, soil and topography is dependent on or influenced by the height and velocity of the fluctuating river currents." Within the streamway lies the river channel itself, which (if not temporarily diked) is constantly adjusting its course within the streamway and floodplain.

Thus the study area is defined as the entire Nooksack Realm and consists of the physical territory within which the river "lives" as well as the visual domain which contributes to the river experience. Not only are all the lands within the Nooksack realm essential to proper management of the river, but within the realm may be found the full range of natural, cultural, and esthetic characteristics which contribute to the Nooksack experience.

Framing the Inventory

In order to effectively gather and record data on the natural processes and forms operative within the river study area it is necessary to establish a hierarchy of river segments which can serve as an immediate framework for inventory as well as a subsequent basis for evaluation. Consider the river realm as a "cosmos": it can be resolved into parts or segments of experience, microcosms of the whole. An assumption is made that the riverscape can be described at different scales based on the minimum distinctive combinations of characteristics that contain no smaller meaningful parts.

Our study proceeds with a river classification system which is based on landscape expression and "sense

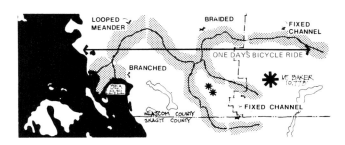

Looped meander, top, of the
Nooksack into Puget Sound. Above,
the Marietta complex area; below,
the Keefe Lake complex area. Opposite, top, the Lawrence complex
area, and below, the Kulshan complex area. Indian words "nook," or
"noot," (people) and "sa-ak," (edible
root of bracken fern) produced
basin's name.

of place." The physiographic region (upland, lowland, coastal) is the minimum distinctive regional area of the river basin. The minimum distinctive sub-region is defined by the major channel course or branch (North Fork, Middle Fork, South Fork, Mainstem, Delta); the minimum distinctive channel pattern (branched, looped-meander, braided, fixed) defines the zone; the minimum distinctive geographic segment of a branch with a given zone defines the reach (Lower South Fork, Upper South Fork, etc.); the minimum distinctive sequence of similar experience (delimited often by a change in stream order) defines the run; the minimum distinctive "sense of space" is the unit (Dye's Canyon, Edfro Creek, etc.). The unit functions as a microcosm of the entire river experience.

A preliminary classification of the Nooksack was accomplished in our office from river maps and aerial photographs, then tested and confirmed by field studies. Names were assigned to each segment for each identification and recall.

Organizing the Pieces
Having established a hierarchy of river segments, data on the intrinsic forms and processes which contribute to the experience of each segment could be effectively gathered and recorded. Initially, the magnitude of occurrence (supply) of each river and riverscape characteristics was recorded relative to each channel pattern zone. A checklist including physical processes (flood proneness, stream flow, etc.); biological elements (wildlife, vegetation, etc.); cultural elements (historic sites, bridges, etc.); and esthetic elements (landmarks, visual contrast, imageability, etc.) was established in a matrix format. This checklist was continuously refined in the field. These characteristics were

26. Hopewell Reach of Lawrence Complex

LYNDEN

KEEFE LAKE

10

A

LAWA

9

FERNDALE

11

BAY

LAKE

MARIETTA

13

12

BELLINGHAM

LAKE WHATCOM

UMMI
ISLAND

LYNDEN

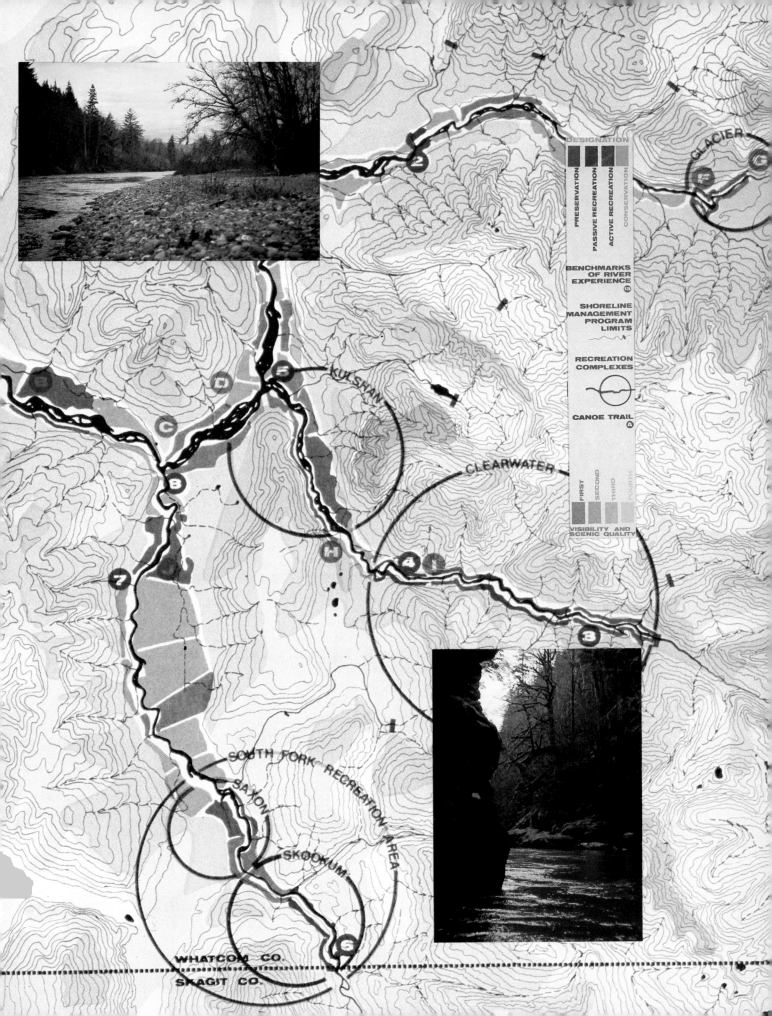

DESIGNATION

PRESERVATION
PASSIVE RECREATION
ACTIVE RECREATION
CONSERVATION

BENCHMARKS
OF RIVER
EXPERIENCE

SHORELINE
MANAGEMENT
PROGRAM
LIMITS

RECREATION
COMPLEXES

CANOE TRAIL

FIRST
SECOND
THIRD
FOURTH

VISIBILITY AND
SCENIC QUALITY

GLACIER

KULSHAN

CLEARWATER

SOUTH FORK RECREATION AREA

SAXON

SKOOKUM

WHATCOM CO.

SKAGIT CO.

recorded at one or more station points for each unit of the river. Once tabulated and summarized in the matrix, the basic supply of characteristics was known. By observing where accumulations of characteristics are most clearly or distinctly illustrated, we could establish priorities in terms of each river unit's possessing a relatively greater or lesser abundance. But, as stated previously, a quantitative level of landscape expression does not comprise the total picture, since the health of the environment affects the quality of the human experience.

Valuing the Indicators

By evaluating the supply according to the dimensions of health, the landscape experience is found to be enhanced, maintained or diminished by certain indicators. For the purpose of this study these indicators are positive: *uniqueness, diversity, fragility,* and *seasonality* and, negative, *encroachment* by man. Each of these indicators was considered relative to the channel zone in which the characteristic is found, except encroachment, considered to be of uniform importance throughout the length of the river. The presence of these indicators was recorded on a matrix for each characteristic and evaluated for preservation, passive recreation, and active recreation. These three recreational-use categories are an expression of potential use impact. The evaluation technique for each of the recreational-use categories is as follows:

PRESERVATION: *In order to locate those areas within the riverscape best suited for preservation, those segments that exhibit the highest magnitude of unique and fragile characteristics that are not encroached by man must be clearly identified. The unique and fragile characteristics are extracted from the magnitude matrix and recorded on a separate matrix for each river unit. An "unadjusted total" is developed by summing the total for each unit, then overlaying the unique and fragile matrix with the encroachment matrix. Since encroachment diminishes the value of that element for preservation, the encroachment totals are subtracted from the unique*

and fragile total, giving the "adjusted total" for each unit. Thus the preservation map displays the relative value of each river unit for preservation by its "adjusted total" (unique + fragile − encroachment).

PASSIVE RECREATION: *Passive recreation implies the use of those areas whose natural resources are more ample and capable of withstanding more human intervention than the preservation areas. For passive recreation those units which exhibit characteristics which are unique and diverse and not encroached upon must be identified. This is accomplished in the same manner as that described for preservation, using the unique and diverse matrices as "adjusted" by the encroachment matrix (unique + diverse − encroachment).*

ACTIVE RECREATION: *Active recreation provides for the use of resources which are found in relative abundance, and are capable of accommodating intensive activities. Those areas which are unique and diverse are recorded as the "unadjusted total" using the matrix prepared for passive recreation. Ecologically sensitive areas can be subtracted from this total by overlaying this matrix with the fragility matrix.*

In this case an additional modifier of "accessibility" is extracted from the magnitude matrix and added to determine the "adjusted total" (unique + diverse − fragility + accessibility).

The passive recreation map and active recreation map reflect the relative value of each river unit for both passive and active recreation by the final adjusted total.

The study summarizes the potential recreational suitability of each unit with a recreation use selection matrix. This matrix shows that some units are highly qualified for all three recreational uses; others are more qualified for only one or two; others are poorly qualified for any recreational use. Priorities are established for each recreation use category according to the scarcity of prime resources found in each unit, the relative recreation suitability, and the level of environmental stress placed on each unit. Initially, preservation units are selected; passive recreation sites are chosen from the

remaining units, and active recreation areas are selected from the balance.

Once the individual units have been evaluated and selected, we then considered the locational relationships. Thus when two or more suitable units group together, an opportunity exists to establish multiple-use complexes to enhance the recreation value to the public and allow for a more effective management of a consolidated stretch of the river.

Aiming at Overall Management

While the method of field inventory is based on the smallest "sense of place" along the river (the unit), the entire river must be tied together as a continuous conservation corridor. The actual degree of conservation required can be identified for each unit by referring to the original matrices of encroached characteristics which are biologically fragile; this is summarized in map form as "fragile areas needing attention."

As an interrelated part of the watershed system, a given river unit drains its immediate surrounding area in addition to the total land area drained upstream. Hence if the river at a given point contains elements that are biologically fragile, conservation is essential, not only of resources within the unit, but the entire natural drainage system upstream.

Of equal importance is the conservation of the riverscape or viewshed which may need protection and management recommendations by Branches for the Delta and Lower Mainstem, the Middle and Upper Mainstem, the North Fork, the Middle Fork and South Fork. The study ends as it began, equating the river as a complete system or realm whose overall management necessitates the management of each part.

Summary

It is apparent that most landscapes (mountains, valleys, deserts, coastal, etc.) can be resolved into minimum distinctive parts, their natural/cultural/esthetic characteristics inventoried, evaluated, then reassembled to manage as an entity.

Subsequent to the adoption of the

Nooksack approach a detailed master recreation plan has been developed for the Skookum Recreation Complex on the South Fork. The master plan provides for further specification of the principles established in the study. In addition the methodology has been adapted and refined in application to other environmental resource studies. The contribution of others was essential to the completion of the study. An annotated bibliography in the appendix attempts to compile the voluminous material related to water ecology, river dynamics, and the growing number of studies attempting to assess tangible and intangible landscape characteristics.

REFERENCES

Bauer, Wolf G., *River Environments: An Interim Report on a Study of Wild, Scenic and Recreational Rivers,* State of Washington, Interagency Committee for Outdoor Recreation, August, 1972.

Dubos, Rene, *A God Within,* New York: Charles Scribner's Sons, 1972.

Horton, R.E., Erosion developments of streams and their drainage basins; hydrophysical approach to quantitative morphology: *Geological Society of America Bulletin,* v. 56.

Jones, Grant R., *Preliminary Report for Classification and Evaluation of Visual Landscapes,* Department of Landscape Architecture, Research Office, Graduate School of Design, Harvard University, 1966.

Leopold Luna, B., "Rivers," *American Scientist,* Vol. 50. December, 1962.

McHarg, Ian, *Design With Nature,* Garden City, New York: The Natural History Press, 1969.

The two dark X lines stretching the length, above and below, of Boulder Creek represent dense stands of Douglas fir. Other symbols mark agricultural area, left, and swimming hole, sandy beach, upper right. Early Dutch settlers created 178 mi. of drainage ditching and canal works within Nooksack Valley.

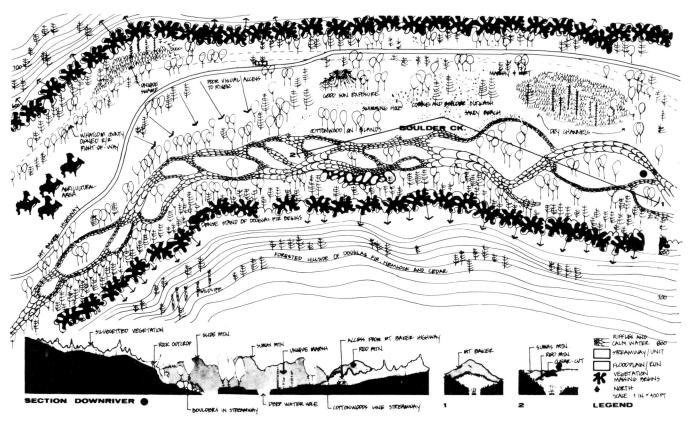

BOULDER CREEK: ANALYSIS OF A UNIT

Destruction Value

How to Charge Developers for the Environmental Destruction They Cause

By ROBERT W. RAMSEY

We have carefully established the destruction value of all components of this landscape, except the underwater habitat, used comparable values wherever available, and tallied up the total.

For example, ground cover. On the Delta land for which the Port has plans, about 625 a. would be covered under many feet of gravel. Accepting only grasses lost, we figure the minimum cost of destruction would be $250,000. Another 300 a. would be stripped for gravel, killing ground cover on some 200 a. which would cost about $5000 per acre to replace, or another $1,500,000. Thus our statement for loss of ground cover comes to $1,750,000.

Trees: the National Shade Tree Conference has established the basic value of trees at $9 per sq. in. of the cross-section at 4½ ft. above grade. For this reforested area, we assume 10 trees of six inch diameter for every 1000 sq. ft. over 200 a. on this site, giving a tree destruction value of $4,428,000.

View: the loss of view value would be large, estimated at $4000 per lot for 370 sites on the west and 160 sites on the east. Total view loss is $2,120,000.

Soil: The Port proposes to cover 1,200 a. of usable soil. Assuming 625 a. excavated three ft. deep for topsoil, or 3,025,000 cu. yds. at 35 cents, this adds a destruction payment for soils of $1,059,000.

Gas exchange: The loss of CO_2 reduction capability can be estimated by noting that 200 a. of forest removes an average of approximately 400 tons of CO^2 from the atmosphere yearly. Assigning a 50-year life to the project, we figure the loss of CO_2 reduction capacity is at $136,000 per year, or $6,800,000 over the the life of the project.

Red Salmon Creek: As a landscape feature it is worth $100 a front foot, or a total of $250,000. Its flow of 5 cu. ft. per second is worth about $12 per day, or $219,000 over the project life. Thus frontage and water together adds $469,000 to the destruction value of the creek.

Birdlife: About 20,000 hunter-days are supported from the Delta at $5.75 per hunter-day, or a total of $115,000. About 125,000 waterfowl use the flats as a flyway stop per year, about 75,000 of them new birds. If we consider these 75,000 as the annual crop loss per year after a One day in 1969 some friends, my partners, and I were discussing the loss of a beautiful oak and fir hillside overlooking a swamp. It was being developed by builders who called themselves "The Preservationists"! Another developer, with us at the time, objected. "Listen, if you'd wanted to save that land, why didn't you buy it, instead of expecting the owner to give it away?"

We had no answer at the moment, but since that time it has begun to come clear. We have watched development, been party to development, and reached conclusions. When developers "finish" a site it is truly finished as far as its original assets are concerned. All have been destroyed, or lost their meaning.

Gradually we became convinced that all land has "destruction value." This can be accurately measured on an economic scale, just as the "location value" of land is traditionally appraised, taxed, and used as a basis for trade.

Every square foot of original natural topography, every cubic foot of soil, every spring, creek, pond, swamp or drainway, every bird and animal, every tree and shrub has value that can be measured.

If the developer eliminates these things by "improving" through clearing, excavating, filling, dredging, refilling, regrading, covering with buildings and pavement, *then he should pay to a public body of jurisdiction a destruction penalty equal to the appraised ecological loss incurred.*

Such funds would then be used only to administer programs for land acquisition, protection, and the development, management and maintenance of greenbelts, parklands, wetlands, shorelands, future living reserves, etc.

We have applied this principle to a remarkable landscape, the Nisqually Delta, an estuary of the Nisqually River which rises on the southern slopes of Mount Rainier and empties into a southern reach of Puget Sound. The site has 4,150 a. and is being hungrily eyed by the City of Tacoma and other interests as the potential site of a new port. Ownership is mixed — public and private — with the U.S. Fish and Wildlife Service having acquired a key tract to help in preservation in January 1974.

In February, 1970, the Washington House of Representatives adopted a document preserving Nisqually Delta — but accepted a reservation promoted by a commerce-minded group saying this not be "inconsistent with the industrial development of said delta." This left the gate open to anything.

Since that time our application of the Landscape Destruction Value Doctrine has shown this land to have a destruction value of over $35,000,000. We have done our homework, supported by the National Audubon Society and local citizens groups determined that this delta shall not go down the development drain as usual and that new thinking and actions are needed to reverse development trend-line processes.

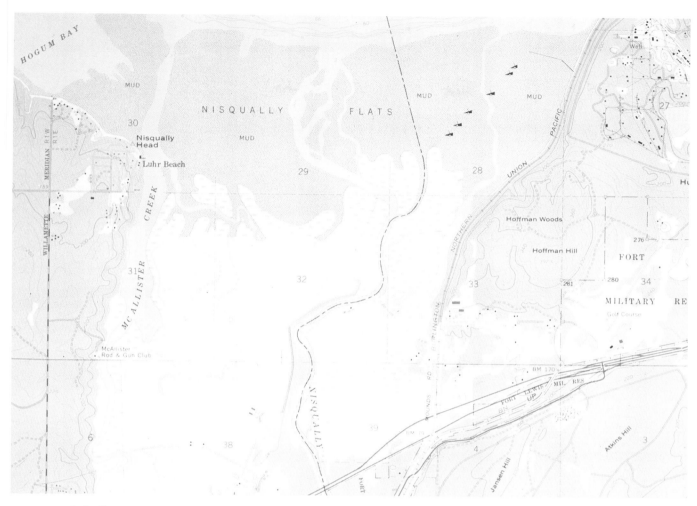

superport is built, we can compute the 50-year loss (at $5 per duck) at $18,750,000.

Combining all these anticipated losses due to development over the 50-year life of the project produces the total destruction payment due of $35,376,000.

How often do the promoters of large developments consider such losses? Hardly ever. It remains for landscape architects, conservationists, and all others dedicated to sound ecosystem preservation to do their studies on their own time, figure the losses as accurately as possible, and thereby put these valuable resources beyond the reach of development, hopefully.

In the long run, this will help establish an accurate measure of value of landscape resources: it could produce large sums for public-landscape purchase and conservation; and divert the forces of necessary development into sites where they do the least harm to our future environment.

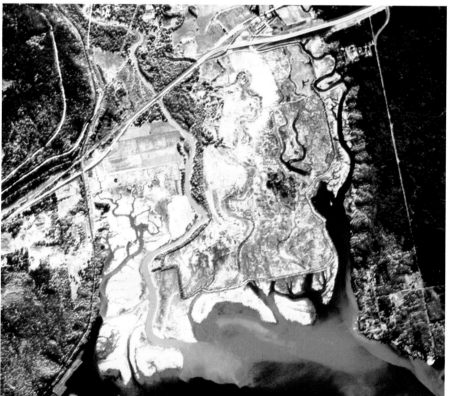

Complex Environmental Plan for 3600 Acre Cooling Ponds at Virginia Nuclear Plant

By THEODORE J. WIRTH, ROD HELLER and BRUCE HOWLETT

prepared for
VIRGINIA COMMISSON OF OUTDOOR RECREATION

prepared by
THEODORE J. WIRTH and ASSOCIATES
environmental planning consultants
billings, montana   chevy chase, maryland

circulation

▪▪▪▪ CIRCUMFERENCIAL HIGHWAY   ●●● MAJOR FEEDER HIGHWAY

▪▪▪▪ SCENIC DRIVE   ●●●● MINOR FEEDER HIGHWAY

– – RAILROAD

recreation

▪ PARK AREA   ⚓ POTENTIAL MARINA SITE

◉ PUBLIC ACCESS AREA   ⫶⫶⫶ POTENTIAL BOAT LAUNCH

▪ CONSERVATION AREA   ✳ POTENTIAL BEACH

residential

▪ HIGH MEDIUM DENSITY
ONE TO TWO D.U. / ACRE

LOW DENSITY, PRESERVE
ONE D.U. / FIVE. ACRES PLUS
NON POLLUTING AGRICULTURE

▪ LOW MEDIUM DENSITY
ONE D.U. / ONE TO FOUR ACRES

commercial

✳ BUSINESS CENTER   ▪ RESORT CENTER

industrial

▪ LIGHT MANUFACTURING   ▪ EXTRACTIVE

▥ UTILITY (VEPCO)   ········ TRANSMISSION LINE

agriculture

CROPLAND,
FOREST LAND, AND VERY LOW DENSITY RESIDENTIAL

north anna reservoir
GENERAL LAND USE PLAN

Between the electric utility and automobile industries, it is difficult to say who gets the lower marks for environmental deterioration. But there are some hopeful signs on the horizon. The following story deals with the problem of hot water — a by-product of the prodigious growth in electric power needed to feed America's increasing affluence — and how one utility sought to solve the problem.

As power demands have grown, utilities have turned to increasingly larger power plants. Larger plants are generally more economic than smaller ones and have helped to keep electric costs down. While plants have grown in size, nuclear generation has been gaining an increasing share of the market, but at some environmental cost. Nuclear plants avoid problems of air pollution (and, indirectly, of strip mining), but they do discharge larger quantities of hot water than do comparable fossil fuel plants and they also emit low levels of radioactivity.

In Virginia, the Virginia Electric Power Company is constructing one of the largest nuclear electric generating complexes in the country — about 4000 megawatts when complete. This facility, unlike most, does not draw its cooling water from a flowing stream or seashore and then pour it directly back. At North Anna the company, by damming the river's main stream, created a large, virtually self-contained reservoir of 9400 a. where the cooling waters could be recirculated, thereby minimizing the impact. Three separate cooling lagoons of 3600 a. (total) are used to pre-cool the water before discharging it back to the reservoir. River temperatures vary during the year; water discharged from the plant will be 14° higher

than at time of withdrawal from the main reservoir. It will be cooled to original reservoir temperature via the cooling lagoons, thus keeping temperature rises to about three degrees. Normal watershed runoff flows into the reservoir and is discharged to the stream below the dam at a predetermined rate.

In the process of providing an environmental solution to their engineering problem, moreover, Vepco also created a massive fresh water recreational resource in a region presently scarce in such opportunities. The reservoir site is a 1½ hour drive from Washington, D.C., via Interstate 95 and less than an hour from Richmond. The small water level fluctuation makes it suitable for most forms of water-oriented recreation, and its rolling, wooded, pastoral setting makes it a natural for recreation and second home development. Without adequate land planning and land use controls, a new and different environmental problem could well occur with rampant subdivisions, silty runoff, septic discharges and polluted ground water supply as only part of the problem. Some form of land use control will be needed.

Although Vepco had little control over how lands adjacent to its reservoir would develop, it was intensely interested in maintaining high water quality for plant operation and other safety considerations associated with a nuclear plant operation. Since the state of Virginia was also concerned with controlling growth adjacent to the reservoir, and with Vepco lacking direct control over development, it was thought that a land use plan was necessary. The Virginia Commission of Outdoor Recreation (VORC) assumed the task of directing a study with the cost paid for by Vep-

co. VORC in turn would try to interest the three counties in which the reservoir lies to adopt the plan and include it in their zoning plans, subdivision regulations, and other land use controls. One of the three has adopted a zoning plan in compliance with the recommendations of our report; the others are now preparing zoning plans and ordinances under a program of co-operative effort with the state.

The recommendations of the report in the field of zoning and land use planning are new to these rural counties and take time and lots of friendly persuasion to get enacted. The state has every hope that the counties will adopt and enforce the zoning regulations and ordinances as recommended by the plan and will assist in such action by legal methods available to them. The state looks upon this project as an opportunity to set a precedent and will exert every effort to help the counties carry out a successful program.

A multi-disciplinary planning group was assembled by the Wirth organization to analyze the problem and produce the plan. Beyond the professions of landscape architecture, architecture, regional planning, civil engineering, ecology and soils engineering, a radiologist, aquatic biologist and chemist were also brought in to evaluate the special problems associated with warm water lagoons, radiation, and maintenance of water quality.

Essentially, the special problems in planning the nuclear facility fell into two categories; safety and water quality. Safety relates primarily to orderly evacuation of the areas in the remote possibility of a nuclear accident. Water quality relates to daily levels of radioactive discharge into the reservoir, set to be well within accepted health standards and cause no limitations on public use of the water resource.

The cooling ponds also required special planning in order to maintain high water quality. Because of their warm water character, any addition of nutrients would result in alga blooms and eventual eutrophication of the ponds. To prevent this, Vepco restricted all direct public access to the cooling ponds by buying all access rights. And in order to maintain the high water quality necessary to the operation of the plant, the introduction of sewage, silt, pesticides and fertilizers is to be kept to a minimum by the state.

To provide a sound base to the plans, all relevant environmental factors were inventoried on maps and evaluated. Topics included vegetation, soils, wildlife habitat, slopes, land use, historic and archaeologic features and similar environmental concerns. From this inventory and analysis, use and density ranges were established for all lands within the reservoir, with particularly sensitive land and water areas delineated. Finally, the potential demand for future land development was estimated and matched against the environmental analysis to determine ranges for the amounts of land required to meet future land development demands.

Maintaining water quality and scenic quality within the context of orderly growth and development became the primary goal of the planning effort. Because of the size and character of the reservoir and the general lack of similar regional resources, maximum public access and provision of recreational opportunities became one of the major land use considerations.

The shoreline development concept that emerged provided a variety of park, recreation and resort opportunities at a number of locations throughout the reservoir, interdispersed with low density (one to four dwelling units per acre) residential developments. Conservation or other protective designations were proposed in the most sensitive areas.

The recommended public outdoor recreation facilities include a 2500 a. state park and two smaller country or regional parks with facilities for camping, picnicking, swimming and boat launching, etc. The state has programmed purchase of these parks in our plan. Interspersed among these three parks are a number of boat and fishing access areas. More intensive recreational development opportunities are to be provided at three resort centers located via zoning maps and regulations enacted by the counties. These would include such facilities as marinas, restaurants, lodges and golf courses. Hiking, canoeing and nature study activities would take place in and along the fingered headwaters of the reservoir. Because of soil conditions, shoreline characteristics and shallow water depth in the headwater areas, they were given a special conservation designation.

The reservoir is to be served by a circumferential road system with three private enterprise business centers located strategically at primary intersection points. Business centers would consist of small retail and service facilities to provide for the basic needs of residents and vacationers. These developments and their sites will be governed by regulations now under consideration by the counties, with state assistance.

As an aid to implementation of the land use plan, minimum impact residential and utility development concepts are indicated. Suggestions were also made to further mitigate other environmental problems including mine drainage, boat pollutants, industrial discharge, erosion control, fertilizer and pesticide control. The problem of implementation was also addressed, and recommendations made for the formation of a regional planning agency with state and Vepco participation in plan implementation. We expect the agency will be established; the area being totally rural now offers an almost textbook opportunity for wise land use and environmental planning.

Bear Swamp Project

By GERD STERN

In the Beginning

New England Power Company in the autumn of 1970 asked Intermedia Systems Corporation of Cambridge, Massachusetts, to recommend an exhibit design for its proposed Visitors' Center at the Bear Swamp Pumped Storage Project in northwestern Massachusetts. After the initial design concept was accepted, Intermedia worked closely with the Boston firm of Chas. T. Main, in charge of the environmental and recreational planning, architecture, engineering and supervision of the Bear Swamp project construction. Herbert Conover, landscape architect, is Chief of the Environmental Site Planning and Recreation Section of Chas. T. Main. The following quotes are from the Environmental Plan for the Bear Swamp project and an interview with Mr. Conover, and from Intermedia Systems' proposals. The Bear Swamp project Visitors' Center opened on Independence Day, 1972.

Environmental Plan

The site selected for the 600,000 kW Bear Swamp Pumped Storage Project is located along an isolated section of the Deerfield River in northwestern Massachusetts close by the licensee's existing 69 kV, 115 kV and 230 kV transmission grid system . . . Over the years few persons have lived in the vicinity and none will be relocated by its development. Of the 1400 a. involved, the licensee has owned all but a small portion for the past 60 years and now owns or has options on all areas required by the project development . . . Development of the major project works will affect some 270 a., or only a small portion of the overall project site; associated facilities, including roads, will only affect

another 20 a. The remaining land will be undisturbed under a forest management program and will be available for public recreational use and for wildlife. The upper reservoir, having a water surface area of 118 a. at maximum elevation (1600 ft.) will be formed by the construction of four impervious core, rock-filled dikes to elevation 1,606 in low saddles on the north, south and east sides of Bear Swamp . . . a portion of the upper reservoir will be visible to travellers along the Mohawk Trail, over three miles away . . . The lower

Tunnel into mound, left, leads to visitors' center at Bear Swamp; interior simulates a power plant, explains power workings graphically.

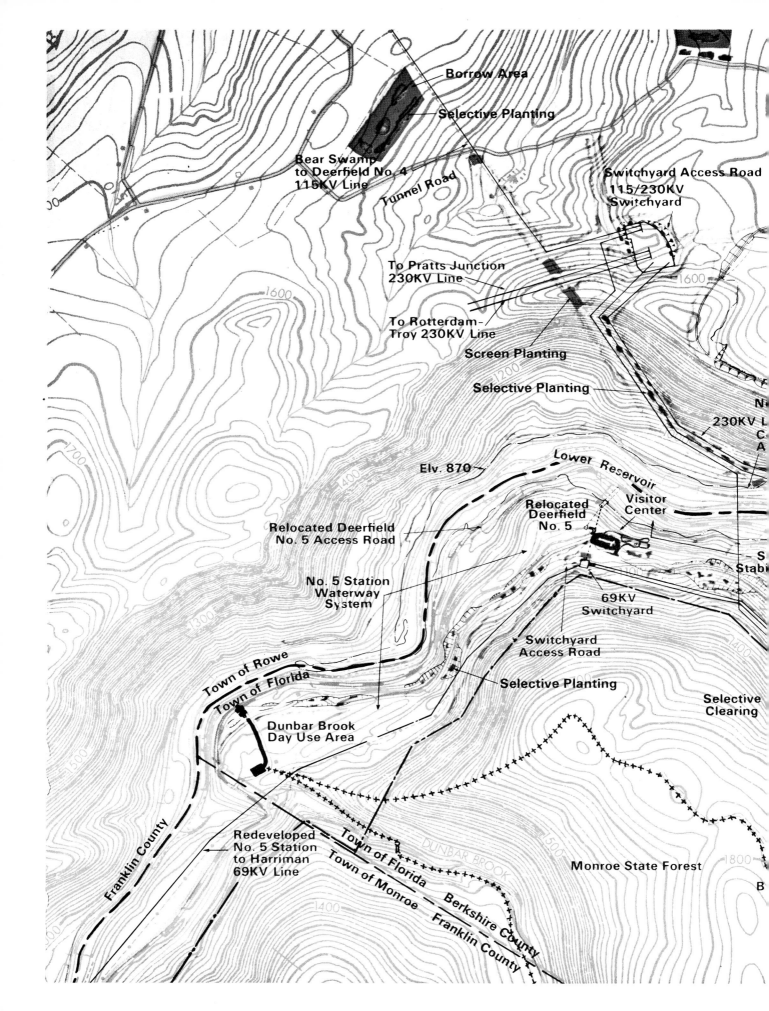

Borrow Area

Selective Planting

Bear Swamp to Deerfield No. 4 115KV Line

Tunnel Road

Switchyard Access Road

115/230KV Switchyard

To Pratts Junction 230KV Line

To Rotterdam-Troy 230KV Line

Screen Planting

Selective Planting

N

230KV L
CA

Elv. 870

Lower Reservoir

Relocated Deerfield No. 5 Access Road

Relocated Deerfield No. 5

Visitor Center

No. 5 Station Waterway System

69KV Switchyard

S
Stabi

Switchyard Access Road

Town of Rowe

Town of Florida

Selective Planting

Selective Clearing

Dunbar Brook Day Use Area

Franklin County

Redeveloped No. 5 Station to Harriman 69KV Line

Town of Florida

Town of Monroe

Town of Florida

Berkshire County

Franklin County

DUNBAR BROOK

Monroe State Forest

B

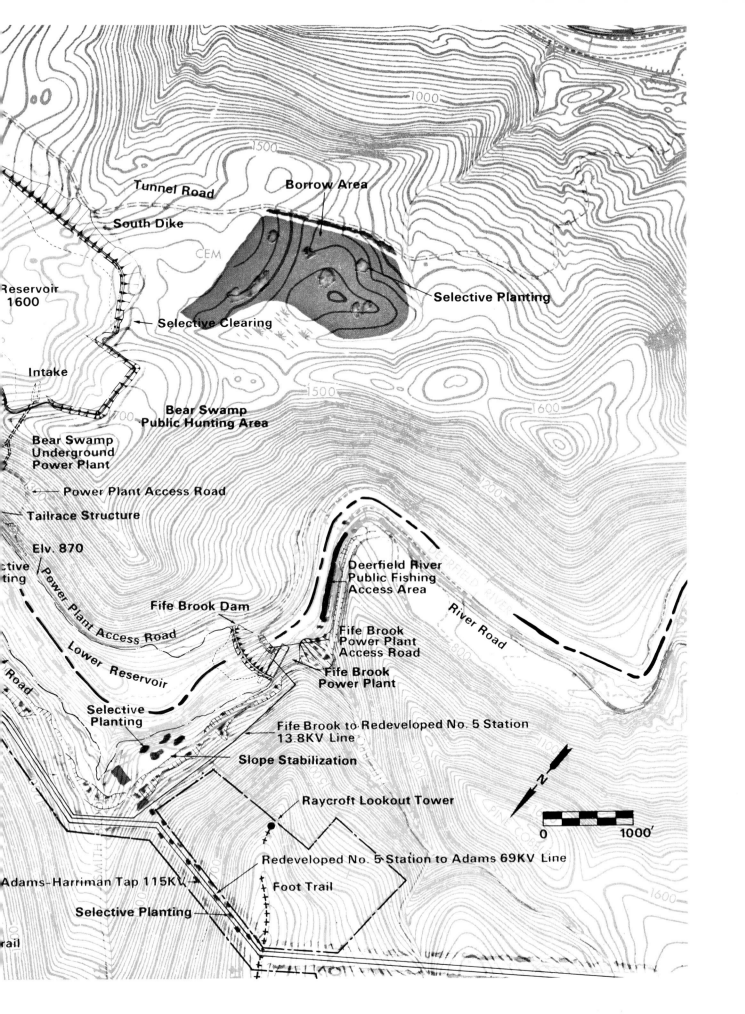

Tunnel Road

Borrow Area

South Dike

Reservoir
1600

CEM

Selective Planting

Selective Clearing

Intake

Bear Swamp
Public Hunting Area

Bear Swamp
Underground
Power Plant

Power Plant Access Road

Tailrace Structure

Elv. 870

Deerfield River
Public Fishing
Access Area

Power Plant Access Road

Fife Brook Dam

Fife Brook
Power Plant
Access Road

River Road

Lower Reservoir

Fife Brook
Power Plant

Selective
Planting

Fife Brook to Redeveloped No. 5 Station
13.8KV Line

Slope Stabilization

Raycroft Lookout Tower

N

0   1000'

Redeveloped No. 5 Station to Adams 69KV Line

Adams-Harriman Tap 115KV

Foot Trail

Selective Planting

rail

reservoir, having a water surface area of 152 a. at maximum operation level 870, will be created by the construction of an impervious core, rock-fill dam across the Deerfield River in the vicinity of Fife Brook. The Bear Swamp power house was (see map) constructed underground 600 ft. into the hillside between the upper and lower reservoirs . . .

Conover

During 1970 we prepared the recreational plan for the Federal Power Commission and the environmental report to be submitted by the commission to the Environmental Protection Agency. The recreation facilities planned around the visitors' center were discussed with the federal agencies and with the Massachusetts State Department of Natural Resources, because we were trying to tie in facilities with the adjoining Monroe State Forest. In addition, we provided picnic areas and parking here and in the Dunbar Brook area with access to hiking and riding trails, sightseeing and camping facilities to be developed jointly with the Natural Resources people. The visitors' center itself was originally an above-ground structure. After the license was granted New England Power Company asked several consultants for recommendations concerning the information and displays to be exhibited. Intermedia Systems proposed that this facility might be placed underground with its interior stimulating a power plant, since visitors could not visit the actual power house.

Intermedia

Until we found a data base around which we could image the architectural space, conceive the information display, manage people flow, we were lost in a slough of traditional exhibit solutions. The key clue was our own need to understand the network of generating plants, power grid, REMVEC and NEPEX (regional computer centers controlling power distribution) the consumer, and the relationship of the "field" experience to the specific Bear Swamp storage project.

The *Six Minute Day* answered our need to simulate a space/time domain which could and would repeat field process without abstracting the flow out of context, without placing it up against the wall, or down on the floor, as separate pieces of demonstrations. In *The Six Minute Day,* symbolic, kinetic, sculptural elements and simulated, modelled, photographed reality are programmed and synchronized with dialogue and music, through our 15-second-hour, a never-ending cycle of morning, day, evening, night, which can be entered and left at any point, experienced once or over and over again.

The network board, hanging from the ceiling vault, represents with colored lamps and kinetic, graphic display symbols the transmission and use of the power environment in New England. In the evening movie marquees scintillate; housing tracts, apartments and hotels illuminate. In the morning factory wheels move. The entire cycle of low and peak load uses are symbolically represented, while the board's center displays the balance of fossil-fuel, hydro, atomic and pumped storage generation. The real images of people going about these uses and controls are told in a series of rear projected slide railings.

This program is also tied in with scale models of the Bear Swamp pumped storage upper and lower reservoirs and power-house with water actually pumped to the upper reservoir during the low-demand night hours and descending through the reversible turbine generators to the lower reservoir at peak day-time hours.

From the visitors' center parking lot a path takes visitors to a tunnel leading down to the display. The ramp winds past the network board and slide railings and the upper reservoir down to the bottom level with the lower reservoir and power-house. From the model one can turn around and exit onto an overlook to see the expanse of the actual lower reservoir. The lower level will also house a Massachusetts Department of Natural Resources, exhibit and information desk, and a New England Power Company display of archeological finds from an archaic-culture Indian hunting and fishing tribe, found by Smithsonian Archeologist William Fitzhugh.

Conover

As things progressed, it was determined that the rock formation was such that it was more economical to build this structure above ground and then build a naturalistic mound over the top of it, using excess fill.

We've found that collecting trees and shrubs in the woods is not successful. The root growth on most collected material is too sparse, and it is difficult to get a sufficient root system to support the tree or shrub. Then the labor is high, so we recommend using material from a qualified nursery, grown for transplanting, with a compact root system.

Intermedia

Our original intent in thinking of the experience underground had to do with the impossibility of simulating the experience in a windowed bungalow, or imposing a display environment on the wooded natural scene. We wanted the descent, the circumambulation and the reentry from the experience into the overlook view of the reservoir. The fact that we managed to "get rid of a building" where none really belonged was a valuable added attraction.

From Yatir to the Negev
Greening the Israeli Landscape

By SHLOMO ARONSON

Desert afforestation in Israel has now reached the point of showing visible results in several places, and offering lessons for other regions of the world with similar challenging conditions.

The Yatir Forest recreation park is an example of the successful establishment of a large park in an area which, for more than a millennium, has been a treeless desert providing at most meager seasonal pasture for more northerly villages and passing Bedouins. The design for the reclamation of the Yatir area has been carefully tailored upon its specific topographical and climatic conditions. Its small, close, rolling hills with deep narrow valleys form an intricate landscape where each configuration may demand its own design solution.

Two other techniques not used in Yatir due to its rocky soil and hilly topography, but used elsewhere in the Negev region with very encouraging results, are the building of bays and erosion control in wadis. These will both be described in detail later.

The semi-arid zone in Israel, the Negev, comprises roughly one-half the country. It has become imperative to encourage ways to allow human settlement and cultivation of the area. To change the harsh and bleak desert into a pleasing, productive green environment had great ideological importance in the eyes of the pioneers at the beginning of the century, as well as tremendous material importance. Fifty years ago Joseph Weiz had the vision of a green and forested desert. He was the "father" and the first head of the Afforestation Department, but many people were involved in this hard and sometimes disappointing work. Among them a major credit goes to Naftali Jaffe, head of the Southern

District of Israel since 1955.

Until recently, visual aspects of afforestation were neglected, as the first necessity was seen to be planting and keeping plants alive. This effort has become more successful, and more recently landscape architects have been called in by the Afforestation Branch of the Jewish National Fund (J.N.F.) to help shape these newly developing landscapes. It is also realized now that while residents of the central and northern regions of the country have forests relatively close to their homes, the inhabitants of the Negev have no such natural areas for recreation. Thus the afforestation program's new goal is to provide recreational areas while maintaining and offsetting the natural beauty of the desert.

Yatir Forest
The southern terminus of the master plan, the Yatir forest is an example of a desert area completely reclaimed, with the planting of millions of trees in a parched region to serve as a cool and green recreation reserve for the people of the Negev.

The Yatir forest is like an oasis situated on the southwestern slopes of the mountains of Hebron at the edge of the vast Judean and Negev deserts, and includes an afforested area of over 5000 a. out of a projected 8000. The landscape of Yatir is a visual accumulation of mountain and desert landscapes, and derives an incredible richness and drama from them. Yet it is not only a gateway to these landscapes, but a place unto itself, composed of undulating forested hills and golden meadows.

Growth conditions are harsh, with temperatures ranging from an average maximum of 32 C. to an average minimum of 7 C. Average rainfall is 250-300 mm. An altitude

of 575-750 m. above sea level provides the forest region with cool winds in the summer, and precipitation sufficient to maintain a green forest without irrigation. The rock outcroppings of the area are mainly limestone, and the soil is light brown with a high loess component. Vegetation is characteristic of the Mediterranean-Irano Turanian border region.

The major influences on tree growth are the steepness of slopes and the depth and composition of soil. On steep southern and eastern slopes the lack of topsoil results in a small carrying capacity for vegetation. On northern and western slopes, the determining factors are the depth of soil and the percentage of ground covered by rocks. There, the steeper the slope the more surface runoff, which brings additional water to trees growing between boulders. Because the southeastern slopes receive more radiation than the northern, they are more arid.

A master plan of Yatir was commissioned after much of it was already planted; thus the main objective in the planning was the integration of an already existing forest into its surroundings. In the north, at the end of the Hebron mountains, the edge of the existing forest is in sharp contrast to the barren desert. The intent in the new afforestation is to soften and ameliorate this explicit edge. In the south and west, cascading wadis (ravines) are to be woven into the forested area, and in the east, a dramatic perspective is accentuated by the steep drop from the Yatir forest to the Arad plateau. The overall visual effect will be to bring out the area's character of "fingers of green" protruding into the desert.

In the planning of the forest, four major elements were used: conifers, the dominant kind of tree in such harsh conditions; broadleaf tree groves, mainly *Pistacia Atlantica,* almonds, and walnuts where soil conditions allow; field crops such as barley and wheat; and areas left in their natural state. The existing coniferous forest of Yatir serves as a nucleus from which the new planted areas will grow, and as a backdrop for other landscape types.

To achieve the desired visual impressions, the following design criteria were recommended: the accentuation of the Dead Sea valley rift in the east with a sharp line marking the edge of the planted forest, giving prominence to the hills by planting forests on the crests rather than in the valleys, delineating the shape of the valleys in the western forest sector by reserving them for field crops which will be surrounded by broadleaf trees, and delineating the shape of the valleys in the eastern forest sector by reserving them exclusively for broadleaf woods. Planted and unplanted areas will overlap throughout the forest, leaving gaps which will let the natural desert scenery intrude and serve as a continuation of the surrounding landscape.

The use of the forest as a public campground calls for special measures to preserve its scenery, especially in camping areas. Thus the plan recommends 14 overnight campsites used in rotation to prevent deterioration of their scenery through overuse. As soon as damage or ruin is spotted at a campsite, it is shut down for rehabilitation and another opened instead.

Likewise, a large number of planned roads can be opened and closed to counter damage through overuse. The roads presently spread into all corners as branches off a main road, and lead back to another main road so as to avoid dead ends. The roads follow contours, thus avoiding expensive cutting and filling which also impairs the scenery. Roads passing through ravines can also be used as fire prevention lanes in broadleaf groves. Such lanes, following the swinging course of the ravine, react to both its sides, in contrast to the usual firelines which run perpendicular to the hillslope and create scars. However, when there is no way to avoid perpendicular fire prevention lines, it is suggested that they be run diagonally over the slopes.

An additional dimension to the forest can be created with the reconstruction of Yatir's two archaeological sites, Yatir and Annim. These ancient towns were inhabited repeatedly through history. Yatir was one of the cities given to the Levites (Joshua 21:14, Chronicles 16:42). Later, in the period of the Second Temple, Yatir was one of the Jewish settlements of Droma. Thereafter, Eusebius writing in the late Byzantine period mentioned that Yatir was a Christian settlement while Annim was Jewish. These sites are awaiting excavations; both can be easily reached.

Bays and Ravines
Another problem particular to arid areas is flash-flooding, where torrential downpours can do extensive damage to dry and dusty areas not prepared to handle a sudden overflow of water. However, the area's floodwaters can be managed, to prevent erosion and irrigate planted areas called bays or "Limans."

A bay is a small grove of trees of ½ to 1½ a., planted in a sunken basin, usually placed not far from roads in order to create a place of rest for the motorist. Being created with heavy machinery, the form given to bays until recently was a simple rectangle with a side channel for overflow during big floods. Bays can also be linked to create a chain of green spots.

As bays only use the floodwater of large catchbasins and do not require additional irrigation, they are planted in arid zones with rainfall ranging from 70-250 mm a year. The size of a catchbasin for a bay varies from 100 to 2-3000 a.

The types of plants used in a bay vary according to the constitution and depth of the soil, size of basin, and dependability of rain. Big Eucalyptus like *E. occidentalis, E. camaldulensis* (Red Gum), *E. brockway;* Jerusalem pine (*Pinus halepensis),* olives and other fruit trees are grown in areas with deep loess soil. In less favorable areas hardier trees like Acacia, Prosopis and small Eucalyptus are used.

It is desirable to shape the bays in a more natural form responding to the surrounding landscape shapes, rather than accepting hardedged bulldozer cuts. Selecting a large variety of plants, using shrubs as well, makes the bay a rich and diverse natural reserve.

When our office was asked to design a series of five bays in the Sde Boker area, the central Negev, where the average rainfall is a harsh 70 mm, we planted 40% of the bays in *Eucalyptus occidentalis* to act as a tall backdrop for the other plants.

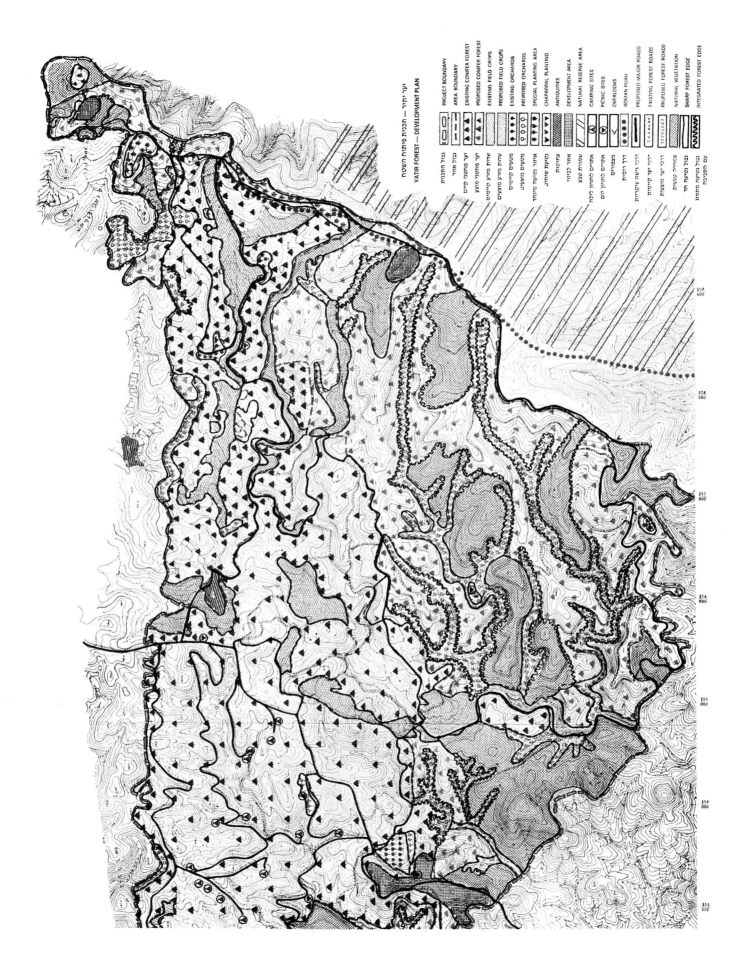

	PROJECT BOUNDARY
	AREA BOUNDARY
	EXISTING CONIFER FOREST
	PROPOSED CONIFER FOREST
	EXISTING FIELD CROPS
	PROPOSED FIELD CROPS
	EXISTING ORCHARDS
	PROPOSED ORCHARDS
	SPECIAL PLANTING AREA
	CHAPAIRAL PLANTING
	ANTIQUITIES
	DEVELOPMENT AREA
	NATURAL RESERVE AREA
	CAMPING SITES
	PICNIC SITES
	OVERLOOKS
	ROMAN ROAD
	PROPOSED MAJOR ROADS
	EXISTING FOREST ROADS
	PROPOSED FOREST ROADS
	NATURAL VEGETATION
	SHARP FOREST EDGE
	INTEGRATED FOREST EDGE

View at bottom of page of totally afforested ravines. Smaller photos, clockwise from top left: regraded, dammed and forested ravine; unreclaimed ravines; closeup of bay at Sde Boker; ravine being regraded; maturing Yatir Forest with field crops; below, portion of Yatir forest region.

Pepper trees, tamarisk, *Pistacia atlantica* and *Acacia cyanophylla* were placed in ascending order of height to produce a grading effect when viewed from the road. We also found that a certain local thorny acacia used in the bays attracted a multitude of birds. These were planted in the periphery of the bays such as not to have thorny plants inside, but still attract birds.

Another method of developing desert areas with afforestation is through erosion control in wadis. In the northern part of the Negev there are hundreds of deep ravines biting and eroding the culturable soil. In the early fifties the J.N.F. tried to plant ravines without soil preparation, the main plant used being *Acacia cyanophylla*. This, after ten years, proved to be too shortlived,

and it became clear that the ravines had to be prepared more thoroughly for better results.

From the '60s until today the procedures have been the following: A bulldozer smooths the banks of the deep ravine and raises its floor with excess soil from the sides, thus creating a shallow depression. Then the new ravine floor is plowed 60 cm deep and planted with a variety of trees such as eucalyptus, pine, cypress, tamarisk, sisifus, etc.

Where the big floods occur, water velocity is reduced by simple damming methods such as laying wooded posts and tree branches across the water course. The length of a manageable ravine can vary up to 3-4 km, its width from 40 to 400 m.

The contribution of these cultivated ravines to the beauty of the landsape is enormous. Besides erosion control, they break the monotonous and vast desert landscape into more graspable units by emphasizing the natural landforms, since they follow the natural line of the ravine. The planted ravine becomes a habitat for animals and birds having a similar effect and function as hedgerows in the British landscape.

The landscape architect's role in arid areas thus has involved a crucial understanding and appreciation of the zone's natural attributes as well as its problems, in order to develop methods which will enable us to use its unique conditions for man's benefit without causing unnecessary ecological damage.

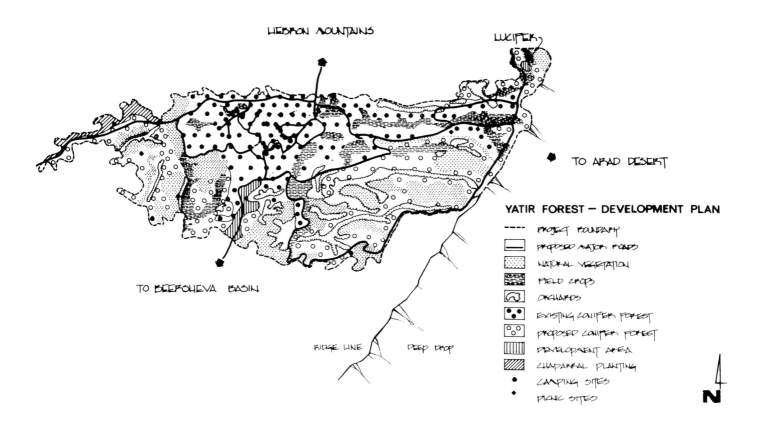

HEBRON MOUNTAINS

LUCIFER

TO ARAD DESERT

TO BEERSHEVA BASIN

RIDGE LINE   DEEP DROP

N

Development plan, above, may be compared with portion of detailed plan on earlier page. Typical water-retention bays in the semi-desert of Sde Boker are shown in author's sketches below.

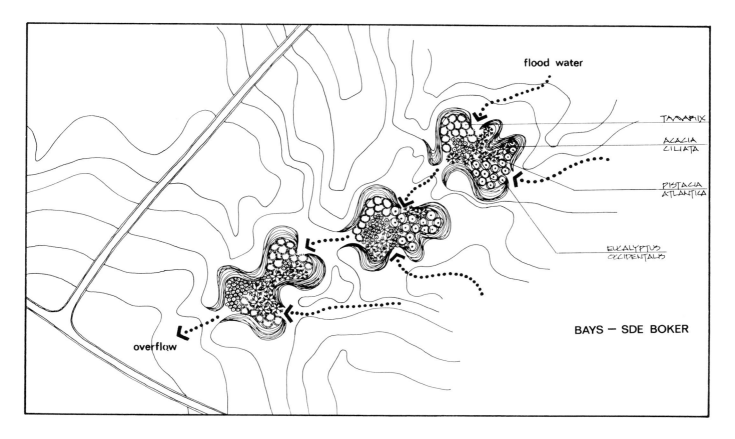

flood water

TAMARIX

ACACIA CILIATA

PISTACIA ATLANTICA

EUCALYPTUS OCCIDENTALIS

BAYS — SDE BOKER

overflow

Joining Forces to Save Damaged Lakes in Sweden and Tunisia

By SVEN BJORK

Since lake restoration research is a very young field, ecologists need opportunities to test their ideas, to apply their theories in nature, to provide concrete examples of ecologically sound methods of tackling the problems created in lake ecosystems by man.

However, responsibility for the restoration of lakes does not rest solely with ecologists. A cooperative effort with public administrators, politicians and technicians is necessary.

There are very few cases on record where these interests have joined forces to save a damaged lake.

This article presents four lake restoration projects, three in Sweden and one in Tunisia, that prove such cooperation is possible. The great interest displayed by the concerned governments in initiating projects such as these to improve the human environment is most encouraging. Two of the projects are completed, and work is progressing on the other two. Each project is an educational experience and provides further knowledge of the structure and function of lake ecosystems.

The four projects were undertaken by a team of limnologists at the University of Lund in Sweden as part of a lake restoration program that has been going on for several years. Now that the initial phase of the program is finished, news of the ideas and methodology is travelling quickly to other parts of the world, and due to a lack of funds for nonroutine limnologic investigations in Sweden, trained limnologists will probably follow.

The aims of the lake restoration research program at the University of Lund can be summarized as follows:

1. To obtain methods of solving some of the severe environmental problems that man has created.

2. To restore certain lakes judged to be of high environmental value.

3. To train limnologists and other ecologists so that they are capable of solving practical problems in applied water management.

4. To contribute additional knowledge to theoretical ecology.

As each water is unique, each one must be investigated and given a tailor-made limnological treatment. It must be stressed that it is impossible to establish a standardized treatment. The lakes investigated in this program represent a wide variety of conditions. Thus three different sets of methods had to be worked out to correct the balance of the three different lake ecosystems. This meant that, among other things, the equilibrium between production and mineralization had to be restored.

A total of about 20 research workers from the Institutes of Limnology, Microbiology, Plant Ecology, Animal Ecology and Quaternary Geology have been active in the project, and there has been close cooperation with technological experts.

The Hornborga Lake project began in the late fall of 1967, the Lake Trummen project in the late winter of 1968, and the Jarla Lake project in the late winter of 1969. The former is still in progress, and the latter two have been completed. Some of the knowledge gained from the Swedish experiment is now being applied in a project to restore the Lake of Tunis in Tunisia.

Lake Trummen

The inland town of Vaxjo (c. 60,000 inhabitants) is surrounded by lakes. Of these, Lake Trummen and Vaxjo Lake became the first recipients of the town's sewage. When these eventually became overexploited, the waste water was diverted to another, South Bergunda Lake. For the past 20 years or so, the sewage has gone through a two-step treatment. A third step, treatment with aluminum sulfate, was added in 1972. At this time, however, South Bergunda Lake is also overexploited. Nearby North Bergunda Lake is therefore being considered as the potential fourth recipient of Vaxjo's waste water.

Helga Lake, which lies north of Vaxjo, became polluted by waste water from a paper pulp plant and is black-listed because of the high mercury content there.

Originally Trummen, Vaxjo, and South Bergunda were low-productivity lakes, but the inflow of waste water eventually converted them into water bodies containing concentrated nutrient solutions and maintaining an enormous growth of algae in the summer.

Lake Trummen (1 km.^{2}, maximum depth 2 m. until 1969) was well fed with sewage, especially from 1936 to 1958. From 1941 to 1957, the lake received waste water from a flax factory. Prior to that, only small quantities of waste water were discharged into the lake. The lake was utilized as a water supply source, at least to some degree, until the 1920s. During that time the bathing places were frequently utilized.

From a water conservationist's point of view, it is a remarkable and important fact that Lake Trummen did not recover after the inflow of waste water was cut off in 1957-58. This meant that the lake maintained the characteristics of an overexploited recipient during the 1960s. In

Seemingly dead, until sewage inflow from Vaxjo was halted, Lake Trummen, above, in southern Sweden did not recover for 12 years. Removal of sedimentary ooze rejuvenated the lake. Diagram, below, shows Lake Trummen's recovery: (1) suction dredger operates with minimal turbidity; (2) settling pond; (3) runoff water; (4) precipitation of phosphorus and suspended matter with aluminum sulfate; (4a) automatic dosage; (5) clarified runoff water; and (6) the dried sediment is used as fertilizer for parks and lawns.

the soup of blue-green algae, the summer transparency in 1969 was only about 20 cm., reeds and water lilies spread and the total oxygen deficiency in the winter killed off the fish. There was no underwater vegetation at all.

Substantial investments are made in sewage treatment plants in order to improve the environment. In Sweden, about 300 million Swedish kronor (c. U.S. $60 million) are invested per year in plants (not including pipes to these). During periods with high unemployment the investments are much larger.

It is common knowledge that waste water treatment methods are still fairly stereotyped, and that very few plants use original combinations of methods specially tailored to the

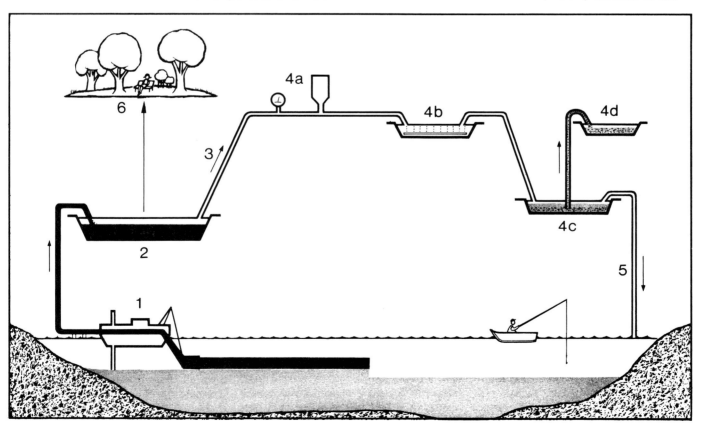

ecosystem of the specific receiving body of water. The efficiency of the treatment is commonly expressed in relation to the raw sewage.

When dealing with a receiving lake's ecosystem, single-factor data are given, e.g., supply of phosphorus or nitrogen per ha./yr. Figures such as these can be evaluated in agriculture when fertilizers containing a few elements are added to monocultures growing in extremely well-known soils. However, no two lake ecosystems are alike, either with respect to environment or to organism communities. Furthermore, the lake ecosystems undergo successive changes as they undergo exploitation, which means that this kind of evaluation is hardly relevant to the measuring of the loading of lakes.

In treatment plants as well as in lakes, physical and chemical parameters are easily recorded automatically. Within the biological sector we must confess that we have great difficulties, even in identifying the organisms chiefly involved in the treatment process and responsible for the variations in the recipient's ecosystems. An enormous investment is necessary if we are to have, decades from now, enough trained limnologists within the biological sector, microbiologists, planktonologists, etc.

The fact that there are great variations in nature means there are also great variations in the influence of different treatment plants on different lakes. Some receiver lakes are exploited to the point where the damage is irreversible; even when the source of pollution is cut off, the lake cannot recover on its own. Other exploited lakes have the capacity for self-recovery, at least to some extent.

In the case of Lake Trummen, the damage was irreversible.

Just before Trummen became a recipient of waste water, the sediment growth rate was 0.4 mm./yr. The onset of pollution and the consequences thereof caused an increase in the growth rate to 8 mm./year. The difference in the quality of the two sediments is striking. During the lake's recipient period, the accumulation per m.[2] of phosphorus was up to 20 times higher and the accumulation of zinc was up to 65 times higher than before the waste waters started pouring in.

The irreversible situation in Lake Trummen was due to the deposition of the loose black "cultural layer" covering the well-consolidated brown sediment of the pre-recipient years. The black mud layer was from 0.2 mm. to 0.4 mm. thick, and the nutrient leakage from this layer caused the high productivity in the spring and summer. Plankton and macroscopic plants grew, died, settled and decayed, maintaining the rapid growth rate of the sediment and supplying it with releasable nutrients.

The limnological plan for the restoration of Lake Trummen was focused on the sediment problem. It was decided that the black cultural mud had to be pumped from the lake up into settling ponds on land. From these, the runoff water would go through a simple treatment plant for phosphorus removal before being discharged back into the lake.

The project was carried out with very stimulating cooperation between the ecologists, town authorities and technological experts. For the sediment-removal part of the project, a suction-dredging method was used. The limnologist requested a nozzle which would make it possible to suck in the sediment without making the lake water turgid and with very little mixing of lake water. The engineerings of the Swedish company Skanska Cementgjuteriet constructed this nozzle.

In 1970 about 0.5 m. of sediment was removed, and in 1971 another 0.5 m. Altogether about 600,000 m.[3] of mud and 300,000 m.[3] of lake water were pumped to the settling ponds. The pond were constructed in an arable land area from which the topsoil had first been removed, exposing a poor moraine suitable for pond dikes. The sediment pumping ended in October 1971. The dried sediment is now being used as fertilizer for lawns and parks in the rapidly growing town of Vaxjo.

The runoff water from the settling ponds was a mixture of lake and interstitial (sediment) water. Its high fertilizing effect was checked by means of bio-assay with algae. The total phosphorus content in the water in Trummen before the restoration was c. 600 ug/1 in the summer, and in the untreated runoff water from the settling ponds, a further increase was brought about by the addition of interstitial water. However, aluminum sulfate was used for precipitation of suspended matter and phosphorus, and thus in the treated water returned to the lake the total phosphorus content was only about 30 ug/1.

The littoral zone of Lake Trummen is fairly rich in stones and boulders. In the landward part, the dense vegetation growing in sediments overlying the stony bottom had to be removed by a dragline. The elimination of the vegetation exposed the original shoreline view. In 1972, the first year after the restoration, a distinct rinsing of the shores took place, thanks to the revived water movements. Until the sedimentation limit has stabilized, a detritus turbidity will be noticeable in the water. The invasion of underwater vegetation and bottom fauna will help to keep the detritus particles confined to the bottom.

Follow-up investigations in Lake Trummen will continue until the summer of 1980. Information will be collected on water and sediment chemistry, phytoplankton, macrophytes, zooplankton, bottom fauna and fish populations.

As was foreseen, the changes in Trummen's ecosystem have been dramatic. The transparency has increased but was, in 1972, still limited by plankton and is highly dependent on the amount of detritus whirled up by the wind, especially from the littoral zone. The phosphorus content has decreased, as has the nitrogen content. During the late winter period which had in the past been the critical time, the oxygen conditions were excellent after the black sediment had been removed. The heavy waterbloom of microcystis spp. (blue-green algae) disappeared, while Pediastrum spp. (green algae) and Anabaena flos aquae (blue-green algae) were the characteristic summer plankters of 1971 and 1972, respectively.

Lake Trummen is now accessible for fishing and bathing and it can be considered to be a valuable recreational asset.

The total cost of bringing Lake

Trummen back to health was Sw. kronor 2.5 million (U.S. $500,000). The cost of adding the third step to the Vaxjo treatment plant was Sw. kronor 20 million (U.S. $4 million).

Now that it has been brought back to health, Lake Trummen is being attacked from another angle. A proposal to build a new motorway across the lake and along the southern shore has been made. None other than the National Swedish Road Administration would be responsible for the realization. It is a remarkably short-sighted proposal, an example of the kind of "progress" envisaged by the forces of exploitation. Another motorway is already built close to the western shore. This new encroachment on the Lake Trummen area would, of course, be an irremediable mistake. The lake has already been restored, yes. But if Trummen is to be framed in by motorways, one could well ask, restored for what? And for whom?

Jarla Lake

Situated near Stockholm, Jarla Lake has an area of 1 km.², is 23 m. deep at its deepest point, and has a distinct thermal stratification in the summer. It is an old recipient for sewage and industrial waste water. Before the restoration project, the oxygen content in the lower water layers was reduced to zero during stagnation periods.

Although it is possible to increase the oxygen content of some lakes by means of artificial total circulation during natural stagnation periods, this method was not advisable in the case of Jarla Lake. Artificial total circulation would have brought about the transport of nutrients from the bottom water layer and their dispersal in the illuminated superficial water layer — thus increasing the productivity — and the cultural sediments would have been warmed up, bringing about an increased consumption of oxygen.

Photo, top, shows helicopter lowering a hypolimnio aerator which restored the oxygen level of the 23-meter-deep Jarla Lake without disturbing thermal stratification. Illustration shows compressed-air oxygenation (250 kg./day) in submerged unit dispersing bubble-free water over large bottom area.

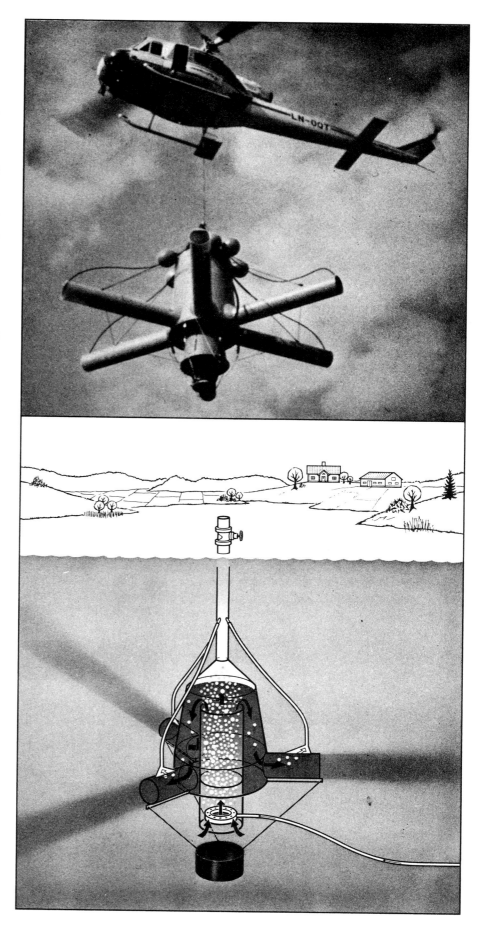

The goal of the Jarla Lake project was to increase the oxygen content of the lower water layers in a limnologically correct way, i.e. without disturbing the thermal stratification. A collaboration between limnologists and technological experts from the Central Laboratory of Physics at the Atlas Copco Company resulted in the ingenious technical solution shown on this page.

In brief, this equipment now makes it possible to increase the oxygen content in deep recipients to the desired degree. In a lake of the Jarla type, the earlier anaerobic water layers could easily be kept at an oxygen level of, say, 7 mg./1.

Because of lack of funds, it has not been possible to carry out long-term studies of limnological changes accompanying the improved oxygen conditions of Jarla Lake. However, after three months' aeration (June-August), the sediment surface was oxidized, the concentrations of phosphate phosphorus and ammonium decreased, and the nitrate concentration increased. In spite of the short experimental period, an invasion of bottom animals was hoped for, but they failed to appear. A search conducted to determine the cause of this and the consequences of the aeration of the sediment led to the discovery that the cultural sediment layer was partly impregnated by oil, which made it impossible for certain organisms to survive.

Experiments are now being carried out in West Germany in which inert phosphate-absorbing substances are added in connection with the aeration. In Sweden, the effect of the so-called "bubble-method" has been checked in a 7 m. deep lake in which a thin layer of bottom water was depleted of oxygen during calm periods. In this lake the proportions between the volumes of water with and without oxygen made it possible to use artificial total circulation. With this method compressed air bubbles out from plastic hoses distributed in a rib pattern in the deepest part of the lake. Anaerobic conditions can thus be avoided. As soon as the oxygen content of the lake starts to decrease, the compressor is started and operates until the oxygen deficiency is eliminated.

Aeration and bubbling are two ways of making recipients more effective and for speeding up the recovery process in old recipients. Irreversible damage can in this way be prevented until a modern sewage treatment plant is built.

Hornborga Lake
Hornborga Lake is a shallow, drained lake. Until man interfered with the well-organized system of components that functioned within this lake, it maintained a rather high degree of productivity without suffering from rapid aging. That is quite remarkable for a lake of this size (30 km.²) and shallowness (3 m. at the deepest point). Most of the lake was much shallower. A constellation of such factors as rapid water renewal, well-situated inlets and outlets, strong water movements, and strong ice movements prevented the lake from becoming overgrown and provided a good system for transporting matter from the lake.

Since 1802 the lake has been lowered five times in attempts to obtain arable land. The last big failure, in 1932-33, resulted in a bottom that was drained in the summer, and which consisted largely of calcareous mud. A hilly land area of about 616 km.² drains into the lake. This area needs the big reservoir Hornborga Lake to catch rainwater and melted snow that rush down the hills to the plain below.

From a nature conservancy point of view, the lake had a very high

Pontoon-borne cutting machine and amphibious front-cutting machine aid in transformation of reed areas to open water at Hornborga Lake, below. Opposite are three views of Lake Trummen before, during and after restoration.

value before it was lowered, especially as a nesting site and resting place for water fowl. After the last lowering, the lake ecosystem's structure and function were definitely destroyed. Monocultures of Phragmites communis (common reed), Carex acuta (sedge) and Salix spp. (willow bushes) crept in and nearly covered the lake area since 1967.

The National Swedish Environmental Protection Board, after being ordered by the government to investigate the possibilities of restoring Hornborga to the status of a waterfowl lake, organized a broad study of the complex of man-made problems concerning the lake. One year of limnological studies made it quite clear — theoretically — that the lake could still be restored. Large-scale field experiments were begun in 1968 to work out practical methods of correcting the irreversible damage. This was made possible because of the cooperation between the National Environment Board, the National Labor Market Board, the National Board of Forestry, Seiga

Lowering Hornborga Lake resulted in large area covered with reeds, sedge and willow bushes. Machinery to mow, cut and cultivate was used to transform some reed area into open water, some sedge-covered as substitute for original marshy areas. Diagram, below, shows changes in composition and colonization of the lake by waterfowl fauna.

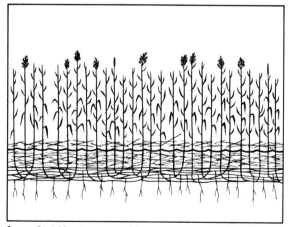

Area: Ca 11 km² covered by common reed until 1967

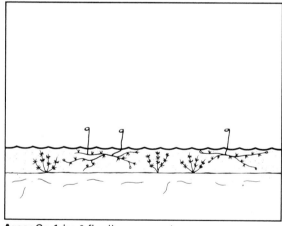

Area: Ca 1 km² finally prepared

Macrophyte detritus:
deposition ↓
decomposition ← →

Bottom fauna:
Chironomidae ind/m² × 1200:

Birds (pairs × 10):
Podiceps auritus, Horned Grebe

Aythya fuligula, Tufted Duck

Aythya ferina, Pochard

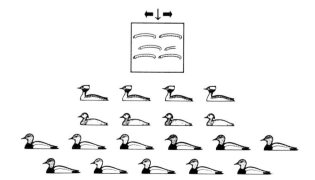

Harvester Co. (manufacturer of amphibious machines), and the Institute of Limnology at Lund.

As the water level had been lowered, emergent vegetation had invaded the colonizable areas and the upper sediment layer had become interwoven by roots. With the two plant species Carex acuta and Phragmites communis covering the main area of the southern and northern parts of the lake, respectively, the sedge had developed a thick, tough and resistant root felt. The sedge root felt posed a problem, as it was impossible to remove. However, the reed root felt could be cut by the amphibious rotor cultivators that were constructed for this project. The development of amphibious and pontoon-equipped machines for the restoration of lower lakes is continuing, and rotor cultivators strong enough to cut the sedge root felt will be constructed.

The project goal for Hornborga Lake is to transform the reed areas to open water (about 11 km.²) and to keep the sedge-covered part (about 18 km.²) for emergent vegetation as a substitute for the originally marshy areas around the lake.

The restoration plans for Hornborga Lake include a raising of the water level for a maximum depth of 1.9 m. or, even better, 2.4 m. It should only take one spring to fill the lake with water, as Hornborga Lake is flooded every year after the melting of the snow. When the water level has been raised, the sedge root felt will float to the water surface. This well-known phenomenon is caused by the gas (mainly methane) that forms in and under the root felt, through which the gas bubbles cannot penetrate. The floating root felt will rapidly be colonized by Phragmitis, Schoenoplectus (bullrush) and Carex.

By means of amphibious excavators, it is possible to break up the monotony of the sedge-covered areas — where the root felt will float up after the water level is raised — and to create a mosaic of open water and biotopes safe for nesting and attractive to birds.

The procedure for achieving the change from production of emergent vegetation to production of submerged vegetation in the reed areas is as follows:

In the winter the dry stems are cut by amphibious harvesters and burned on the ice. In the spring the stubble mats are shortened to about 40 cm. by pontoon-equipped mowers. During the low water period in the summer and autumn, amphibious machines are again utilized, first for cutting the green shoots and then for rotor cultivating the stubble mats and root felts. The requisite time per hectare is 8-10 machine hours. Enormous masses of accumulated coarse detritus are loosened from the bottom and transported by the spring high water to the shores where they are burned in the summer.

With the detritus out of the way, the consolidated mud again becomes the bottom and the reed monoculture is replaced by an underwater vegetation of Chara (charophytes), Potamogeton (pondweeds) and Myriophyllum (water milfoils). A rich bottom fauna, microbenthos and periphyton, is also reestablished.

Altogether, the biotope changes during the experimental period have resulted in a very obvious improvement of the waterfowl fauna. Of the nesting species, 70% have increased in number. Larus ridibundus (blackheaded gull) increased from 5000 to 8500 couples, Podiceps cristatus (the great crested grebe) from five to 50 and Aythya ferina (the pochard) from 20 to 110 couples. These are results of the limited experimental activity that has taken place in a small diked area of the lake where the maximum summer water depth is 80 cm. A definitive raise of the water level must include the whole lake area.

The Lake of Tunis

Experiences gained in the Swedish restoration projects — with aeration, sediment pumping and vegetation removal — were all useful in drawing up plans for the restoration of the Lake of Tunis. The city of Tunis has long suffered from the bad breath of the polluted lake. The stench is most repelling close to the population center, and it is there that the Tunisian authorities want to create an attractive environment. The planning of the Lake of Tunis restoration project has been organized and sponsored by the Tunisian government in cooperation with the

Swedish International Development Authority (S.I.D.A.) and the Institute of Limnology at Lund.

The Lake of Tunis is divided into the north and south lakes. Increasing volumes of raw sewage and increasing amounts of industrial waste water have been discharged into the north and south lakes, respectively. The north lake is the object of the restoration project dealt with here. It has an area of 29.5 km.², but contains only 27.6 million m.³ of water. Tunis is surrounded by very shallow, highly saline lakes. As the Lake of Tunis is connected with the Mediterranean, it does not dry up as the other lakes do. The water level, however, is dependent upon that of the sea.

The north lake is still receiving raw sewage (the westernmost part) and effluent from a treatment plant (the northwestern part). Thanks to the high salinity of the lake water (specific conductivity ranges from about 45 mS_{20} in early June to about 65 mS_{20} in early August), the coagulation and precipitation of particles is good. The sewage sludge deposits are, therefore, concentrated to restricted areas.

The self-purification capacity of the lake is still extremely good. This is apparent from the compressed zonation and steep gradients of environmental conditions and organism communities east of the outlets. In the summer the turbid zones of bacteria and phytoplankton can be very narrow in the western part, while the water in the rest of the lake is clear. In the clear area, luxuriant meadows of Ulva (sea lettuce) cover the bottom from shore to shore (Enteromorpha is also common), with the exception of the eastern part where brown algae are numerous, and there are open bottom areas that consist of pure shell gravel. Reefs of Mercierella enigmatica (tube worm) are common. The reefs are problematic from a hydrological point of view. However, the animals perform a filtration function, and thus play an important role in the lake's self-purification process.

The direct discharge of nutrients and the release of nutrients from the sewage sludge deposits speed up the growth of Ulva and other algae in the warm, shallow lake, and condi-

How Lake Tunis can be restored: (A) Sewage sludge suction-dredged from basin nearest city; runoff water treated. (B) Basin aerated until sludge removed. (C) Montplaisir and Cherguia sewage outlets: runoff treatment. (D) Waste water from Cherguia plant collected in two ponds until removal of outfall sludge. (D1) Pond aeration. (E) Intake of Mediterranean Sea water controlled by lock, passes into North lake, then into harbor and via channel, out to sea. (F&G) Removal of algae by pontoon and amphibious skimmers.

tions are similar to those prevailing in a very effective algal culture. Due to the efficient photosynthesis, gas bubbles form in Ulva leaves, and large amounts of Ulva are set afloat. Thus, green mats of loosened algae periodically cover vast areas of the water surface. When the weather is warm and the water stagnant, the crop of Ulva and other algae decomposes and the water becomes oxygen-deficient. As the consequences of primary and secondary pollution, a nasty stench of raw sewage and hydrogen sulfide is apparent, and fish kills can occur. At times the waters of the Lake of Tunis become wine-red, and it looks as though the lake has been visited by one of the "seven plagues." This wine-red color is caused by the mass development of planktonic micro-organisms, a common phenomenon in salines and highly saline lakes in North Africa.

According to present plans, the sewage will be diverted from the north lake when a more effective treatment plant is completed. The preliminary aims of the project are to eliminate the most disturbing effects of the pollution, to break the trend toward progressively worsening conditions, and at the same time to prepare for the final restoration. In line with these aims, a working program has been presented to the concerned authorities.

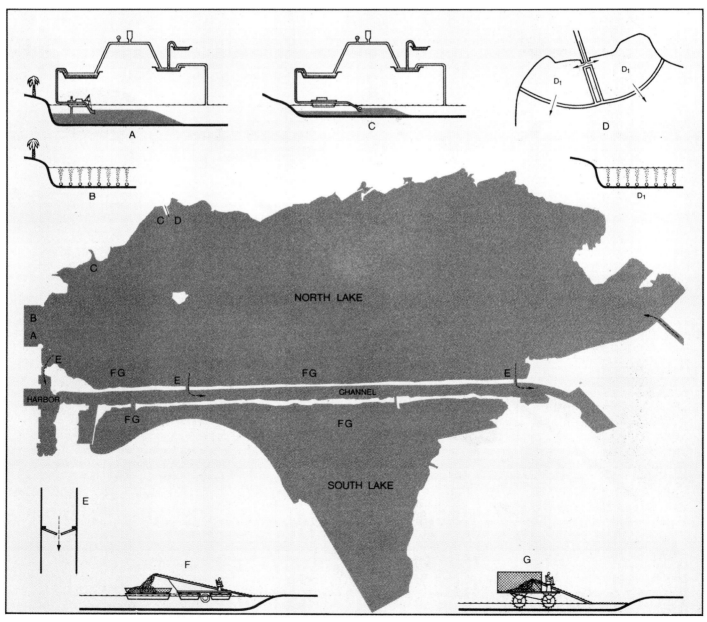

The c. 20-hectare water basin closest to the beautiful palm-lined Avenues Mohammed V and Curtelin is filled with sewage sludge and the water sparkles with gas convection. Within the areas around the sewage outlets of Montplaisir and Cherguia, the situation is about the same. In laboratory tests it was found that the release of NH_4-N is 500-900 and of PO_4-P, 25-30 mg./m.^{2}/day from the sewage sludge sediment to the water. The corresponding figures from Lake Trummen were 75 and 15 mg./m.^{2}/day, respectively.

The method used in the restoration of Lake Trummen can be adopted for use in the Lake of Tunis project. Land areas perfectly suited for sediment deposition are available close to the parts of the lake where the sewage sludge is concentrated. Until now, these land areas, enveloped in the evil-smelling gas from the polluted lake, were considered to be a no-man's land.

The runoff water from the sediment ponds will be a highly concentrated nutrient solution. It must therefore be treated in a simple plant before being discharged into the lake, and experiments are presently being carried out with different coagulents.

When the restoration project is finished and the western and northwestern parts of the lake are accessible, the dewatered sludge should be quite useful when parks and gardens are laid out in the land areas adjoining the lake.

Until the new treatment plant is finished, sewage will continue to be discharged into the lake. In order to overcome the problems presently caused by anaerobic conditions in the water nearest the population centers, and in order to keep the fertilizing effect of the sewage at a minimum during the construction period, it has been proposed that the following measures be taken.

Sewage sludge should be removed from the Esplanade basin; leaving a water depth of 2.0-2.5 m. "Bubble" equipment should be installed here to aerate the well-defined basin. At Montplaisir and Cherguia, the outlets in the northwest, simple ponds should be constructed in the littoral zone of the lake. These ponds should also be aerated.

Nutrients transported to the lake are efficiently concentrated in the large-leaved algae *Ulva* and *Enteromorpha*. After some alterations, the equipment designed to deal with the vegetation in Hornborga Lake should be used to skim off floating algae at different water depths in the Lake of Tunis. This activity would result in losses in nutrients and gains in oxygen for the lake.

Longer-range plans for the lake's restoration ought to include the creation of a water inflow at Khereddine and an outflow to the harbor at Tunis Marine. This should not be considered solely as an hydro-mechanical undertaking, but should be seen as a means of achieving a

nutrient budget suitable for the lake.

By making use of short-term, wind-caused water level variations of at least 50 cm. at Tunis Marine, a large-scale export of nutrients could be secured from the lake to the harbor, to the canal and finally to the Mediterranean, bringing about self-purification. In July-August 1972, for example, nutrient-loaded water with 400-700 ug PO_4-P/1 rushed out from the north lake at Tunis Marine, and then the same water, with an addition of oil from the harbor, flowed back the same way into the north lake. At Khereddine, the proposed intake of water for the north lake, there was at the time only about 20 ug PO_4-P/1.

In its present unbalanced state, the Lake of Tunis ecosystem represents an interesting case of illness. After active therapy it will be a marvelous water. At present, it is understandable that most visitors don't pay too much attention to the large flocks of flamingos that can be seen in the lake, very close to the capital. However, when the lake has been restored to health, the malodorous pollution barrier will be down, and I am sure that the scene of water flamingos set against the picturesque ruins in the island of Chekli and the sundrenched mountains beyond will become an attraction.

Despite sewage sludge and stench, the Lake of Tunis can be recovered.

6
Recreational Water Use

Water as a Low-Class Problem

Drinking water and sewage, being necessitous to us, we have managed not to think about them. They are "being taken care of" by experts. Out of sight, out of mind, the water pipe and sewer pipe in our society have been cast aside, thrust underground, not thought upon, subconsciously *socialized*. We do this with many necessities; we assume "they will take care of it," and — we always add, "We pay taxes, don't we?"

Gradually, without realizing it, we have come to classify almost all activities and objects having to do with water delivery and disposal not only as Problems but as Low-Class Problems. (Such exceptions as gold-plated bathroom faucets have become merely part of an expensive exhibitionary routine, carefully merchandized by fixture manufacturers.)

Thus we have relegated one of the most beautiful of all basic elements in life — water — to an intellectual ghetto. "Useful" water is piped, engineered, bond-issued, distributed, used, dirtied, made to stink, and then piped away to be treated and discarded.

Other water — that is to say, useless water — is made to stand in ponds, lakes, pools, or to squirt and jet through fountains, where it is made to perform aesthetic acts and routines; it reflects light, mirrors the sky, becomes "an eye in the landscape," and titillates the fancy of artists, and enhances the prestige of the owners who can use the Alhambra, Tivoli and Villa D'Este as their aesthetic models.

However, we have discovered that in some cases, "useful" water can be made clean — sanctified by the application of time to its surroundings. Take the water-powered mill, which from the 17th through the 19th century was a necessary adjunct of the industrial revolution, an essential predecessor of the steam-powered mill. (Where would millers have got their training without the early water mills?) The water mill was a place of work and some risk of injury. Women shunned them, wisely. Then, within two generations, after the introduction of steam power, water mills were outmoded. Only now are the few surviving mills revered and protected as aesthetic objects in the landscape, and the waters that keep them splashing are the object of environmentalists' agitations.

Since the mill and its waters are no longer seen as efficient power sources and machines, they can be safely kept in the landscapes as picturesque elements. To protect an old mill now reflects credit upon the protectors, who are seen as persons of sensibility. Thus time casts over the mill and its flow the sweet odor of sanctification, and today we see well-tended specimen mills appearing in four-color ads for cigarettes, suggesting natural coolness — and aesthetic joy.

But all the while we in the United States, for at least the last century, have been turning our backs on useful water, assuming that all its associated problems could be solved by science, engineering and bond issues. The waters themselves, however, did a most inconsiderate thing indeed. They grew scarce. Waters where we wanted them, in pristine condition, became "short." An increasing population was drinking them up, using them up, processing, contaminating, wasting and otherwise disposing in quantities undreamed of by the most lavish of pagan water gods.

Along the way, those people who persisted in nestling their homes, their vacation places, their resorts and retreats at some lovely waters' edges discovered that they, too, were confronting a shortening supply. Fun and games at the water's edge were using up a diminishing resource; the pleasureful use of the water's surface for sport, games and unalloyed leisure had become a flawed exercise, beset with disappointments and rising expenses.

So, during the past decade, it came as no surprise to those already grappling with the planning and design of waterfront recreation places to find that each place needed more care, more study and more expensive improvements to make it enjoyable for human uses. As the following examples were to show, the rush of population to recreational waterfronts would increasingly demand public policies to protect the waters, and private initiatives to see that the edge was developed with care and affection.

The Editor

A Leisure Park Near Paris . . . Innovative Design at Cergy-New Town

By THE API TEAM

The new town of Cergy-Pontoise some 25 km. west of Paris is being developed around a unique series of natural and man-made water bodies. Among them, sandpits, both old and new, dug from a great bend of the Oise River, are becoming the essential ingredients of a new waterscape called Cergy-Neuville Ponds.

A major purpose of the master plan and first-stage development of this new leisure park is to stop the anarchical digging of sandpits, and to harmonize the future exploitation of the rich sand deposits with the creative development of an attractive leisure landscape.

Consequently, one of the early steps in the planning of Cergy-Neuville Ponds was the drawing up of a general plan for an outdoor recreation complex, occupying most of the great bend of the Oise. Once this was done, the API Team, a group of landscape architects including the writer, was retained to propose a detailed plan of development. As a result of long consultations with local groups, the plans shown on these pages were completed and are now being carried out in the landscape. Major elements were completed and in full use during the summer of 1977.

The detailed site studies and master plan were required by the Agence Fonciere et Technique de la Region Parisienne (real estate and technical agency for the suburbs of Paris), which was also the contractor. The client is the Syndicat Mixte d'Etude d'Amenagement et de Gestion (development and management study committee).

---

*The members of the API (Association de Paysagistes et D'Ingenieurs): Paul Brichet, Michele Delaigve, Michel Massot, Jean Francois Morel, Claire Sullerot, Michel Viollet, Andreas Jaeggli, and Bernard Cavalie.

Densely vegetated, the first area completed includes the Welcome Center, providing a restaurant, cloakrooms and restrooms.

Some of the slopes, which are concrete covered with colored plastic resin, have proven too slippery around the paddling pool, and will be modified.

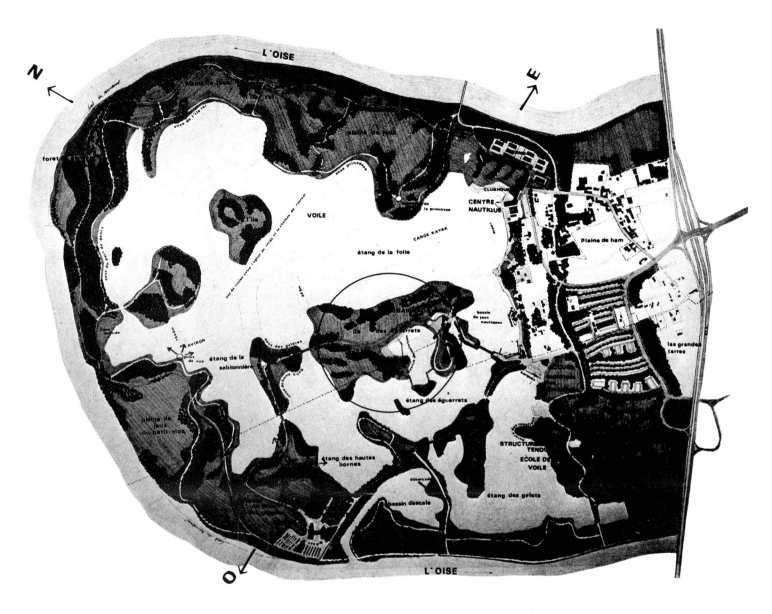

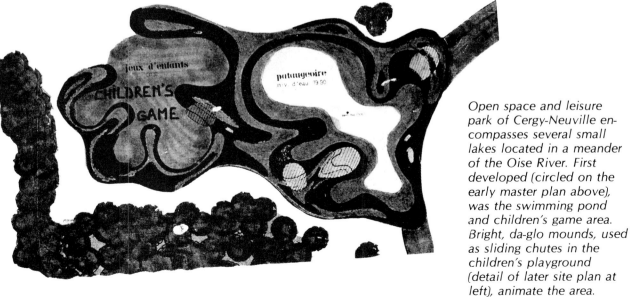

Open space and leisure park of Cergy-Neuville encompasses several small lakes located in a meander of the Oise River. First developed (circled on the early master plan above), was the swimming pond and children's game area. Bright, da-glo mounds, used as sliding chutes in the children's playground (detail of later site plan at left), animate the area.

The Cergy-Neuville Ponds are part of the municipality of Cergy-Pontoise, a fast-growing new town arising on the opposite side of the great bend of the Oise.

It was first considered essential to recognize the land's potentials. On the eastern half of the territory, rich alluvial soils of the Oise were favorable for agriculture, and should continue in that open-field use. On the west, the exploitation of sand deposits had already given birth to a very different landscape: old digging pits have become ponds, separated by narrow earth mounds bearing a dense vegetation: willow, ash, aune, etc., overgrowing the banks. Poplars line the footpaths, and there are groves of oak and dying elm. Fishing has become a favorite sport here, with many picturesque fishing cabins on the banks.

Keeping the view open to local landmarks was important so that the sight axis between the castle of Vaureal and the bell tower of Cergy's church was preserved in the plan.

In keeping with the plan, development is proceeding for an intensive-use area around the swimming ponds, and a wilder, nature-like park close to the great bend.

It would have been cheap and simple to continue digging out the rich sand, using one large mound for the leftover dirt, and ending with one giant pond with linear banks. However, during meetings with local officials and the sand-dealers, our team proposed a different layout to create more diversified landscapes.

Our goals were: to stress the visual effect of spreading water areas; and to create a visual link be-tween one extremity and the other of the water areas, by emphasizing a feeling of depth. (This was done by forming foreground knolls, over which to view the scene; and by preserving an island and peninsula in the existing lakes. Thus the unpleasant feeling created by a uniform stretch of water was avoided.) Gulfs and bays allowed us to mark out small spaces, to be viewed either from the pond or from the bank, giving pleasant changes of scale.

We further sought an enhanced level of complexity, in order to maximize the variety of paths which wind through a very attractive labyrinth-like atmosphere. Also, the design made the most of co-existence, allowing boats to sail from one pond to the next.

Consequently, the master-plan has been followed so that a formerly flat

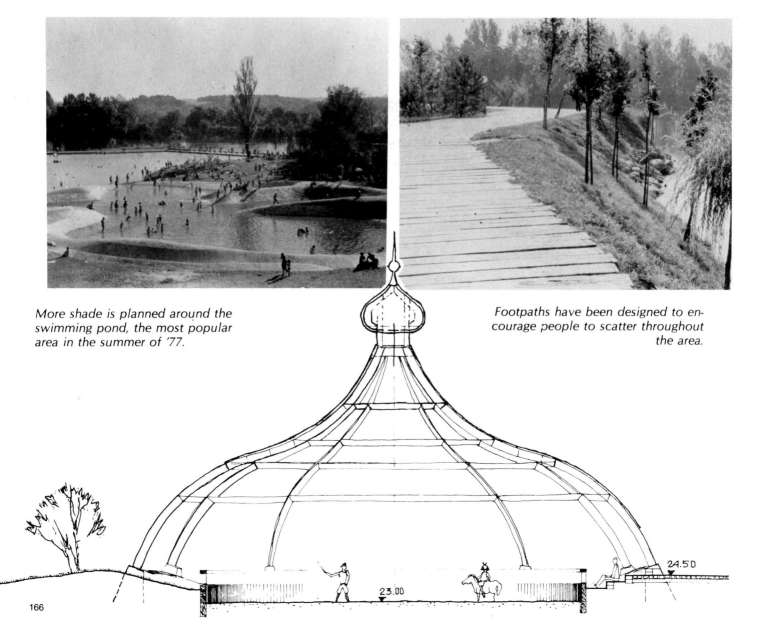

More shade is planned around the swimming pond, the most popular area in the summer of '77.

Footpaths have been designed to encourage people to scatter throughout the area.

river plain (with its random piles of old sand refuse) has been transformed into a landscape of manmade knolls, hills, crests, valleys, slopes and prairies. Much of the material came from sites abandoned by the sand-dealers.

A development plan for new planting has been carried out, following these principles:

1. Establishment of several wooded areas densely planted with seedlings.

2. Establishment of sapling and shrub clusters in areas which continually receive large numbers of people.

3. Planting of young trees and malls or avenues near the restaurant, swimming pool and other heavily-populated areas.

4. Creation of marshy areas on some banks, allowing the establishment and development of aquatic animal life — these being restricted to observation tours only.

5. Development of wild prairies open to the public only in summer and spring; and playgrounds for large numbers of people all year long.

Having worked out the details and phasing of the master plan with local groups, it was easier to proceed with development — the first and most prominent being the swimming park. This area was opened June 1977 and includes a 16,000 m.^{2} swimming pond, solaria or sunning-terraces, playgrounds, sports fields, prairies for walks, picnic ground and welcome centers (with restaurant, cloakrooms, toilets).

The site of the pond was chosen for its relief, its planted banks and poplars, and the possibility of creating an island to be linked with a footbridge from the main entrance.

The main pond is 1.8 m. (approximately 5 ft. deep), and has a smooth slope to provide a non-swimmers' area along the shore. Water is recirculated. Next to this a paddling pool was created with brick and masonry-covered mounds and slopes that are used for sliding and water jets that are popular with the children.

The success of the project, evidenced by fairly large attendance (3000 per day) in its opening season, despite a rainy summer, has been clear proof to all associated with it of the usability of sand-pit areas once thought to be useless and blighting upon the landscape.

Leading directly from the main entrance of the water-park, the footbridge, above, provides a pleasant and unusual access.

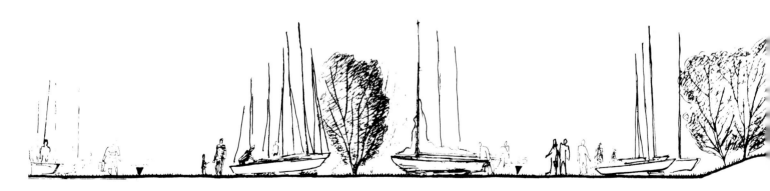

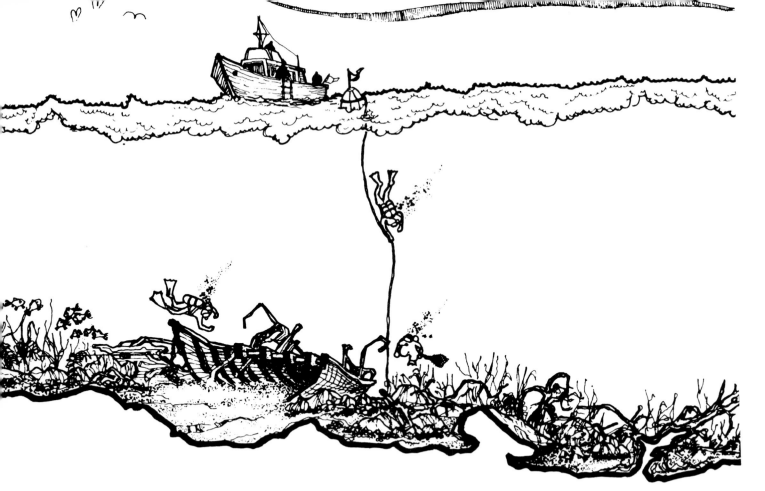

Fathom Five Underwater Park

Ontario's Rich Marine Heritage to Become Recreation Preserve Under Georgian Bay and Lake Huron

By STEVEN MOORHEAD

The emergence of underwater parks around the world is a relatively new phenomenon. Only recently has man realized that the aquatic and marine environments of our world must be protected from exploitation and abuse.

The enormous values to be protected in marine parks and preserves embrace a full range of scientific, scenic, economic, and cultural elements. At present there are numerous marine reserves, particularly in temperate regions of the United States and the Caribbean, the Mediterranean and Japan. In undertaking the study on Ontario's Fathom Five Provincial Park, two basic sets of facts emerged. Fathom Five as an aquatic park is uniquely related to its location in northern waters; and the process of analysis,

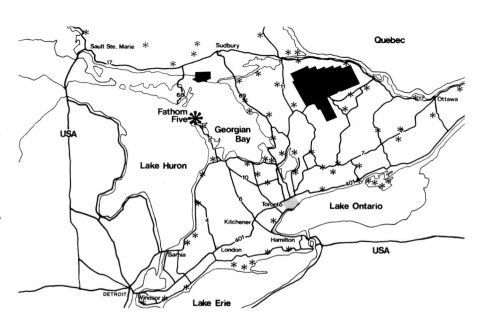

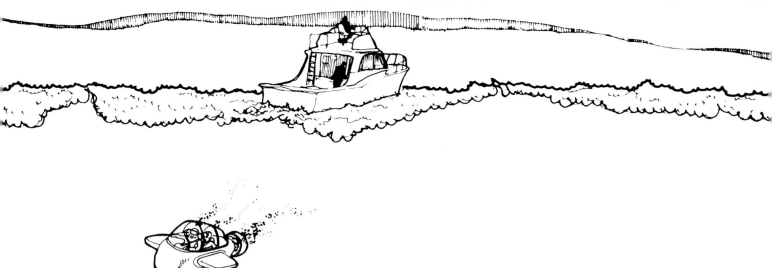

development of plannng, recommendations, and logical management objectives had few if any precedents. The resulting study became a pioneering, research-oriented effort encompassing 42 sq. mi. of water and 450 a. of land.

Background
In an outlying peninsula of Southern Ontario, unhurried by the rush of the 20th century, may be found some of Ontario's richest marine heritage. Beneath the waters of Georgian Bay and Lake Huron which surround the Bruce Peninsula, and within sight of Tobermory, lie the "Shipwrecks of the Bruce." With them are stories of trade and commerce, of men and the sea, and a silent unsung saga of Ontario history. This rich marine history and the many natural resources of both the aquatic and terrestrial environment with respect to geology, limnology, biology and climate make this a superb setting for an underwater park.

For many years and with ever-increasing volume, scuba divers began to discover the pleasures and interest of diving in this unique aquatic environment. Primarily due to potential deterioration of the resource and the avid support of interested scientific and recreational users, the Province of Ontario in 1970 designated a water area at the tip of Ontario's Bruce Peninsula as Fathom Five Provincial Park, thereby immediately establishing a legislative protection for the resources within the park boundary.

Having taken these steps, the next objective was to look at the park in terms of long-range planning,

management and visitor use. This was the point at which our firm was engaged by the Province to undertake a development study. A stated objective was to organize this as a park for all visitors, not just specifically scuba divers, and to satisfy the potentially diverse interests of several groups including cottage owners, local tour boat operators, commercial fishermen, the Ontario Underwater Council, and the local government, most of these groups already having chosen to live here for the rugged beauty of both the aquatic and terrestrial environ-

ment. Other planning factors included the desire to preserve the character and charm of the historical village of Tobermory, the existence of a Canadian National Park (Flower Pot Island) and other islands within the park boundary, the expansion of ferry services to Northern Ontario from Tobermory, and an ever-increasing influx of visitors from urban centers within easy driving distance of the site in both Canada and the United States.

Approach
The basic objective in developing a

Fathom Five park, at end of the Bruce peninsula between Georgian Bay and Lake Huron (sketch, opposite) is 190 mi. from Toronto, 290 from Detroit. Below: circles with names, dates are shipwrecks (1850-1920); asterisks indicate historic sites, circled numbers are potential historic sites.

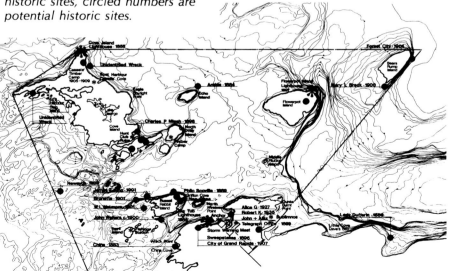

master plan was, up to a point, similar to more normal processes well-known in terrestrial analysis and design. Two distinct differences were the lack of data on underwater resources (including the obvious difficulties of even looking at "the resource") and the realization that a master plan on water is meaningless, at least in traditional context.

With the assistance of an aquatic biologist, data accumulated by the Provincial Parks Branch, record data, and numerous discussions with local residents and fishermen intimately familiar with the region and the water, we compiled a systematic inventory and conducted an analysis.

Climate and underwater topography are the principal factors which have led to the concentration of shipwrecks, to the water clarity and to the historic quality of the area. A resulting richness of aquatic biology adds to the appeal.

The combination of these factors revealed five basic planning units within the waters of the park. These subsequently determined various recreation and management recommendations. This breakdown, in effect, comprised the basis for a master plan of the park.

The Park
Large expanses of open water on Georgian Bay and Lake Huron with resulting currents, varying water temperatures, and weather systems converge within the Fathom Five Park area with a glacier-carved dolomite lake bed, fractured by the submersion of the Niagara Escarpment, a major geological feature. This combination of violent, unpredictable storms, and rugged, island-studded shoreline produces some of the most treacherous waters in the Great Lakes. In addition to being a graveyard for shipping, particularly in the schooner period of the late 19th century and early 20th century, the area has a rich cultural history centered on the natural deep water harbor and village at Tobermory. Within the park area two distinct aquatic ecosystems, Georgian Bay, with precipitous shore lines, colder water and water depths to 550 ft. and Lake Huron with gradually sloping shore lines, warmer waters, and maximum depths of 100 ft. have been formed by glacial activity and subsequent fluctuations in lake level. The resulting underwater geomorphology is a fascinating record of geological history featuring underwater caves, cliffs, till, and other groupings which are more ob-

vious underwater because of the lack of overburden. These factors also combine to create sheltered water areas, dense pockets of aquatic flora and a resulting concentration and variety of fish life.

Recommendations
We chose a land base which allows divers and non-divers to experience and gain a significant understanding of the underwater environment. It is also intended that this facility absorb and subtly disperse visitor demands on the area, thereby preserving and maintaining the physical qualities which, when combined, make this area an exciting and valuable Provincial Park.

The land base is also the jumping-off place for scuba diving and snorkling which will originate at the Dive Center. More conventional day-use activities and boat tours of the park area also organize within the land base.

The major planning exercise related to Fathom Five involved the development of administration and management guidelines.

Diving in northern waters is a more demanding undertaking and involves more equipment than its temperate-zone and tropical counterparts. To establish a diver's capabilities and to control overuse and conflict at popular diving areas

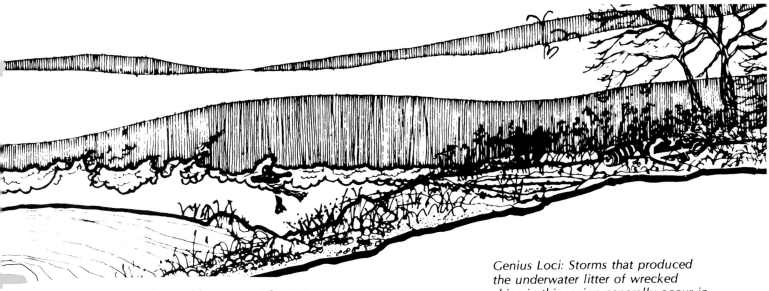

presents many complex problems. Controlling quantity and condition of charter dive boats, and the use of private boats in diving is also essential because of the often dangerous, unpredictable weather and water conditions. These conditions conspire to give the park the qualities it now possesses, but also conspire to make experiencing these qualities potentially dangerous.

Based on the five basic park units, the main design effort became the articulation of administrative considerations, non-diving activities and diving activities relative to each unit. Differences included such things as water depth, water temperature, exposure, quantity of shipwrecks, navigational hazards and underwater visibility.

The Future

The development report was submitted to the Province of Ontario in 1973. Despite many other demands on Provincial Park budgets, Fathom Five, because of its unique qualities and potential, has the total commitment of the Ontario provincial parks administrative and design staff. The land will be acquired by the end of 1974 and changes to the water base boundary as recommended in the report have been re-established. Since submission of the report, the provincial parks staff concentrated on establishing the legislation and management package which will become the legal basis of park definition and use.

Genius Loci: Storms that produced the underwater litter of wrecked ships in this region generally occur in October and November. Fishermen report seeing whirlpools, one 30 ft. deep, 40 ft. across. A rare summer visitor is the "Black Fog" (thunderhead clouds) that descend to cover boats with ice.

Pavilion at lower left includes meeting and washrooms, sauna, etc.; main body of building is for exhibitions, administration, shops.

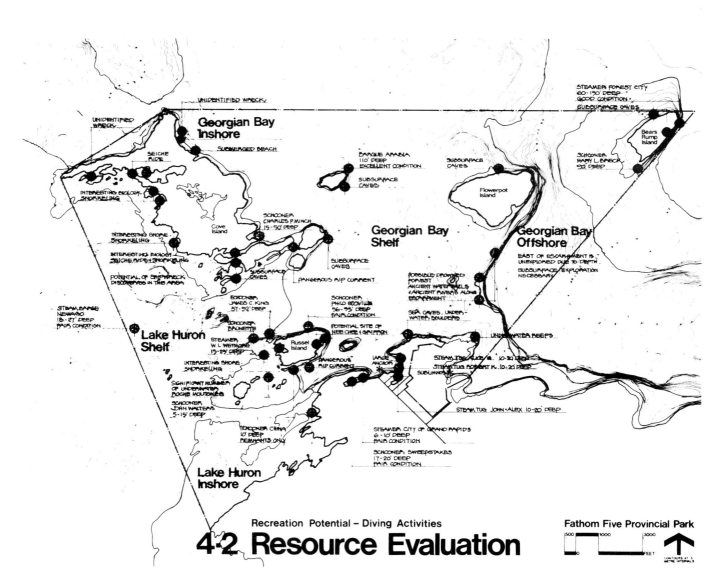

Recreation Potential – Diving Activities

4-2 Resource Evaluation

Fathom Five Provincial Park

Finally, the Park Center and the Dive Center, the two structural facilities essential to achieving the desired objectives of park use, are now being designed and given feasibility tests. It was felt that a significant initial expenditure, particularly on the Park Center, was necessary to have the desired impact and effect consistent with the park planning objectives. Accordingly the funding for development has been budgeted for the next three to five years. From all indications the province will proceed with Fathom Five as a high priority project.

Fathom Five now has generated what we believe to be the most complete and comprehensive plan for an underwater recreation resource in the world. The report has attracted attention throughout North America and inquiries from many other parts of the world. It is hoped that this interest will stimulate the orderly planning and sensitive use of underwater resources in general, one of man's last unexploited frontiers.

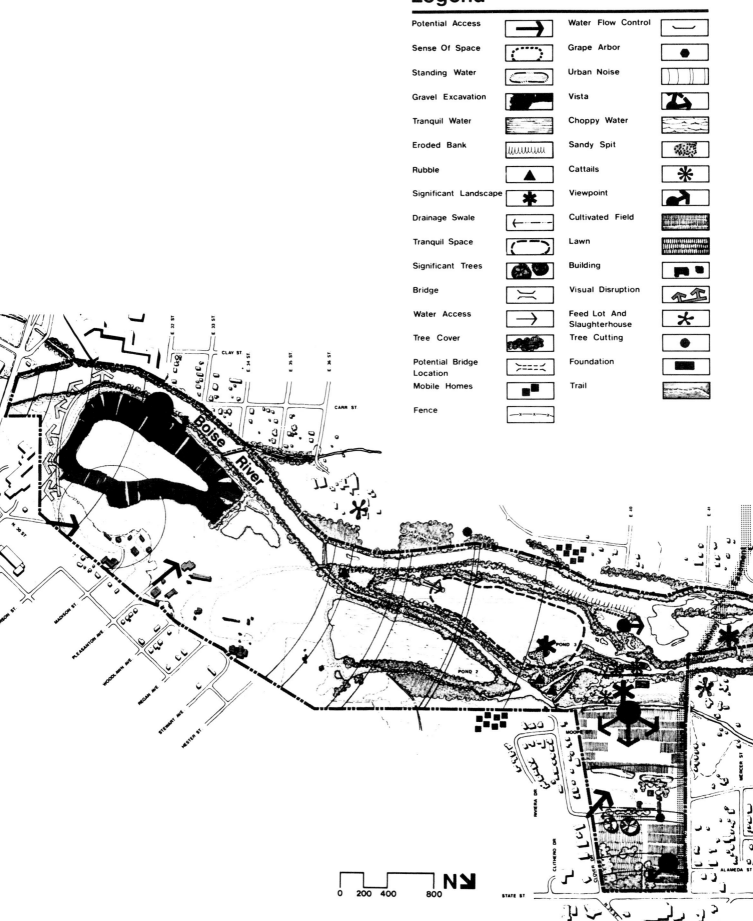

Legend

Potential Access		Water Flow Control	
Sense Of Space		Grape Arbor	
Standing Water		Urban Noise	
Gravel Excavation		Vista	
Tranquil Water		Choppy Water	
Eroded Bank		Sandy Spit	
Rubble		Cattails	
Significant Landscape		Viewpoint	
Drainage Swale		Cultivated Field	
Tranquil Space		Lawn	
Significant Trees		Building	
Bridge		Visual Disruption	
Water Access		Feed Lot And Slaughterhouse	
Tree Cover		Tree Cutting	
Potential Bridge Location		Foundation	
Mobile Homes		Trail	
Fence			

Boise River

0 200 400 800 N

Boise Oasis

By FRED L. BECK and RICHARD A. CAROTHERS

After much controversy, Idaho is about to realize its first urban state park.

Enveloped by the city of Boise, this project may become an oasis of calm within the urban fabric, where city dwellers can experience a natural environment.

Classified a state "Natural Park," the purpose of the park is to protect and perpetuate the resources typical of Idaho's natural heritage. The concept of Veteran's Memorial State Park relates not only to environmental issues, but to the war veterans of Idaho, for the Idaho Old Soldiers Home has been on the site for 71 years. At the turn of the century, the home housed men involved in the Civil War, Spanish-American War, the Boxer Rebellion and various Indian wars. In 1971 the Idaho State Legislature passed a bill providing for the exercise of eminent domain and created the park from the Old Soldiers Home.

The study approach utilized by Richard Carothers Associates is based on natural systems analysis, using this information to establish the direction for the master planning process.

Site investigations began in early December 1973, yielding detailed studies of microclimatology, topography, slopes, geology and soils, flora, fauna, hydrology, acoustics, and a perceptual inventory. Members of the planning team discussed their findings at an informal seminar which capped the investigation. Subsequent visits identified the site's history, potential,

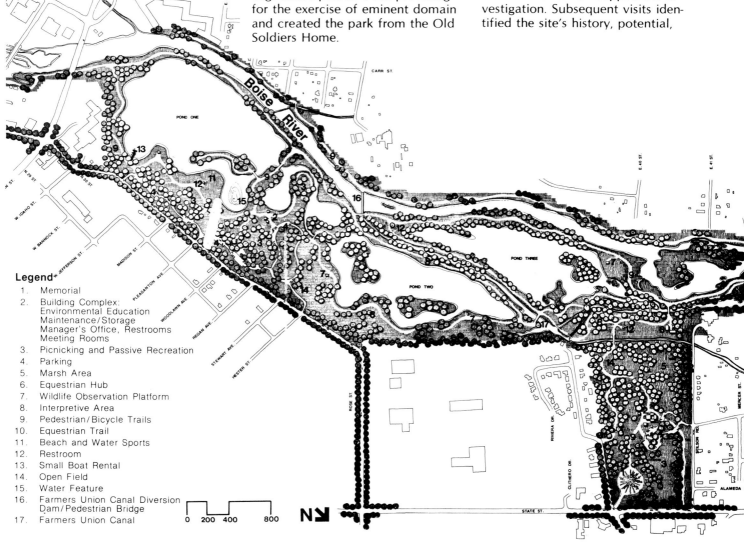

Legend

1. Memorial
2. Building Complex: Environmental Education Maintenance/Storage Manager's Office, Restrooms Meeting Rooms
3. Picnicking and Passive Recreation
4. Parking
5. Marsh Area
6. Equestrian Hub
7. Wildlife Observation Platform
8. Interpretive Area
9. Pedestrian/Bicycle Trails
10. Equestrian Trail
11. Beach and Water Sports
12. Restroom
13. Small Boat Rental
14. Open Field
15. Water Feature
16. Farmers Union Canal Diversion Dam/Pedestrian Bridge
17. Farmers Union Canal

0 200 400   800

N

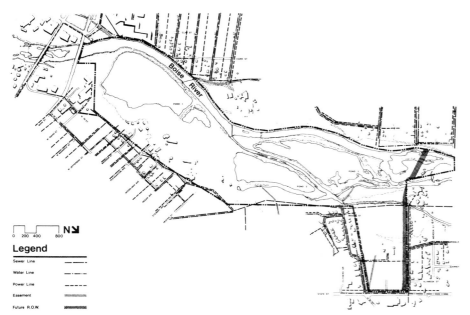

Legend

Sewer Line	——————
Water Line	—·—·—·—
Power Line	— — — —
Easement	▨▨▨▨▨
Future R.O.W.	▧▧▧▧▧

0 200 400 800   N↘

Boise River's potential is recognized by city's plan which tries to balance demands for water supply, sewage disposal and recreation. Park trails for walking and wheeling, below, provide barrier-free access for the handicapped. Map, opposite, shows city and park locations.

problems of access, surrounding land use, and development programs. Public meetings and staff workshops then helped to determine the public's reaction to the proposed park and to encourage citizen participation in the planning process.

Development of the park's natural areas will be minimal since much of the site already has been subjected to gravel excavations. New plantings of native materials will provide food for bird, animal and aquatic life, while dead trees and underbrush will shelter wildlife. Selective shaping of the ponds and island construction will foster better aquatic plant growth and fish habitat. Island construction will also encourage use of the park by birds and water fowl.

Interpretive/educational programs will focus on the natural areas adjacent to waters where boating and swimming will be prohibited. Wildlife observation towers, bridge crossings and self-contained restroom facilities are the only structures planned here.

Programs to involve people in environmental projects will be developed by the State Parks Department. The handicapped will be encouraged to utilize a barrier-free access throughout the park. Students of all ages may use the park facilities. A full-time naturalist is slated for the park's staff. An environmental center will include exhibit space, audio-visual facilities, classrooms, labs and a lecture hall. The lecture hall is also intended to serve as a community meeting center.

The park had become a front-page controversy in 1972 because of the proposed extension of a roadway across the northern portion of the site by the Ada County Highway District. Several hundred people attended the hearing. A western roadway realignment completely bypassing the proposed park won public support and in 1974 county and state officials met to agree on the new alignment. After several years of conflict the roadway and park are now in a state of peaceful coexistence.

The Cancun Strip: Mexico's Bid for Touristic Dollars

By MARIO SCHJETNAN G.

In 1969 Mexico's Territory of Quintana Roo* had less than 45,000 inhabitants in an area of 50,350 km.[2] That was the year the Mexican government started a development plan for the territory looking at several alternatives as a development strategy: to promote agriculture, enlarge the fishing industry, create a major international port, organize industry, and/or to develop a major tourist complex.

Of all these activities, given the economic, technologic and existing

conditions of the region, tourism resulted as the most suitable in relation to generation of jobs, type of development, natural conditions, resources (existence of water, quality of soils, climate, etc.), and to the capitalization of pesos invested in a time span.

Therefore, Banco de Mexico, S.A., the Mexican central bank, started a feasibility study, looking primarily into market and locational studies. The market study contemplated the existing situation of Caribbean sites and places to compete with: i.e., San Juan, Puerto Rico; Jamaica, the

*Achieved statehood on Sept. 20, 1974.

Floating between the Caribbean and a lagoon on Cancun's touristic strip, hotels such as the stunning Camino Real contribute dramatically to Mexico's development strategy for the new state of Quintana Roo. Opposite, viewing the Cancun model from the northeast, with Caribbean at left. Inland (at top of model), the city of Cancun has space to grow in several directions.

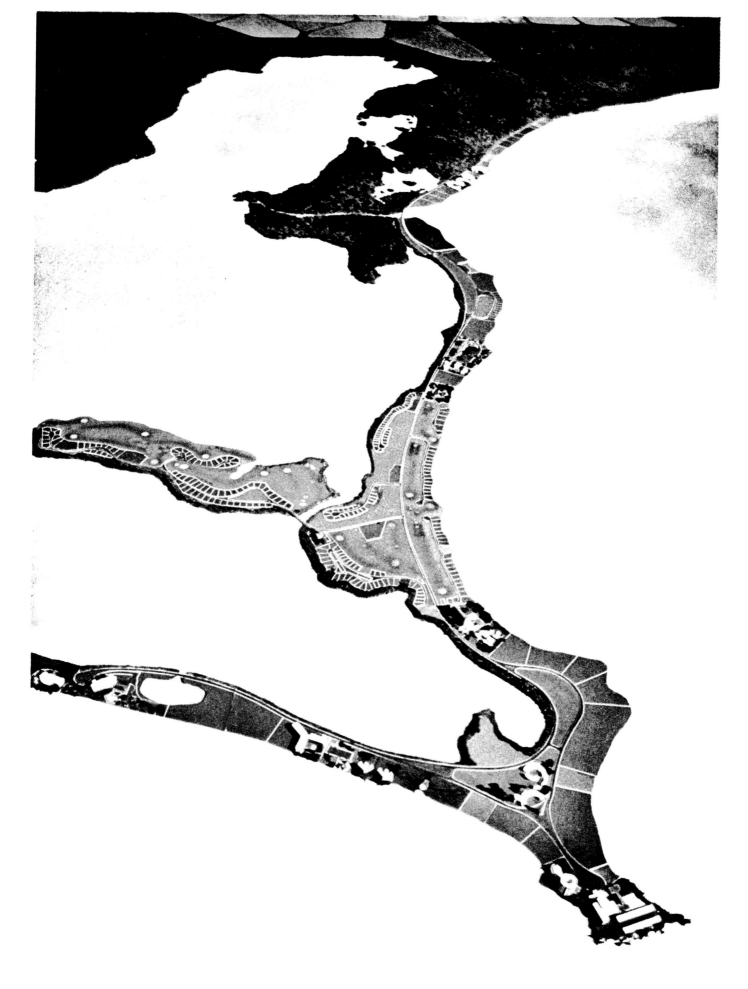

Fueled by rapid population growth, the town is developing in strip fashion. The Commercial Center Plaza, above, for which the author was landscape consultant, is one area which utilizes the more humanized plaza/portico/pedestrian pattern. Accessibility of Mayan ruins such as the coastal city of Tulum was a major criterion considered in the locational study.

Bahamas; in short, the whole spectrum of the Antilles resort complex. The most important factors of comparison were, of course, the types and quality of services and amenities provided. The main clientele of the development plan was geared toward the U.S. East Coast and Canadian tourist plus a minor fraction to the European and Mexican tourist. It is important to mention that one of the key economic goals was to absorb as many foreign tourists as possible in order to balance Mexico's highly deficient balance of payments with U.S. and European countries.

The locational study considered several alternatives along the Mexican Caribbean coast (see map), from Chetumal to Puerto Juarez and both Mujeres and Cozumel islands. The criteria for decision included: the quality of beaches, the costs of infrastructure and services, connection to an existing highway in order to provide food and services, the availability of an international jet-port, the quality of the natural environment, the existence of Mayan ruins easily accessible and the possibility of establishing a town and food industries either adjacent to or within the project.

The final alternatives considered were Isla Mujeres, an existing small island resort; Puerto Morelos, a small fishing settlement; Tulum, the old marine Mayan sacred walled city; the Xel-ha inlets, a group of mangrove and coraline lagoons; Cozumel island, an existing resort several miles off the coast, and Cancun. Of all these alternatives, Cancun is an island only 100 m. offshore, a strip of land 21 km. long by 400 m. in its widest portion; completely flat except for a dune six m. high along the Caribbean coast. It is a 90° degree wedge which faces on one side Bahia de Mujeres and Nichupte Lagoon; and on the other the Caribbean sea, Bojorquez Lagoon and Cancun Lagoon. All the lagoons are connected with each other and with the sea through narrow mouths.

Cancun's advantages include easy access to the mainland, beautiful beaches and the opportunity to enjoy the lagoon on one side and the ocean on the other. Also, the town could be established in the mainland with sufficient space to grow and connections to the existing highways. A considerable disadvantage was having to build a new international jetport as compared with Cozumel island which already had one. But, on the other hand, to provide infrastructure (mainly water), food and construction materials to Cozumel would in the long run be very costly.

The Mexican government owned part of the land; the rest was acquired and within the Banco de Mexico structure a trust company was named. Infratur was created as a decentralized agency whose objective was to develop tourism. (Infratur was renamed Fonatur in 1976.)

When established, it actually worked as a full development agency: planning, building, promoting, advertising, selling and leasing concessions. However, Fonatur has now been turned into a bank to support tourism mainly concentrating on hotels.

Considering the market shown by economic studies, plus the capacity of the island's resources (land, water and beaches) and the corresponding impact of the town to provide services, Fonatur established a target of 10,000 hotel rooms by 1994. At present there are 2000 rooms in use. The average occupancy rate in 1977 has been 85%, which is considered very good for a resort town as a whole. The Mexican government established a seed capital of 588 million pesos, with a 50% loan of 269 million pesos provided by the Inter American Development Bank (BID).

A master plan was prepared by Landa y Asoc., a Mexican planning firm, and by Fonatur, contemplating two areas for development: the resort and the nearby town and food industries. These were separated for obvious reasons, since the town could not fit in the small island. The tourist area would have various hotel types and densities, depending on the quality of beaches, sand, vistas and waves. Following a traditional speculative system, the best beach fronts were the most expensive, so they were acquired by the top level hotel companies. However, eight public beaches were set apart adjacent to those unique places.

Filling in remaining spaces are areas for individual houses, clusters and horizontal condominiums. These are well located to take advantage of existing forested areas (palms and casuarina) and soft topography, hiding as much as possible; since in Mexico architecture of individual houses in high-priced subdivisions is an extravagant cacophony of bad taste.

Other activities accommodated within the resort were commercial facilities, convention center, restaurants, night clubs, public beaches, marina and yacht club, 18-hole golf course and tennis club, mini parks and plazas, bike and pedestrian path and the location and preservation of the archaeological site of Laguna de San Miguel. An important accomplishment of the plan declared almost all mangrove areas around the lagoons to be natural parks and ecological sanctuaries; and an aviary is being studied and prepared in one of the mangrove lagoon islands. Three submarine parks were also declared: Punta Cancun, Punta Nizuc and one in Isla Mujeres called Punta Garrafon — splendid coraline areas for submarine observation.

Not in Cancun but within the Cancun region, extensive archaeological work was done by the Instituto Nacional de Antropologia e Historia (INAH) restoring part of Tulum. At present, work is being accomplished on the Cancun island strip in the Laguna de San Miguel archaeological site.

Xavier Solorzano, project coordinator from Fonatur since the beginning, recalls that Fonatur acted at first only as planner-financier but ended up being a developer. Due to the immense impact of a population move into the region since construction started, Fonatur had to provide housing, schools, clinics, roads and utilities, accelerating the town's construction since the population was growing at a much faster rate than originally expected. Immediately afterwards came people wanting to put up stores, restaurants, cinemas, night clubs, even a bullring and churches.

The town grew from zero to 40,000 inhabitants in four years and is still attracting people at a fast rate. In the middle of this rush, land uses and construction controls as devised by the planners — actually very rigidly — could not be preserved. Some families would buy a lot, start to build a house and convert the garage into a store, beauty parlor or restaurant. Others who came as carpenters, masons, etc., would become established definitely and at once their wives and family would start an improvised store, restaurant or shop.

Such a development pattern is an extraordinary experience to be recorded and studied more deeply, as a way to orient planning theory and criteria in new towns of rapid growth in developing countries. For instance, materials and labor had to be brought from Merida, while specialized items and labor came from Mexico City.

The total circulation pattern of the town has been very difficult to understand and read, so that even people who worked on the plans find it difficult to orient themselves.

However, the barrio superblock form (something close to the pentagon) has proven successful, discouraging through traffic and giving an inward feeling and a recognizable coherence to the barrio. It is large enough to give flexibility to various layouts, thus providing choice and giving opportunity for different urban design solutions.

A major point to regret in the communication system is that there was no provision for a major bike path through the urban area, making trips from the hotels to town or vice versa by bike difficult. Many workers do ride bikes or small motor bikes from home to work and also tourists go to town for all sorts of errands.

The development of the town center has evolved in a strip fashion, losing a unique opportunity to explore for a more humanized town center in a tropical situation, such as a pedestrian or plaza-portico pattern. Such an urban form would take advantage of the climate, vegetation and resort feeling of the town and this strong feeling one has in the old Caribbean "triangle" of Veracruz-Habana-Merida, — which have so much in common — at the same time being so different. There would be people drinking cold tea and playing dominoes, strolling in the plaza or sitting in the portals in the late afternoon and night.

Unlike the town area, the linear pattern resulting from the island's touristic strip has proven successful for a tourist development town, taken from the experience of Mazatlan and Cancun. This is so because the infrastructure is more economical to implement; the standard of infrastructure, road, landscaping and urban furniture which can be provided is higher; the development relatively easy to control and implement in successive stages; and a finished, rather than "in-construction" feeling can be accomplished sooner, especially in terms of roads, public services and landscaping.

One interesting device is the linear right-of-way which incorporates all utilities: water, electricity, gas, sewage, telephone, all running underground between the bike path and the road. This separates the bike path from the road by pleasant landscaping and furthermore separates the road from the property line by the landscaped bike path.

Cancun is a plausible example of regional development centered around tourism, as a major element to develop a new state.

In my opinion that is being accomplished fully, and quite successfully. It is interesting now to see all sorts of public agencies, such as INFONAVIT, building houses for the workers; the Social Security Institute building clinics; and CAPFCE, the school board system, building schools. The private sector from Mexico city, Yucatan and elsewhere is investing in hotels, travel agencies, boutiques and restaurants. This is important in a country such as Mexico, its past development having been so pathologically centered around the high plateau. This is an effort of decentralization both to the southeast and to the coast.

Certainly many problems have emerged — of population, politics, administration, etc. These are inevitable in this type of frontier situation. But the general quality of the development is good, both from the ecological and the human point of view.

The Kagerzoom Competition

Water Skis and Farm Tractors: A New Agri-Recreation Mix on Dutch Polders

By CHRIS BLANDFORD, ROBERT HOLDEN and XAVER MONBAILLIU

One of Holland's most beautiful polder landscapes — the Kager Lakes near Leiden — is under increasing pressure from "day recreation" — the onset of thousands of one-day visitors from nearby towns and cities.

By 1980, at least 35,000 persons will come daily, about 10,000 for watersports, bringing 3600 of their own or rented sailboats onto the water at one time.

To create a complex new landscape that would accommodate this surge of people, yet retain its great polder quality was the object of the Kagerzoon Competition. This was organized in 1973 by the V.T.L. (Vereniging voor Tuin en Landschaparchitekten), the Dutch equivalent of the American Society of Landscape Architects or the (British) Institute of Landscape Architects.

The polder landscape — unique in the western world — is composed of silhouetted villages, treed farmsteads set in flat grasslands, with everything viewed over a wide field of vision extending from dike to dike.

The authors' joint proposal was one first prize winner; the other was by the Ontwerpgroep Adviesbureau of Arnhem. It evolved around a proposed framework to maintain visual

qualities of the area, conserve wildlife, and still meet the pressure of recreation needs. It is designed to fit into both scale and pattern of existing villages and farmsteads, combine transportation routes, consolidate future expansion of town and villages, and maintain the greenbelt continually.

For instance: no new forest-planting, for that would interrupt the wide vistas so characteristic of Holland. The existing large new lake of 300 ha. will be reproduced in 45 ha. versions, each with peninsulas and islands to maintain the local landform character; and interconnected to provide plenty of moorings, and to maintain a water connection between the Kager lakes and the neighboring large lakes (i.e. the Braasemer).

Furthermore, farming practices will be carefully controlled in the western part of the Kagerzoom to make modern farming co-exist peacefully with recreation. For example, restrictions will be placed on the use of fertilizers, and on drainage improvements; the present farm size (average 12 ha.) and land parcel size would be retained, and there would be no new land consolidations. Thus the picturesque old field system would be maintained.

These precautions are essential,

for the western part is an important area for meadowbirds and includes small areas of blue grassland (Caricion canescentis-fuscae). The meadowbird areas will be affected by large-scale recreational development and the blue grasslands are already threatened by change in farming practice: Van Leeuwen has estimated that the present 80 ha. of existing Caricion canescentis-fuscae in the Netherlands would need to be increased to 500 ha. to ensure survival of this plant association whose sub-associations and geographical gradients differ markedly with habitat.

Farmers would be compensated for the above restrictions by funds dispensed from a public agency administering relations between farming, conservation, and tourism in the reserve and promoting recreational development throughout the area as provided for by a proposed agricultural policy of the European Communities.

The farmer's economy would be supported by his produce, compensation payments, and recreation. Such a policy complements tourism development by maintaining the picturesque landscape as well as a local community to support tourist facilities. Such support by local farmers already exists.

Water skiing and houseboats would be banned, except that there would be a new houseboat harbor near Warmond where sewage can be handled. Sailing craft would have access to all the main bodies of water; restrictions to bays and inlets would be by floating booms.

The more intensely used areas will have car parks, picnic sites and foot access, to be sited in areas of highly varied habitat, such as marginal polderland, lakeshores, and farmsteads. Around them will be medium

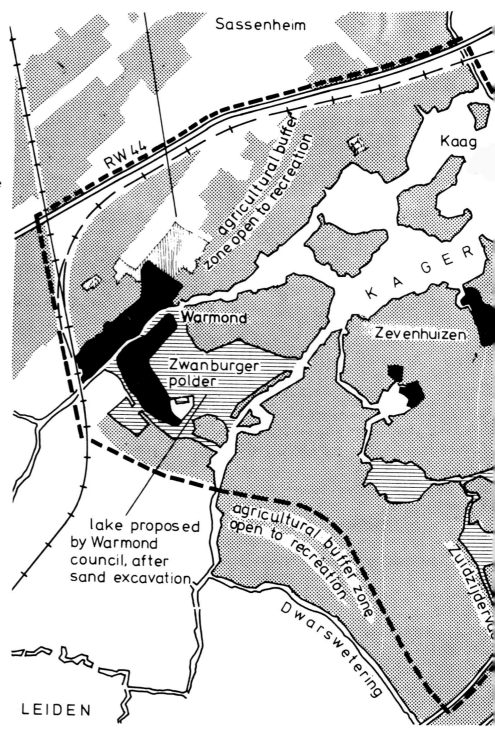

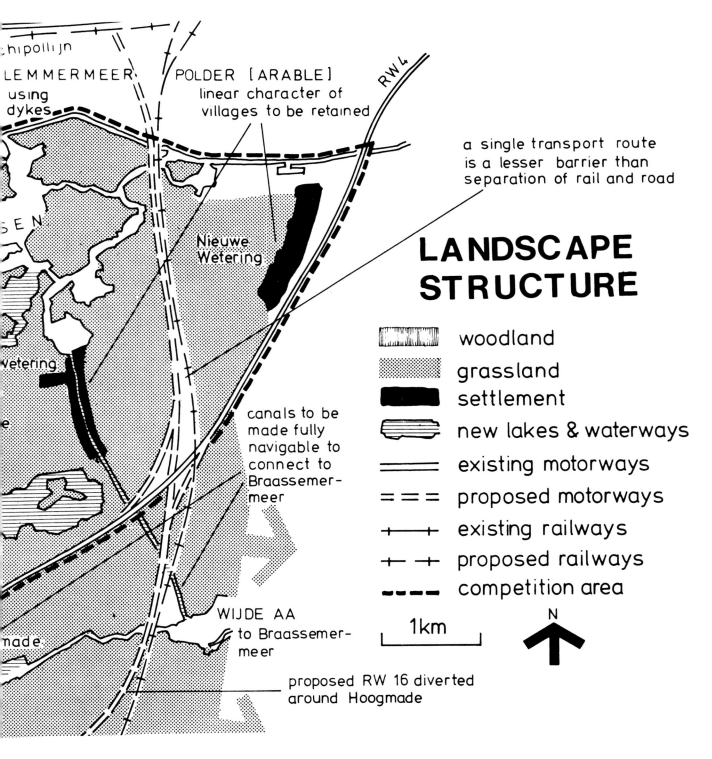

hipollijn

LEMMERMEER,
using
dykes

POLDER [ARABLE]
linear character of
villages to be retained

RW 4

a single transport route
is a lesser barrier than
separation of rail and road

S E N

Nieuwe
Wetering

LANDSCAPE
STRUCTURE

Wetering

woodland

grassland

settlement

new lakes & waterways

existing motorways

= = = proposed motorways

+——+ existing railways

+ — + proposed railways

- - - - competition area

canals to be
made fully
navigable to
connect to
Braassemer-
meer

1km

N

WIJDE AA
to Braassemer-
meer

nade

proposed RW 16 diverted
around Hoogmade

recreation use areas where agricultural production would be of equal importance; here only traffic routes — roads, cycle tracks, and footpaths — will be provided. Farther away, on the margins of the competition area or on islands, will be areas for nature conservation or maximum agricultural production.

The designed integration and co-existence of these activities is the key to the success of this cultural recreation center.

With an existing farm as a basis, a new "landmark" cultural and center has been created at Zevenhuizen. This functions as a living settlement: footpaths and tracks lead through the farm yards, where campers buy food, visitors enjoy refreshment, children get to know farm animals, tourists learn local history, people learn the physical planning of the area so that new changes are subject to public comment.

The eastern lake edge was designed with a maximum shore length and optimal differentiation in shape by creating new peninsular elements. Peak summer-period car traffic is restricted by one-way systems and the 500-space capacity of the evenly distributed car parks. Dispersal from the parks is structured by the bike track and footpath systems.

Three meadowland links through the center maintain the flow of the polders, crucial to the overall unity of the Kagerzoom landscape. Afforested areas of Zevenhuizen gradually penetrate the surrounding landscape rather than forming a wall or block effect. This establishes a transition from meadowland to small clusters of shrubs to denser tree groups in the landmark center area.

The Kagerzoom Competition was sponsored by the Dutch government, by the local councils, the province of South Holland, and the Prince Bernhard fund. It was a two-stage competition, entry to the second stage being by selection.

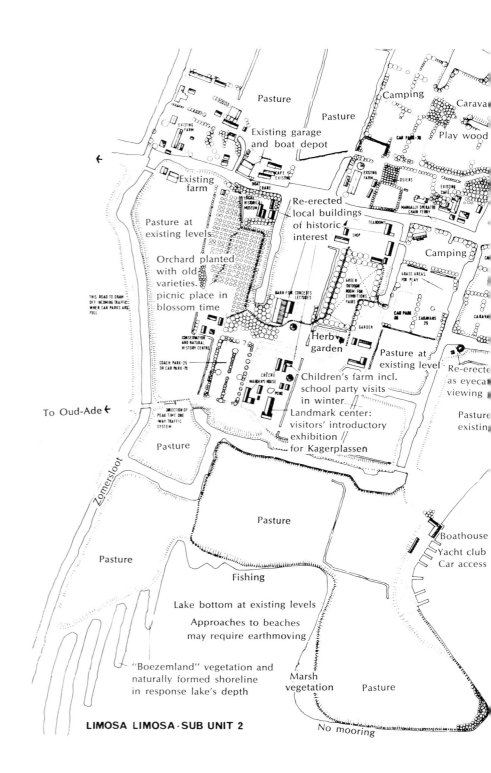

LIMOSA LIMOSA · SUB UNIT 2

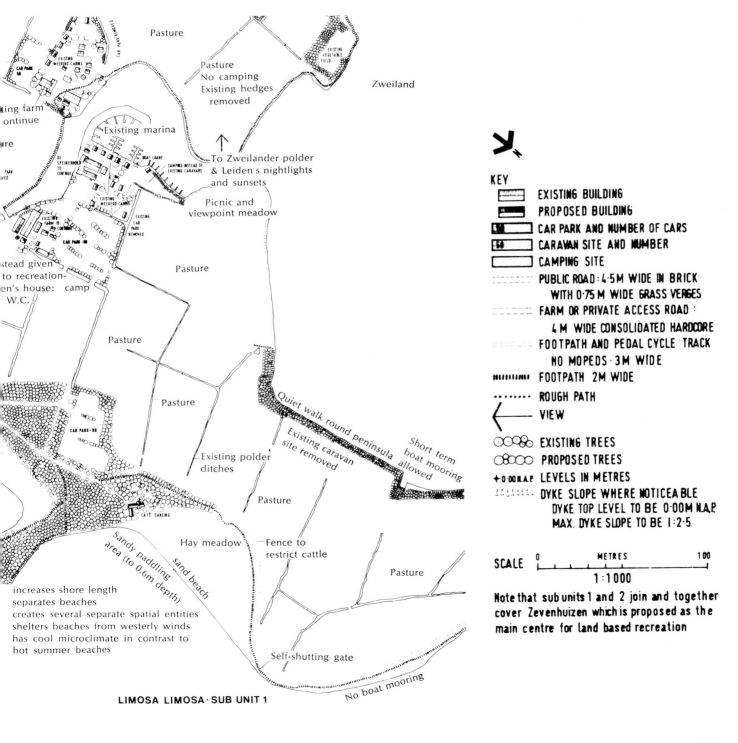

Pasture

Pasture
No camping
Existing hedges
removed

EXISTING
VEGETABLE
FIELD

Zweiland

Existing marina

BOAT CRANE

CAMPING INSTEAD OF
EXISTING CARAVANS

↑
To Zweilander polder
& Leiden's nightlights
and sunsets

ing farm
ontinue

re

EXISTING
WEEKEND CABINS

Picnic and
viewpoint meadow

stead given
to recreation-
en's house: camp
W.C.

Pasture

Pasture

Pasture

Existing polder
ditches

Quiet walk round peninsula

Short term
boat mooring
allowed

Existing caravan
site removed

Pasture

CAFÉ DANCING

Sandy paddling
area (to 0.6m depth)

sand beach

Hay meadow

Fence to
restrict cattle

Pasture

increases shore length
separates beaches
creates several separate spatial entities
shelters beaches from westerly winds
has cool microclimate in contrast to
hot summer beaches

Self-shutting gate

No boat mooring

LIMOSA LIMOSA · SUB UNIT 1

KEY

▭	**EXISTING BUILDING**
▪	**PROPOSED BUILDING**
▭	**CAR PARK AND NUMBER OF CARS**
▭	**CARAVAN SITE AND NUMBER**
▭	**CAMPING SITE**

······· **PUBLIC ROAD : 4·5M WIDE IN BRICK**
　　　　WITH 0·75 M WIDE GRASS VERGES

‑‑‑‑‑‑‑ **FARM OR PRIVATE ACCESS ROAD :**
　　　　4 M WIDE CONSOLIDATED HARDCORE

‑‑‑‑‑ **FOOTPATH AND PEDAL CYCLE TRACK**
　　　　NO MOPEDS · 3M WIDE

┉┉┉ **FOOTPATH 2M WIDE**

······· **ROUGH PATH**

←── **VIEW**

○○○○○ **EXISTING TREES**

○○○○○ **PROPOSED TREES**

+0·00N.A.P **LEVELS IN METRES**

┉┉┉┉ **DYKE SLOPE WHERE NOTICEABLE**
　　　　DYKE TOP LEVEL TO BE 0·00M N.A.P.
　　　　MAX. DYKE SLOPE TO BE 1:2·5

SCALE 0 ┠─┴─┴─┴─┴─┨ METRES 100
　　　　　　　1:1000

Note that sub units 1 and 2 join and together
cover Zevenhuizen which is proposed as the
main centre for land based recreation

Index

Credits

"Drainage Plans with Environmental Benefits" first appeared in *Civil Engineering ASCE,* October 1973. The work upon which this publication is based was supported in part by funds provided by the U.S. Department of the Interior as authorized under the Water Resources Research Act of 1964, Public Law 88-379, as amended.

"Joining Forces to Save Damaged Lakes in Sweden and Tunisia" first appeared in AMBIO 5/72 and is published with permission of its publisher, Royal Swedish Academy of Sciences.

Photographs: p. 58, right center, by Rick Graft; p. 57 and lower right and upper left on p. 58 by Richard Matlock; pp. 88-92 by Peter M. Harvard; maps on pp. 99-101 provided by the U.S. Department of the Interior, Fish and Wildlife Service, and prepared by Bather, Ringrose, Wolsfield, Jarvis, Gardner, Inc., Edina, Minnesota; drawings on p. 151 by Ronald Lovinger; aerial view on p. 178 by Mr. Buzulier; photos on pp. 178-182 by Bob Schalkwijk, courtesy of Fonatur.